The Persuasive Pen

The Jones and Bartlett Series in Logic, Critical Thinking, and Scientific Method

Gary Jason, Consulting Editor

First-Order Logic: A Concise Introduction
John Heil, Davidson College

Introduction to Logic
Gary Jason, San Diego State University

The Persuasive Pen: An Integrated Approach to Reasoning and Writing
Nancy Carrick and Lawrence Finsen, University of Redlands

*Reading and Writing Arguments: A Primer for Beginning Students of
    Philosophy*
John F. Petrik, Rockhurst College

Writing Science through Critical Thinking
Marilyn F. Moriarty, Hollins College

Other Titles of Interest

Getting Funded: It Takes More Than Just a Good Idea (Videos),
Liane Reif-Lehrer, Tech-Write Consultants/ERIMON Associates

Grant Application Writers Handbook, Third Edition, Liane Reif-Lehrer,
Tech-Write Consultants/ERIMON Associates

The Winning Writer: Studies in the Art of Self-Expression, Robin White,
California State Polytechnic University, Pomona

Writing and Speaking for Excellence: A Guide for Physicians, Deborah St.
James, Medical Editor with Howard Spiro, Yale University School of
Medicine

The Persuasive Pen

An Integrated Approach
to
Reasoning and Writing

Nancy Carrick and Lawrence Finsen
University of Redlands
Redlands, California

Jones and Bartlett Publishers
Sudbury, Massachusetts

Boston   London   Singapore

Editorial, Sales, and Customer Service Offices
Jones and Bartlett Publishers
40 Tall Pine Drive
Sudbury, MA 01776
1-508-443-5000   info@jbpub.com
1-800-832-0034   http://www.jbpub.com

Jones and Bartlett Publishers International
Barb House, Barb Mews
London W67PA
UK

Library of Congress Cataloging-in-Publication Data

Carrick, Nancy.
    The persuasive pen : an integrated approach to reasoning and writing / Nancy Carrick and Lawrence Finsen.
        p.   cm. — (The Jones and Bartlett series in philosophy)
    Includes bibliographical references and index.
    ISBN 0-7637-0234-X
    1. English language Rhetoric.   2. Persuasion (Rhetoric)
3. Critical thinking.   4. Reasoning.   I. Finsen, Lawrence.
II. Title.   III. Series.
PE1431.C37   1997
808´.042—dc20   96-43142
                                                                       CIP

Credits
Acquisitions Editors: Arthur C. Bartlett and Nancy E. Bartlett
Manufacturing Manager: Dana L. Cerrito
Editorial Production Service: Diane Ratto, Michael Bass & Associates
Typesetting: Devlin Graphics
Cover Design: Hannus Design Associates
Printing and Binding: Edwards Brothers, Inc.
Cover Printing: Henry N. Sawyer Company, Inc.
Cover Artist: Katsushika H. Kusai

Printed in the United States of America

01 00 99 98 97   10 9 8 7 6 5 4 3 2 1

To the memory of our fathers:

G. Rayner Carrick
(1908–1994)

and

Irving Finsen
(1918–1995)

Contents

Preface

Thinkers and writers wear two hats. On the one hand they must generate ideas, arguments, contexts, ways of presenting material to others; on the other they must evaluate those ideas, arguments, contexts, and strategies for being heard. They must generate abundantly and reject all but the best. The interplay between these two processes varies greatly among writers, but however complementary they may be, they are in one important sense mutually exclusive. Generating requires that one keep an open mind; evaluating too soon can prevent the seed of an idea from reaching fruition. But unfettered generating will not, by itself, however imaginative, produce the carefully reasoned writing that persuades others to see things from the writer's point of view—much less the truth.

The Persuasive Pen seeks to provide detailed and helpful assistance in both the writing process and critical thinking because both sets of skills are indispensable in persuasive writing. One who wishes to write persuasively and with integrity must learn both how to think critically and clearly and how to shape ideas convincingly for readers with varying expectations and responses.

More important, *The Persuasive Pen* seeks to balance these two activities. In part, it integrates them. For example, if thinkers and writers know the expectations of their readers and if they understand the situation that raises an important question, they will be better able to generate useful ideas and hypotheses. And as they generate new ideas, they may in turn redefine their central question or offer an alternative approach to it. At some point, however, writers and thinkers must generate ideas while restraining the temptation to evaluate. Generating, after all, requires open space, whereas evaluating requires a text to consider. To attempt synthesizing too early diminishes both, subduing activities that, individually, ought to be intense and sustaining. In fact, the two processes—generating one's own text and evaluating a text (one's own or another's)—make use of strategies that differ in interesting ways.

The Persuasive Pen, therefore, does not lead its readers through a single process, either from conception to final text or through an analysis of argumentation. Rather, it opens in Part I by defining and illustrating the dual nature of the task (Chapter 1) and introducing means to conceive as fully as possible the issues at hand (Chapters 2 and 3); shifts in Part II to special strategies for clarifying and evaluating arguments (Chapters 4 through 8); and returns in Part III to show how to reconceive the task in order to make one's case public (Chapters 9 and 10). The parts need not be used in sequence. By no means do we wish to imply a three-part "process" of thinking and writing. Instead, we seek to shift the focus of instruction, first bearing primarily on generating, then primarily on evaluation, and then on structuring for a public hearing. Students and their teachers are free to move among the strategies as they are useful to them.

Nonetheless, the twin skills of reasoning and writing are integral throughout. They work collaboratively throughout generating, and they interact as one critiques arguments and text. Clear thinking and clear writing are inseparable, and practicing the two together—recursively—aids in the study of both.

Throughout, *The Persuasive Pen* focuses on what students can do to reason and write more effectively, rather than on errors to avoid. Too often students mistake error-free work for good work and complain (justifiably) that they do not know what to do to improve their work once they remedy the errors. Therefore, although we do discuss fallacies and writing errors, primarily we emphasize what works well in reasoning and writing, and when we introduce errors, we do so in the context of considering strategies for creating well-reasoned, persuasive writing. We classify fallacies, for instance, in the same terms we use to construct a case.

Among the many texts from which we have learned much, we wish especially to acknowledge a few that figured significantly in the development of our thinking, including Howard Kahane's *Logic and Contemporary Rhetoric*, Howard Munson's *The Way of Words*, Brian Skyrms's *Choice and Chance*, Kathleen Dean Moore's *Inductive Arguments: A Field Guide*, David Hitchcock's *Critical Thinking: A Guide to Evaluation*, Linda Flower's *Problem-Solving Strategies for Writing*, Peter Elbow's *Writing with Power*, Richard Lanham's *Analyzing Prose*, and Toby Fulwiler's many articles.

Over a number of years many students at the University of Redlands have helped us test *The Persuasive Pen*. Their responses contributed enormously to our reflection on drafts leading to this publication. A number of those students—Gillian Thackeray, Scott Hengesbach, Janet Grenda, and Mary Daniels—kindly allowed us to use materials they had written for the class. Many individuals have given us valuable comments and suggestions. In particular, Philip Glotzbach, Gary Jason, Catherine Choate, James W. Slinger, Michael Small, and Daniel Bahner all read the text in manuscript and made helpful observations. We are blessed with a very helpful staff at the University of Redlands Armacost Library; we are especially grateful to Les Canterbury, whose unselfish assistance in hunting elusive sources was crucial. Robert Ginsberg offered wise advice. Penny McElroy helped prepare some illustrations for publication. Rhesa Pontti helped by typing the manuscript. A special thanks is due to Art and Nancy Bartlett, our publishers, who guided us skillfully and with good humor through the publication process.

Our daughters Caitlin, Amy, and Thalia have been helpful in ways they don't even know. Their wit (in both senses) has stimulated us along the way. But above all, we wish to thank Susan Finsen and Dwight Yates. In addition to providing many valuable insights from their experience teaching critical thinking and writing, our spouses have been enormous sources of support and help at all stages of writing this book.

PART I

Discovering the Issues

1

Introduction:
A Case Study of Holmes

What does it mean to think fully and carefully about an issue? How might you write yourself into understanding, and how can you then explain that understanding to someone else? We will begin to probe these, the basic questions underlying this book, by considering how Sherlock Holmes attempts to solve the mystery of Silver Blaze. First you must read the story. As you do, keep the following study questions in mind. They will help you focus on strategies of reasoning and writing.

1.1 "Silver Blaze" Study Questions

1. Write a brief summary of the story. Keep your summary to about half a page.
2. Sherlock Holmes is reputed to be a good reasoner. Is he? If so, explain what stands out most prominently—what things he does, which characteristics—to make you think he is. If not, where does his skill fail him?
3. What differences are there between Holmes's theory and Inspector Gregory's theory?
4. What clue sets Holmes onto the line of reasoning he eventually favors? Explain how he was able to recognize the importance of this clue.
5. Consider each of the following data from the story. Explain how each item fits into the overall picture: what it shows or does not show, whether it suggests a line of thought or confirms a hypothesis, how it contributes to the final explanation of the mystery.
   A. The dog that did not bark.
   B. The lame sheep.
   C. The millinery bill.
   D. The cataract knife.
   E. Silver Blaze's presence at Mapleton.

F. Computing the speed of the train.

G. The curried mutton.

6. Present two arguments, the first with the conclusion that Holmes solved the mystery, the second concluding that he did not solve it successfully. Make both as strong as you can. Then explain which argument you think is more believable and why.

1.2 "The Adventure of Silver Blaze" *

by Arthur Conan Doyle

"I am afraid, Watson, that I shall have to go," said Holmes, as we sat down together to our breakfast one morning.

"Go! Where to?"

"To Dartmoor—to King's Pyland."

I was not surprised. Indeed, my only wonder was that he had not already been mixed up in this extraordinary case, which was the one topic of conversation through the length and breadth of England. For a whole day my companion had rambled about the room with his chin upon his chest and his brows knitted, charging and re-charging his pipe with the strongest black tobacco, and absolutely deaf to any of my questions or remarks. Fresh editions of every paper had been sent up by our newsagent only to be glanced over and tossed down into a corner. Yet, silent as he was, I knew perfectly well what it was, over which he was brooding. There was but one problem before the public which could challenge his powers of analysis, and that was the singular disappearance of the favourite for the Wessex Cup and the tragic murder of its trainer. When, therefore, he suddenly announced his intention of setting out for the scene of the drama, it was only what I had both expected and hoped for.

"I should be most happy to go down with you if I should not be in the way," said I.

"My dear Watson, you would confer a great favour upon me by coming. And I think that your time will not be mis-spent, for there are points about this case which promise to make it an absolutely unique one. We have, I think, just time to catch our train in Paddington, and I will go further into the matter upon our journey. You would oblige me by bringing with you your very excellent field-glass."

And so it happened that an hour or so later I found myself in the corner of a first-class carriage, flying along, on route for Exeter, while Sherlock Holmes, with his sharp, eager face framed in his earflapped traveling cap, dipped rapidly into the bundle of fresh papers which he had procured at Paddington. We had left Reading far behind us before he thrust the last of them under the seat, and offered me his cigar case.

"We are going well," said he, looking out of the window, and glancing at his watch. "Our rate at present is fifty-three and a half miles an hour."

*The Strand Magazine 4 (1892): 83ff.

"I have not observed the quarter-mile posts," said I.

"Nor have I. But the telegraph posts upon this line are sixty yards apart, and the calculation is a simple one. I presume you have already looked into this matter of the murder of John Straker and the disappearance of Silver Blaze?"

"I have seen what the *Telegraph* and the *Chronicle* have to say."

"It is one of those cases where the art of the reasoner should be used rather for the sifting of details than for the acquiring of fresh evidence. The tragedy has been so uncommon, so complete, and of such personal importance to so many people that we are suffering from a plethora of surmise, conjecture, and hypothesis. The difficulty is to detach the framework of fact—of absolute, undeniable fact—from the embellishments of theorists and reporters. Then, having established ourselves upon this sound basis, it is our duty to see what inferences may be drawn, and which are the special points upon which the whole mystery turns. On Tuesday evening I received telegrams, both from Colonel Ross, the owner of the horse, and from Inspector Gregory, who is looking after the case, inviting my co-operation."

"Tuesday evening!" I exclaimed. "And this is Thursday morning. Why did you not go down yesterday?"

"Because I made a blunder, my dear Watson—which is, I am afraid, a more common occurrence than anyone would think who only knew me through your memoirs. The fact is that I could not believe it possible that the most remarkable horse in England could long remain concealed, especially in so sparsely inhabited a place as the north of Dartmoor. From hour to hour yesterday I expected to hear that he had been found, and that his abductor was the murderer of John Straker. When, however, another morning had come and I found that, beyond the arrest of young Fitzroy Simpson, nothing had been done, I felt that it was time for me to take action. Yet in some ways I feel that yesterday has not been wasted."

"You have formed a theory then?"

"At least I have got a grip of the essential facts of the case. I shall enumerate them to you, for nothing clears up a case so much as stating it to another person, and I can hardly expect your co-operation if I do not show you the position from which we start."

I lay back against the cushions, puffing at my cigar, while Holmes, leaning forward, with his long forefinger checking off the points upon the palm of his left hand, gave me a sketch of the events which had led to our journey.

"Silver Blaze," said he, "is from the Isonomy stock, and holds as brilliant a record as his famous ancestor. He is now in his fifth year, and has brought in turn each of the prizes of the turf to Colonel Ross, his fortunate owner. Up to the time of the catastrophe he was first favourite for the one Wessex Cup, the betting being three to one on. He has always, however, been a prime favourite with the racing public, and has never yet disappointed them, so that even at those odds enormous sums of money have been laid upon him. It is obvious, therefore, that there were many people who had the strongest interest in preventing Silver Blaze from being there at the fall of the flag next Tuesday.

"This fact was, of course, appreciated at King's Pyland, where the Colonel's training stable is situated. Every precaution was taken to guard the

"HOLMES GAVE ME A SKETCH OF THE EVENTS."

By Sidney Paget. Originally published in *Strand Magazine*, 1892.

favourite. The trainer, John Straker, is a retired jockey, who rode in Colonel Ross's colours before he became too heavy for the weighing chair. He has served the Colonel for five years as a jockey, and for seven years as a trainer, and has always shown himself to be a zealous and honest servant. Under him were three lads, for the establishment was a small one, containing only four horses in all. One of these lads sat up each night in the stable, while the others slept in the loft. All three bore excellent characters. John Straker, who is a married man, lived in a small villa about two hundred yards from the stables. He has no children, keeps one maid-servant, and is comfortably off. The country round is very lovely, but about a half a mile to the north there is a small cluster of villas which have been built by a Tavistock contractor for the use of invalids and others who may wish to enjoy the pure Dartmoor air. Tavistock itself lies two miles to the west, while across the moor, also about two miles distant, is the larger establishment of Mapleton, which belongs to Lord Blackwater, and is managed by Silas Brown. In every other direction the moor is a complete wilderness inhabited by only a few roaming gipsies. Such was the general situation last Monday night when the catastrophe occurred.

"On that evening the horses had been exercised and watered as usual, and the stables were locked up at nine o'clock. Two of the lads walked up to the trainer's house, where they had supper in the kitchen, while the third, Ned Hunter, remained on guard. At a few minutes after nine the maid, Edith Baxter, carried down to the stables his supper, which consisted of a dish of curried mutton. She took no liquid, as there was a water-tap in the stables, and it was the rule that the lad on duty should drink nothing else. The maid carried a lantern with her, as it was very dark, and the path ran across the open moor.

"Edith Baxter was within thirty yards of the stables when a man appeared out of the darkness and called to her to stop. As he stepped into the circle of the yellow light thrown by the lantern she saw that he was a person of gentlemanly bearing, dressed in a grey suit of tweed with a cloth cap. He wore gaiters, and carried a heavy stick with a knob to it. She was most impressed, however, by the extreme pallor of his face and by the nervousness of his manner. His age, she thought, would be rather over thirty than under it.

" 'Can you tell me where I am?' he asked. 'I had almost made up my mind to sleep on the moor when I saw the light of your lantern.'

" 'You are close to King's Pyland training stables,' she said.

" 'Oh, indeed! What a stroke of luck!' he cried. 'I understand that a stable boy sleeps there alone every night. Perhaps that is his supper which you are carrying to him. Now I am sure that you would not be too proud to earn the price of a new dress, would you?' He took a piece of white paper folded up out of his waistcoat pocket. 'See that the boy has this to-night, and you shall have the prettiest frock that money can buy!'

"She was frightened by the earnestness of his manner, and ran past him to the window through which she was accustomed to hand the meals. It was already open, and Hunter was seated at the small table inside. She had begun to tell him of what had happened, when the stranger came up again.

" 'Good evening,' said he, looking through the window, 'I wanted to have a word with you.' The girl has sworn that as he spoke she noticed the corner of the little paper packet protruding from his closed hand.

" 'What business have you here?' asked the lad.

" 'It's business that may put something into your pocket,' said the other. 'You've two horses in for the Wessex Cup—Silver Blaze and Bayard. Let me have the straight tip, and you won't be a loser. Is it a fact that at the weights Bayard could give the other a hundred yards in five furlongs, and that the stable have put their money on him?'

" 'So you're one of those damned touts,' cried the lad. 'I'll show you how we serve them in King's Pyland.' He sprang up and rushed across the stable to unloose the dog. The girl fled away to the house, but as she ran she looked back, and saw that the stranger was leaning through the window. A minute later, however, when Hunter rushed out with the hound he was gone, and though the lad ran all round the buildings he failed to find any trace of him."

"One moment!" I asked. "Did the stable-boy, when he ran out with the dog, leave the door unlocked behind him?"

"A MAN APPEARED OUT OF THE DARKNESS."

By Sidney Paget. Originally published in *Strand Magazine,* 1892.

"Excellent, Watson; excellent!" murmured my companion. "The importance of the point struck me so forcibly, that I sent a special wire to Dartmoor yesterday to clear the matter up. The boy locked the door before he left it. The window, I may add, was not large enough for a man to get through.

"Hunter waited until his fellow grooms had returned, when he sent a message up to the trainer and told him what had occurred. Straker was excited at hearing the account, although he does not seem to realize its true significance. It left him, however, vaguely uneasy, and Mrs. Straker, waking at one in the morning, found that he was dressing. In reply to her inquiries, he said that he could not sleep on account of his anxiety about the horses, and that he intended to walk down to the stables to see that all was well. She begged him to remain at home, as she could hear the rain pattering against the windows, but in spite of her entreaties he pulled on his large mackintosh and left the house.

"Mrs. Straker awoke at seven in the morning, to find that her husband had not yet returned. She dressed herself hastily, called to the maid, and set off for the stables. The door was open: inside, huddled together upon a chair, Hunter was sunk in a state of absolute stupor, the favourite's stall was empty, and there were no signs of his trainer.

"The two lads who slept in the chaff-cutting loft above the harness-room were quickly aroused. They had heard nothing during the night, for they are both sound sleepers. Hunter was obviously under the influence of some powerful drug; and, as no sense could be got out of him, he was left to sleep it off while the two lads and the two women ran out in search of the absentees. They still had hopes that the trainer had for some reason taken out the horse for early exercise, but on ascending the knoll near the house, from which all the neighboring moors were visible, they not only could see no signs of the favourite, but they perceived something which warned them that they were in the presence of a tragedy.

"About a quarter of a mile from the stables, John Straker's overcoat was flapping from a furze bush. Immediately beyond there was a bowl-shaped impression in the moor, and at the bottom of this was found the dead body of the unfortunate trainer. His head had been shattered by a savage blow from some heavy weapon, and he was wounded in the thigh, where there was a long, clean cut, inflicted evidently by some very sharp instrument. It was clear, however, that Straker had defended himself vigorously against his assailants, for in his right hand he held a small knife, which was clotted with blood up to the handle, while in his left he grasped a red and black silk cravat, which was recognized by the maid as having been worn by the stranger who had visited the stables.

"Hunter, on recovering from his stupor, was also quite positive as to the ownership of the cravat. He was equally certain that the same stranger had, while standing at the window, drugged his curried mutton, and so deprived the stables of their watchman.

"As to the missing horse, there were abundant proofs in the mud which lay at the bottom of the fatal hollow, that he had been there at the time of the struggle. But from that morning he has disappeared; and although a large reward has been offered, and all the gipsies of Dartmoor are on the alert, no news has come of him. Finally an analysis has shown that the remains of his supper, left by the stable lad, contain an appreciable amount of powdered opium, while the people of the house partook of the same dish on the same night without any ill effect.

"Those are the main facts of the case, stripped of all surmise and stated as badly as possible. I shall now recapitulate what the police have done in the matter.

"Inspector Gregory, to whom the case has been committed, is an extremely competent officer. Were he but gifted with imagination he might rise to great heights in his profession. On his arrival he promptly found and arrested the man upon whom suspicion naturally rested. There was little difficulty in finding him, for he inhabited one of those villas which I have mentioned. His name, it appears, was Fitzroy Simpson. He was a man of excellent birth and education, who had squandered a fortune upon the turf, and who lived now by doing a little quiet and genteel bookmaking in the sporting clubs of London. An examination of his betting-book shows that bets to the amount of five thousand pounds had been registered by him against the favourite.

"On being arrested he volunteered the statement that he had come down to Dartmoor in the hope of getting some information about the King's Pyland horses, and also about Desborough, the second favourite, which was in [the] charge of Silas Brown, at the Mapleton Stables. He did not attempt to deny that he had acted as described upon the evening before, but declared that he had no sinister designs, and had simply wished to obtain first-hand information. When confronted with his cravat he turned very pale, and was utterly unable to account for its presence in the hand of the murdered man. His wet clothing showed that he had been out in the storm of the night before, and his stick, which was a Penang lawyer, weighted with lead, was just such a weapon as might, by repeated blows, have inflicted the terrible injuries to which the trainer had succumbed.

"On the other hand, there was no wound upon his person, while the state of Straker's knife would show that one, at least, of his assailants must bear his mark upon him. There you have it all in a nutshell, Watson, and if you can give me any light I shall be infinitely obliged to you."

I had listened with the greatest interest to the statement which Holmes, with characteristic clearness, had laid before me. Though most of the facts were familiar to me, I had not sufficiently appreciated their relative importance, nor their connection to each other.

"Is it not possible," I suggested, "that the incised wound upon Straker may have been caused by his own knife in the convulsive struggles which follow any brain injury?"

"It is more than possible; it is probable," said Holmes. "In that case, one of the main points in favour of the accused disappears."

"And yet," said I, "even now I fail to understand what the theory of the police can be."

"I am afraid that whatever theory we state has very grave objections to it," returned my companion. "The police imagine, I take it, that this Fitzroy Simpson, having drugged the lad, and having in some way obtained a duplicate key, opened the stable door, and took out the horse, with the intention, apparently, of kidnapping him altogether. His bridle is missing, so that Simpson must have put this on. Then, having left the door open behind him, he was leading the horse away over the moor, when he was either met or overtaken by the trainer. A row naturally ensued, Simpson beat out the trainer's brains with his heavy stick without receiving any injury from the small knife which Straker used in self-defence, and then the thief either led the horse on to some secret hiding-place, or else it may have bolted during the struggle, and be now wandering out on the moors. That is the case as it appears to the police, and improbable as it is, all other explanations are more improbable still. However, I shall very quickly test the matter when I am once upon the spot, and until then I really cannot see how we can get much further than our present position."

It was evening before we reached the little town of Tavistock, which lies, like the boss of a shield, in the middle of the huge circle of Dartmoor. Two gentleman were awaiting us at the station; the one a tall fair man with lion-like hair and beard, and curiously penetrating light blue eyes, the other a small alert person, very neat and dapper, in a frock-coat and gaiters, with trim little side-whiskers and an eye-glass. The latter was Colonel Ross, the well-known sportsman, the other Inspector Gregory, a man who was rapidly making his name in the English detective service.

"I am delighted that you have come down, Mr. Holmes," said the Colonel. "The Inspector here has done all that could possibly be suggested; but I wish to leave no stone unturned in trying to avenge poor Straker, and in recovering my horse."

"Have there been any fresh developments?" asked Holmes.

"I am sorry to say that we have made very little progress," said the Inspector. "We have an open carriage outside, and as you would no doubt like to see the place before the light fails, we might talk it over as we drive."

A minute later we were all seated in a comfortable landau and were rattling through the quaint old Devonshire town. Inspector Gregory was full of his case, and poured out a stream of remarks, while Holmes threw in an occasional question or interjection. Colonel Ross leaned back with his arms folded and his hat tilted over his eyes, while I listened with interest to the dialogue of the two detectives. Gregory was formulating his theory, which was almost exactly what Holmes had foretold in the train.

"The net is drawn pretty close around Fitzroy Simpson," he remarked, "and I believe myself that he is our man. At the same time, I recognise that the evidence is purely circumstantial, and that some new development may upset it."

"How about Straker's knife?"

"We have quite come to the conclusion that he wounded himself in his fall."

"My friend Dr. Watson made that suggestion to me as we came down. If so, it would tell against this man Simpson."

"Undoubtedly. He has neither a knife nor any sign of a wound. The evidence against him is certainly very strong. He had a great interest in the disappearance of the favourite, he lies under the suspicion of having poisoned the stable boy, he was undoubtedly out in the storm, and his cravat was found in the dead man's hand. I really think we have enough to go before a jury."

Holmes shook his head. "A clever counsel would tear it all to rags," said he. "Why should he take the horse out of the stable? If he wished to injure it, why could he not do it there? Has a duplicate key been found in his possession? What chemist sold him the powdered opium? Above all, where could he, a stranger to the district, hide a horse, and such a horse as this? What is his own explanation as to the paper which he wished the maid to give to the stable-boy?"

"He says that it was a ten-pound note. One was found in his purse. But your other difficulties are not so formidable as they seem. He is not a stranger to the district. He has twice lodged at Tavistock in the summer. The opium was probably bought from London. The key, having served its purpose, would be hurled away. The horse may lie at the bottom of one of the pits or old mines along the moor."

"What does he say about the cravat?"

"He acknowledges that it is his, and declares that he had lost it. But a new element has been introduced into the case which may account for his leading the horse from the stable."

Holmes pricked up his ears.

"We have found traces which show that a party of gipsies encamped on Monday night within a mile of the spot where the murder took place. On Tuesday they were gone. Now, presuming that there was some understanding between Simpson and these gipsies, might he not have been leading the horse to them when he was overtaken, and may they not have him now?"

"It certainly is possible."

"The moor is being scoured for these gipsies. I have also examined every stable and outhouse in Tavistock, and for a radius of ten miles."

"There is another training stable quite close, I understand?"

"Yes, and that is a factor which we must certainly not neglect. As Desborough, their horse, was second in the betting, they had an interest in the disappearance of the favourite. Silas Brown, the trainer, is known to have had large bets upon the event, and he was no friend to poor Straker. We have, however, examined the stables, and there is nothing to connect them with the affair."

"And nothing to connect this man Simpson with the interests with the Mapleton Stables?"

"Nothing at all."

Holmes leaned back in the carriage and the conversation ceased. A few minutes later our driver pulled up at a neat little red-brick villa with overhanging eaves, which stood by the road. Some distance off, across a paddock, lay a long grey-tiled out-building. In every other direction the low curves of the moor, bronze-coloured from the fading ferns, stretched away to the skyline, broken only by the steeples of Tavistock, and by a cluster of houses away to the westward, which marked the Mapleton stables. We all sprang out with the exception of Holmes, who continued to lean back with his eyes fixed upon the sky in front of him, entirely absorbed in his own thoughts. It was only when I touched his arm that he roused himself with a violent start and stepped out of the carriage.

"Excuse me," said he, turning to Colonel Ross, who had looked at him in some surprise. "I was day-dreaming." There was a gleam in his eyes and a suppressed excitement in his manner which convinced me, used as I was to his ways, that his hand was upon a clue, though I could not imagine where he had found it.

"Perhaps you would prefer at once to go on to the scene of the crime, Mr. Holmes?" said Gregory.

"I think that I should prefer to stay here a little and go into one or two questions of detail. Straker was brought back here, I presume?"

"Yes, he lies upstairs. The inquest is to-morrow."

"He has been in your service some years, Colonel Ross?"

"I have always found him an excellent servant."

"I presume that you made an inventory of what he had in his pockets at the time of his death, Inspector?"

"I have the things themselves in the sitting-room if you would care to see them."

"I should be very glad."

We all filed into the front room and sat round the central table, while the Inspector unlocked a square tin box and laid a small heap of things before us. There was a box of vestas, two inches of tallow candle, an A.D.P. briar-root pipe, a pouch of sealskin with half an ounce of long-cut Cavendish, a silver watch with a gold chain, five sovereigns in gold, an aluminum pencil-case, a few papers, and an ivory-handled knife with a very delicate inflexible blade marked Weiss and Co., London.

"This is a very singular knife," said Holmes, lifting it up and examining it minutely. "I presume, as I see bloodstains upon it, that it is the one which was found in the dead man's grasp. Watson, this knife is surely in your line."

"It is what we call a cataract knife," said I.

"I thought so. A very delicate blade devised for very delicate work. A strange thing for a man to carry with him upon a rough expedition, especially as it would not shut in his pocket."

"The tip was guarded by a disc of cork which we found beside his body," said the Inspector. "His wife tells us that the knife had lain for some days upon the dressing-table, and that he had picked it up as he had left the room. It was a poor weapon, but perhaps the best that he could lay his hand on at the moment."

"Very possibly. How about these papers?"

"Three of them are receipted hay-dealers' accounts. One of them is a letter of instruction from Colonel Ross. This other is a milliner's account for thirty-seven pounds fifteen, made out by Madame Lesurier, of Bond Street, to William Darbyshire. Mrs. Straker tells us that Darbyshire was a friend of her husband's, and that occasionally his letters were addressed here."

"Madame Darbyshire had somewhat expensive tastes," remarked Holmes, glancing down the account. "Twenty-two guineas is rather heavy for a single costume. However, there appears to be nothing more to learn, and we may now go down to the scene of the crime."

As we emerged from the sitting-room a woman who had been waiting in the passage took a step forward and laid her hand upon the Inspector's sleeve.

Her face was haggard, and thin, and eager; stamped with the print of a recent horror.

"Have you got them? Have you found them?" she panted.

"No, Mrs. Straker; but Mr. Holmes, here, has come from London to help us and we shall do all that is possible."

"Surely I met you in Plymouth, at a garden party, some little time ago, Mrs. Straker," said Holmes.

"No, sir; you are mistaken."

"Dear me; why, I could have sworn it. You wore a costume of dove-coloured silk, with ostrich feather trimming."

"I never had such a dress, sir," answered the lady.

"Ah; that quite settles it," said Holmes; and, with an apology, he followed the Inspector outside. A short walk across the moor took us to the hollow in which the body had been found. At the brink of it was the furze bush upon which the coat had been hung.

"There was no wind that night, I understand," said Holmes.

"None; but very heavy rain."

"In that case the overcoat was not against the furze bushes, but placed there."

"Yes, it was laid across the bush."

"You fill me with interest. I perceive that the ground has been trampled up a good deal. No doubt many feet have been there since Monday night."

"A piece of matting has been laid here at the side, and we have all stood upon that."

"Excellent."

"In this bag I have one of the boots which Straker wore, one of Fitzroy Simpson's shoes, and a cast horseshoe of Silver Blaze."

"My dear Inspector, you surpass yourself!" Holmes took the bag, and descending into the hollow he pushed the matting into a more central position. Then stretching himself upon his face and leaning his chin upon his hands he made a careful study of the trampled mud in front of him.

"Halloa!" said he, suddenly, "what's this?"

It was a wax vesta, half burned, which was so coated with mud that it looked at first like a little chip of wood.

"I cannot think how I came to overlook it," said the Inspector, with an expression of annoyance.

"It was invisible, buried in the mud. I only saw it because I was looking for it."

"What! You expected to find it?"

"I thought it not unlikely." He took the boots from the bag and compared the impressions of each of them with marks upon the ground. Then he clambered up to the rim of the hollow and crawled about among the ferns and bushes.

"I am afraid that there are no more tracks," said the Inspector. "I have examined the ground very carefully for a hundred yards in each direction."

"Indeed!" said Holmes, rising, "I should not have the impertinence to do it again after what you say. But I should like to take a little walk over the moor before it grows dark, that I may know my ground to-morrow, and I think that I should put this horseshoe into my pocket for luck."

Colonel Ross, who had shown some signs of impatience at my companion's quiet and systematic method of work, glanced at his watch.

"I wish you would come back with me, Inspector," said he. "There are several points on which I should like your advice, and especially as to whether we do not owe it to the public to remove our horse's name from the entries for the Cup."

"Certainly not," cried Holmes, with decision: "I should let the name stand."

The Colonel bowed. "I am very glad to have had your opinion, sir," said he. "You will find us at poor Straker's house when you have finished your walk, and we can drive together into Tavistock."

He turned back with the Inspector, while Holmes and I walked slowly across the moor. The sun was beginning to sink behind the stables of Mapleton, and the long sloping plain in front of us was tinged with gold, deepening into rich, ruddy brown where the faded ferns and brambles caught the evening light. But the glories of the landscape were all wasted upon my companion, who was sunk in the deepest thought.

"It's this way, Watson," he said at last. "We may leave the question of who killed John Straker for the instant, and confine ourselves into finding out what has become of the horse. Now, supposing that he broke away during or after the tragedy, where could he have gone to? The horse is a very gregarious creature. If left by himself his instincts would have been to return to King's Pyland, or go over to Mapleton. Why should he run wild upon the moor? He would surely have been seen by now. And why should gipsies kidnap him? These people always clear out when they hear of trouble, for they do not wish to be pestered by the police. They could not hope to sell such a horse. They would run a great risk and gain nothing by taking him. Surely that is clear."

"Where is he, then?"

"I have already said that he must have gone to King's Pyland or to Mapleton. He is not at King's Pyland, therefore he is at Mapleton. Let us take that as a working hypothesis and see what it leads to. This part of the moor, as the Inspector remarked, is very hard and dry. But it falls away toward Mapleton, and you can see from here that there is a long hollow over yonder, which must have been very wet on Monday night. If our supposition is correct, then the horse must have crossed that, and there is the point where we should look for his tracks."

We had been walking briskly during this conversation, and a few more minutes brought us to the hollow in question. At Holmes's request I walked down to the bank to the right and he to the left, but I had not taken fifty paces before I heard him give a shout, and saw him waving his hand to me. The track of a horse was plainly outlined in the soft earth in front of him, and the shoe which he took from his pocket exactly fitted the impression.

"See the value of imagination," said Holmes. "It is the one quality which Gregory lacks. We imagined what might have happened, acted upon the supposition, and find ourselves justified. Let us proceed."

We crossed the marshy bottom and crossed over a quarter of a mile of dry, hard turf. Again the ground sloped and again we came upon the tracks. Then we lost them for half a mile, but only to pick them up once more quite close to

Mapleton. It was Holmes who saw them first, and he stood pointing with a look of triumph upon his face. A man's track was visible beside the horse's.

"The horse was alone before," I cried.

"Quite so. It was alone before. Halloa, what is this?"

The double track turned sharp off and took the direction of King's Pyland. Holmes whistled, and we both followed along after it. His eyes were on the trail, but I happened to look a little to one side, and saw to my surprise the same tracks coming back again in the opposite direction.

"One for you, Watson," said Holmes, when I pointed it out; "you have saved us a long walk which would have brought us back on our own traces. Let us follow the return track."

We had not to go far. It ended at the paving of asphalt which led up to the gates of the Mapleton stables. As we approached a groom ran out from them.

"We don't want any loiterers around here," he said.

"I only wished to ask a question," said Holmes, with his finger and thumb in his waistcoat pocket. "Should I be too early to see your master, Mr. Silas Brown, if I were to call at five o'clock to-morrow morning?"

"Bless you, sir, if anyone is about he will be, for he is always the first stirring. But here he is, sir, to answer your questions for himself. No, sir, no; it's as much as my place is worth to let me see him touch your money. Afterwards, if you like."

As Sherlock Holmes replaced the half crown which he had drawn from his pocket, a fierce-looking, elderly man strode out from the gate with a hunting-crop swinging in his hand.

"What's this, Dawson?" he cried. "No gossiping! Go about your business! And you—what the devil do you want here?"

"Ten minutes' talk with you, my good sir," said Holmes, in the sweetest of voices.

"I've no time to talk to every gadabout. We want no strangers here. Be off, or you may find a dog at your heels."

Holmes leaned forward and whispered something in the trainer's ear. He stared violently and flushed to the temples.

"It's a lie!" he shouted. "An infernal lie!"

"Very good! Shall we argue about it here in public, or talk it over in your parlour?"

"Oh, come in if you wish to."

Holmes smiled. "I shall not keep you more than a few minutes, Watson," he said. "Now, Mr. Brown, I am quite at your disposal."

It was quite twenty minutes, and the reds had all faded into greys before Holmes and the trainer reappeared. Never have I seen such a change as had been brought about in Silas Brown in that short time. His face was ashy pale, beads of perspiration shone upon his brow, and his hands shook until the hunting-crop wagged like a branch in the wind. His bullying, overbearing manner was all gone too, and he cringed along at my companion's side like a dog with its master.

"Your instructions will be done. It shall be done," said he.

"There must be no mistake," said Holmes, looking round at him. The other winced as he read the menace in his eyes.

"Oh, no, there shall be no mistake. It shall be there. Should I change it first or not?"

Holmes thought a little and then burst out laughing. "No, don't," said he. "I shall write to you about it. No tricks now or—"

"Oh, you can trust me, you can trust me!"

"Yes, I think I can. Well, you shall hear from me to-morrow." He turned upon his heel, disregarding the trembling hand which the other held out to him, and we set off for King's Pyland.

"A more perfect compound of the bully, coward and sneak than Master Silas Brown I have seldom met with," remarked Holmes, as we trudged along together.

"He has the horse, then?"

"He tried to bluster out of it, but I described to him so exactly what his actions had been upon that morning, that he is convinced that I was watching him. Of course, you observed the peculiarly square toes in the impressions, and that his own boots exactly corresponded to them. Again, of course, no subordinate would have dared to have done such a thing. I described to him how when, according to his custom, he was the first down, he perceived a strange horse wandering over the moor; how he went out to it, and his astonishment at recognising from the white forehead which has given the favourite its name that chance had put in his power the only horse which could beat the one upon which he had put his money. Then I described how his first impulse had been to lead him back to King's Pyland, and how the devil had shown him how he could hide the horse until the race was over, and how he had led it back and concealed it at Mapleton. When I told him every detail he gave it up, and thought only of saving his own skin."

"But his stables had been searched."

"Oh, an old horse-faker like him has many a dodge."

"But are you not afraid to leave the horse in his power now, since he has every interest in injuring it?"

"My dear fellow, he will guard it as the apple of his eye. He knows that his only hope of mercy is to produce it safe."

"Colonel Ross did not impress me as a man who would be likely to show much mercy in any case."

"The matter does not rest with Colonel Ross. I follow my own methods, and tell as much or as little as I choose. That is the advantage of being unofficial. I don't know whether you observed it, Watson, but the Colonel's manner has been just a trifle cavalier to me. I am inclined now to have a little amusement at his expense. Say nothing to him about the horse."

"Certainly not, without your permission."

"And, of course, this is all quite a minor point compared to the question of who killed John Straker."

"And you will devote yourself to that?"

"On the contrary, we both go back to London by the night train."

I was thunderstruck by my friend's words. We had only been a few hours in Devonshire, and that he should give up an investigation which he had begun so brilliantly was quite incomprehensible to me. Not a word more could I draw from him until we were back at the trainer's house. The Colonel and the Inspector were awaiting us in the parlour.

"My friend and I return to town by the midnight express," said Holmes. "We have had a charming little breath of your beautiful Dartmoor air."

The Inspector opened his eyes, and the Colonel's lip curled in a sneer.

"So you despair of arresting the murderer of poor Straker," said he.

Holmes shrugged his shoulders. "There are certainly grave difficulties in the way," said he. "I have every hope, however, that your horse will start upon Tuesday, and I beg that you will have your jockey in readiness. Might I ask for a photograph of Mr. John Straker?"

The Inspector took one from an envelope in his pocket and handed it to him.

"My dear Gregory, you anticipate all my wants. If I might ask you to wait here for an instant, I have a question which I should like to put to the maid."

"I must say that I am rather disappointed in our London consultant," said Colonel Ross, bluntly, as my friend left the room. "I do not see that we are any further than when he came."

"At least, you have his assurance that your horse will run," said I.

"Yes, I have his assurance," said the Colonel, with a shrug of his shoulders. "I should prefer to have the horse."

I was about to make some reply in defence of my friend, when he entered the room again.

"Now, gentleman," said he, "I am quite ready for Tavistock."

As we stepped into the carriage one of the stable-lads held the door open for us. A sudden idea seemed to occur to Holmes, for he leaned forward and touched the lad upon the sleeve.

"You have a few sheep in the paddock," he said. "Who attends to them?"

"I do, sir."

"Have you noticed anything amiss with them of late?"

"Well, sir, not of much account; but three of them have gone lame, sir."

I could see that Holmes was extremely pleased, for he chuckled and rubbed his hands together.

"A long shot, Watson; a very long shot," said he, pinching my arm. "Gregory, let me recommend to your attention this singular epidemic among the sheep. Drive on, coachman!"

Colonel Ross still wore an expression which showed the poor opinion which he had formed of my companion's ability, but I saw by the Inspector's face that his attention had been keenly aroused.

"You consider that to be important?" he asked.

"Exceedingly so."

"Is there any other point to which you would wish to draw my attention?"

"To the curious incident of the dog in the night-time."

"The dog did nothing in the night-time."

"That was the curious incident," remarked Sherlock Holmes.

Four days later Holmes and I were again in the train bound for Winchester, to see the race for the Wessex Cup. Colonel Ross met us, by appointment, outside the station, and we drove in his drag to the course beyond the town. His face was grave and his manner was cold in the extreme.

"I have seen nothing of my horse," said he.

"HOLMES WAS EXTREMELY PLEASED."

By Sidney Paget. Originally published in *Strand Magazine,* 1892.

"I suppose that you would know him when you saw him?" asked Holmes.

The Colonel was very angry. "I have been on the turf for twenty years, and never was asked such a question as that before," said he. "A child would know Silver Blaze with his white forehead and his mottled off fore leg."

"How is the betting?"

"Well, that is the curious part of it. You could have got fifteen to one yesterday, but the price has become shorter and shorter, until you can hardly get three to one now."

"Hum!" said Holmes. "Somebody knows something, that is clear!"

As the drag drew up in the inclosure near the grand stand, I glanced at the card to see the entries. It ran:—

Wessex Plate. 50 sovs. each, h ft, with 1,000 sovs. added, for four- and five-year olds. Second L300. Third L200. New course (one mile and five furlongs).

1. *Mr. Heath Newton's The Negro (red cap, cinnamon jacket).*
2. *Colonel Wardlaw's Pugilist (pink cap, blue and black jacket).*
3. *Lord Backwater's Desborough (yellow cap and sleeves).*
4. *Colonel Ross's Silver Blaze (black cap, red jacket).*
5. *Duke of Balmoral's Iris (yellow and black stripes).*
6. *Lord Singleford's Rasper (purple cap, black sleeves).*

"We scratched our other one and put all hopes on your word," said the Colonel. "Why, what is that? Silver Blaze favourite?"

"Five to four against Silver Blaze!" roared the ring. "Five to four against Silver Blaze! Fifteen to five against Desborough! Five to four on the field!"

"There are the numbers up," I cried. "They are all six there."

"All six there! Then my horse is running," cried the Colonel, in great agitation. "But I don't see him. My colours have not passed."

"Only five have passed. This must be he."

As I spoke a powerful bay horse swept out from the weighing inclosure and cantered past us, bearing on its back the well-known black and red of the Colonel.

"That's not my horse," cried the owner. "That beast has not a white hair upon its body. What is this that you have done, Mr. Holmes?"

"Well, well, let us see how he gets on," said my friend, imperturbably. For a few minutes he gazed through my field-glass. "Capital! An excellent start!" he cried suddenly. "There they are, coming round the curve!"

From our drag we had a superb view as they came up the straight. The six horses were so close together that a carpet could have covered them, but half way up the yellow of the Mapleton stable showed to the front. Before they reached us, however, Desborough's bolt was shot, and the Colonel's horse, coming away with a rush, passed the post a good six lengths before its rival, the Duke of Balmoral's Iris making a bad third.

"It's my race anyhow," gasped the Colonel, passing his hand over his eyes. "I confess that I can make neither head nor tail of it. Don't you think that you have kept up your mystery long enough, Mr. Holmes?"

"Certainly, Colonel. You shall know everything. Let us all go round and have a look at the horse together. Here he is," he continued, as we made our way into the weighing inclosure where only owners and their friends find admittance. "You have only to wash his face and his leg in spirits of wine and you will find that he is the same old Silver Blaze as ever."

"You take my breath away!"

"I found him in the hands of a faker, and took the liberty of running him just as he was sent over."

"My dear sir, you have done wonders. The horse looks very fit and well. It never went better in its life. I owe you a thousand apologies for having doubted your ability. You have done me a great service by recovering my horse. You would do me a greater still if you could lay your hands on the murderer of John Straker."

"I have done so," said Holmes, quietly.

The Colonel and I stared at him in amazement. "You have got him! Where is he, then?"

"He is here."

"Here! Where?"

"In my company at the present moment."

The Colonel flushed angrily. "I quite recognise that I am under obligations to you, Mr. Holmes," said he, "but I must regard what you have just said as either a very bad joke or an insult."

Sherlock Holmes laughed. "I assure you that I have not associated you with the crime, Colonel," said he; "the real murderer is standing immediately behind you!"

He stepped past and laid his hand upon the glossy neck of the thoroughbred.

"The horse!" cried both the Colonel and myself.

"Yes, the horse. And it may lessen his guilt if I say that it was done in self-defence, and that John Straker was a man who was entirely unworthy of your confidence. But there goes the bell; and as I stand to win a little on this next race, I shall defer a more lengthy explanation until a more fitting time."

We had the corner of a Pullman car to ourselves that evening as we whirled back to London, and I fancy that the journey was a short one to Colonel Ross as well as to myself, as we listened to our companion's narrative of the events which had occurred at the Dartmoor training stables upon that Monday night, and the means by which he had unraveled them.

"I confess," said he, "that any theories which I had formed from the newspaper reports were entirely erroneous. And yet there were indications there, had they not been overlaid by other details which concealed their true import. I went to Devonshire with the conviction that Fitzroy Simpson was the true culprit, although, of course, I saw that the evidence against him was by no means complete.

"It was while I was in the carriage, just as we reached the trainer's house, that the immense significance of the curried mutton occurred to me. You may remember that I was distrait, and remained sitting after you had all alighted. I was marveling in my own mind how I could possibly have overlooked so obvious a clue."

"I confess," said the Colonel, "that even now I cannot see how it helps us."

"It was the first link in my chain of reasoning. Powdered opium is by no means tasteless. The flavour is not disagreeable, but it is perceptible. Were it mixed with any ordinary dish, the eater would undoubtedly detect it, and would probably eat no more. A curry was exactly the medium which would disguise this taste. By no possible supposition could this stranger, Fitzroy Simpson, have caused curry to be served in the trainer's family that night, and it is surely too monstrous a coincidence to suppose that he happened to come along with powdered opium upon the very night when a dish happened to be served which would disguise the flavour. That is unthinkable. Therefore Simpson becomes eliminated from the case and our attention centres upon Straker and his wife, the only two people who could have chosen curried mutton for supper that night. The opium was added after the dish was set aside for the stable-boy, for the others had the same for supper with no ill effects. Which of them, then, had access to that dish without the maid seeing them?

"Before deciding that question I had grasped the significance of the silence of the dog, for one true inference invariably suggests others. The Simpson incident had shown me that a dog was kept in the stables, and yet, though someone had been in and had fetched out a horse, he had not barked enough to arouse the two lads in the loft. Obviously the midnight visitor was someone whom the dog knew well.

"I was already convinced, or almost convinced, that John Straker went down to the stables in the dead of the night and took out Silver Blaze. For what purpose? For a dishonest one, obviously, or why should he drug his own stable-boy? And yet I was at a loss to know why. There have been cases before now where trainers have made sure of great sums of money by laying against their own horses, through agents, and then preventing them from winning by fraud. Sometimes it is a pulling jockey. Sometimes it is some surer and subtler means. What was it here? I hoped that the contents of his pockets might help me to form a conclusion.

"And they did so. You cannot have forgotten the singular knife which was found in the dead man's hand, a knife which certainly no sane man would choose for a weapon. It was, as Dr. Watson told us, a form of a knife which is used for the most delicate operations known in surgery. And it was to be used for a delicate operation that night. You must know, with your wide experience of turf matters, Colonel Ross, that it is possible to make a slight nick upon the tendons of a horse's ham, and to do it subcutaneously so as to leave absolutely no trace. A horse so treated would develop a slight lameness which would be put down to a strain in exercise or a touch of rheumatism, but never to foul play."

"Villain! Scoundrel!" cried the Colonel.

"We have here the explanation of why John Straker wished to take the horse out on the moor. So spirited a creature would have certainly roused the soundest of sleepers when it felt the prick of a knife. It was absolutely necessary to do it in the open air."

"I have been blind!" cried the Colonel. "Of course that was why he needed the candle, and struck the match."

"Undoubtedly. But in examining his belongings, I was fortunate enough to discover, not only the method of the crime, but even its motives. As a man of the world, Colonel, you know that men do not carry other people's bills about in their pockets. We have most of us quite enough to do to settle our own. I at once concluded that Straker was leading a double life, and keeping a second establishment. The nature of the bill showed that there was a lady in the case, and one who had expensive tastes. Liberal as you are with your servants, one hardly expects that they can buy twenty-guinea walking dresses for their women. I questioned Mrs. Straker as to the dress without her knowing it, and having satisfied myself that it had never reached her, I made a note of the milliner's address, and felt that by calling there with Straker's photograph, I could easily dispose of the mythical Darbyshire.

"From that time on all was plain. Straker had led out the horse to a hollow where his light would be invisible. Simpson, in his flight, had dropped his cravat, and Straker had picked it up with some idea, perhaps, that he might use it in securing the horse's leg. Once in the hollow he had got behind the horse, and had struck a light, but the creature, frightened at the sudden glare, and with the strange instinct of animal's feeling that some mischief was intended, had lashed out, and the steel shoe had struck Straker full on the forehead. He had already, in spite of the rain, taken off his overcoat in order to do his delicate task, and so, as he fell, his knife gashed his thigh. Do I make it clear?"

"Wonderful!" cried the Colonel. "Wonderful! You might have been there."

"My final shot was, I confess, a very long one. It struck me that so astute a man as Straker would not undertake this delicate tendon-nicking without a little practice. What could he practise on? My eyes fell upon the sheep, and I asked a question which, rather to my surprise, showed that my surmise was correct."

"You have made it perfectly clear, Mr. Holmes."

"When I returned to London I called upon the milliner, who at once recognised Straker as an excellent customer, of the name Darbyshire, who had a very dashing wife with a strong partiality for expensive dresses. I have no doubt that this woman had plunged him over head and ears in debt, and so led him into this miserable plot."

"You have explained all but one thing," cried the Colonel. "Where was the horse?"

"Ah, it bolted and was cared for by one of your neighbours. We must have an amnesty in that direction, I think. This is Clapham Junction, if I am not mistaken, and we shall be in Victoria in less than ten minutes. If you care to smoke a cigar in our rooms, Colonel, I shall be happy to give you any other details which might interest you."

By Sidney Paget. Originally published in *Strand Magazine*, 1892.

1.3 Holmes as a Reasoner

We all know of Sherlock Holmes's reputation: outstanding reasoner, master at the "art of deduction," as his creator, Arthur Conan Doyle, puts it. But what is this skill that Holmes so proudly exhibits? Can we use Holmes as a model, his thinking an example useful to us as reasoners?

1.3.1 The Gift of Imagination

Throughout "Silver Blaze" Holmes's strategies for investigating the mystery are set against Inspector Gregory's. Holmes himself says of the difference, "Inspector Gregory, to whom the case has been committed, is an extremely competent officer. Were he but gifted with imagination he might rise to great heights in his profession." According to Holmes, Gregory lacks what presumably Holmes possesses: the gift of imagination. But what is imagination?

Imagination is a term we often use when we don't really know (or don't think we know) how someone comes up with a new idea. Moreover, when we use the term *imagination*, we often assume that the ability to discover a new idea is inborn—something, as Holmes puts it, we are either "gifted with" or not. But if we believe that the difference between Holmes and Gregory is simply talent, we may give up too soon in our attempt to understand what makes Holmes a successful reasoner. And if we believe that imagination (and its cousin, inspiration) are gifts, we could easily give up on ourselves, thinking—erroneously—that if we are not so gifted, we cannot improve our reasoning skills. Instead, let us watch what Holmes actually does that is so successful—what makes him "imaginative." Let us consider Holmes's reasoning a skill that we can learn and emulate.

Holmes, in fact, hints at an important point when he uses the term *imagination:* at times he comes upon an important insight without having observed anything new, anything those around him had missed. Instead he grasps the importance of information already known. How?

One thing Holmes does is to remain open-minded, unbiased about the solution of the mystery. That does not mean he simply gathers all the evidence with no idea of what to expect. Certainly he does not begin by emptying his mind. Consider his explanation for not becoming involved in the investigation when he was first invited to join:

> The fact is that I could not believe it possible that the most remarkable horse in England could long remain concealed, especially in so sparsely inhabited a place as the north of Dartmoor. From hour to hour yesterday I expected to hear that he had been found, and that his abductor was the murderer of John Straker.

Clearly he was making some important assumptions (assumptions the reader probably shares throughout most of the story): that Straker was murdered and the horse abducted. When he does leave for Dartmoor two days later, he explains that initially he had blundered. However, he blundered not by making assumptions, but by holding the wrong ones. Holmes never empties his mind; rather he takes a certain attitude toward his assumptions: he readily reexamines them when the evidence suggests doing so.

But a willingness to reexamine one's assumptions proves, by itself, insufficient. Inspector Gregory is also ready to revise his beliefs in light of further evidence. For example, when he outlines his case against Fitzroy Simpson, he concludes, "The net is drawn pretty close around Fitzroy Simpson, . . . and I believe myself that he is our man. At the same time I recognize that the evidence is purely circumstantial, and that some new development may upset it."

In one sense, Gregory is right: some new development may (and presumably does) upset the case against Fitzroy Simpson. What is important, though, is not *what* those developments are but *how* they are obtained. Holmes succeeds in his thinking to a far greater extent than Gregory because he doesn't wait for these developments to occur. He makes them happen. Whereas Gregory says, "Some new development may upset this," Holmes says, "Let's test this idea; how can I produce a new development that would upset it?" How does he produce such developments? In one way, the answer is deceptively simple: he asks himself questions, and then seeks the answers.

1.3.2 The Questioning Mind

Let's look in some detail at what Holmes actually does in the story to produce such developments. Recall that Holmes began thinking about the mystery by adopting the same view of the "crime" as did Inspector Gregory. He assumed that Silver Blaze had been abducted and that John Straker had been murdered somehow in the process. So Holmes began thinking about the case by asking:

1. Who killed John Straker and abducted Silver Blaze?

    The evidence initially points to Fitzroy Simpson. Gregory's case against Simpson has many strong points, and most of the objections Holmes initially voices to Gregory are easily answerable. After their discussion of the hypothesis, Holmes's objections to it, and Gregory's answers to these, the two investigators arrive at something of an impasse. It is at this point that Holmes tries to produce developments that might upset the case against

Simpson. He reasons that if Simpson is the culprit, all the known facts of the case must fit this hypothesis. So he proceeds by testing whether in fact they do.

As Holmes points out, the turning point in the case occurs when he begins thinking about the significance of the curried mutton. Remember that the stable boy, Hunter, was drugged with opium powder placed in curried mutton. Relying on his past knowledge that powdered opium has a strong flavor, Holmes reasons that it is unlikely someone seeking to drug a person with opium would put it in just any food; the culprit would want to put it in food with a strong enough flavor (such a curry) to mask the opium. As a result, Holmes rules out the possibility that the opium was administered coincidentally on the evening that curried mutton was served. And since Simpson was a stranger, his administering the drug to the curry would have been a coincidence. Holmes therefore eliminates Simpson from the case.

Notice that the new development comes not from new information, but rather from careful thinking and testing of the proposed solution. If Simpson is out of the picture, though, where might Holmes turn? He proceeds by building on the progress he has just made. He can now limit the suspects by questioning the drugging:

2. Who drugged Hunter?

Since the person who drugged Hunter knew that curried mutton was being served, the culprit must have been in a position to select the menu for dinner. Who could make such a choice? Holmes answers, John Straker and his wife. Thus Holmes is led to ask:

3. Did Straker or his wife drug Hunter?

If Holmes knew who had access to the dish without the maid's finding out, he would know which of them drugged Hunter. Unfortunately, he has no way of discovering the answer directly; instead he has to proceed indirectly, by grasping the significance of another clue: the dog didn't bark.

4. Why didn't the dog bark?

Remembering that the dog barked wildly when Simpson first approached the stable, Holmes finds it particularly interesting that the dog did not bark late that night when someone removed Silver Blaze from the stable. Holmes figures, of course, that the dog didn't bark because it was well acquainted with the person who entered the stable. He concludes, then, that it was Straker rather than his wife who drugged Hunter. This conclusion suggests the next question:

5. Why would Straker want to drug Hunter?

    Most likely, Straker did not want Hunter to see him removing the horse from the stable later that night. But, then,

6. Why wouldn't Straker want Hunter to see him removing Silver Blaze from the stable?

    Surely, as the trainer, he rightfully had access to the horse. Holmes decides that most likely Straker had some dishonest purpose in mind, one he would not want to be observed carrying out. So he must ask,

7. What dishonest purpose might Straker have had?

    Knowing that other trainers have, on occasion, bet against their own horses and then fixed the race, Holmes hypothesizes that Straker may have planned to do the same. Of course Holmes recognizes that he must test this hypothesis to see if it accords well with all the known facts of the case. For example, if his hypothesis is correct, he must ask,

8. How could Straker have prevented Silver Blaze from winning?

    A trainer cannot throw a race by himself the way a jockey can. Here Holmes's background knowledge proves crucial to solving the case. He knows that one can cut a tendon subcutaneously so that the horse appears simply to be strained. If Straker had indeed intended to cut Silver Blaze's tendon, he would have need of the cataract knife, which is, after all, a very unlikely weapon. (Holmes's hypothesis thereby explains this piece of evidence better than Gregory's.) And he simply may have laid his coat on a bush, accounting for its peculiar placement. Later, the discovery of the lame sheep further confirms this hypothesis. But we still have a loose thread, for

9. Why would Straker need to take Silver Blaze out of the stable to cut the tendon?

    Being a spirited horse, Silver Blaze would not have stood quietly while being cut; therefore, to avoid detection, Straker may have wanted him far from the stable.

    Holmes's hypothesis that it was Straker who drugged Hunter and removed the horse from the stable seems so far to account for the details of the crime and how it was allegedly committed. But Holmes presses the matter further, looking for something that might suggest his hypothesis wrong. For instance, Straker's motivation for the crime is not clear, so Holmes asks,

10. Why would Straker want to defraud Colonel Ross?

    After all, Straker, a long-time, trusted employee, would need a strong motive for such a daring crime as this. The milliner's bill suggests to Holmes that Straker may have been leading a double life, with a wife and a mistress, which required more money than he made. Holmes points out that even a generous salary from Colonel Ross would not have satisfied demands for dresses as expensive as the one in the milliner's bill. (Holmes verifies also that the dress was not ordered for Straker's wife by questioning her about the "dove-coloured silk with ostrich-feather trimming," a dress she claims she never owned.) So Straker appears to have had ample motivation to seek a quick profit by defrauding his employer. What we need to know now is

11. How did Straker die?

That Straker removed Silver Blaze from the stable seems pretty certain, but unless Holmes can explain Straker's own death, he cannot consider the mystery satisfactorily solved. Again Holmes must answer this question indirectly by asking related questions. Noticing that the tracks lead away from the depression in the moor where Straker was found dead, Holmes concludes that the horse either got away or was set loose. And since he could find no incision when he located Silver Blaze, Holmes concludes that the horse got loose before Straker could cut the tendon. However, he knows that Straker was an experienced horse trainer, so he must ask,

12. How did Silver Blaze get away from Straker?

Recalling the burnt match and candle found at the scene, Holmes hypothesizes that the horse bolted when Straker lit the match. Because Silver Blaze was not wearing a bridle, he could have escaped, and in the process he could have kicked Straker in the head, causing fatal wounds.

1.3.3 Scrutinizing the Master's Reasoning

Holmes is indeed a model reasoner from whom we may learn much. But a model reasoner need not be a perfect reasoner. Perhaps we would not trust Sherlock's (fictional) humanity if he were too perfect! In fact, a reader interested in how well the mystery has been solved should be asking a few questions.

For instance, should Holmes have ruled out suspicion of the maid? Holmes reasons that whoever drugged Hunter must have had control of the menu, or else the element of coincidence could not be ruled out. But is *control* of the menu necessary to eliminate the coincidence, or just *prior knowledge*? If simple knowledge were sufficient, the circle of suspects in the drugging would have widened to include the maid as well as the

Strakers. It seems Holmes eliminates a suspect on the basis of a faulty assumption. The omission of the maid may seem a minor flaw; after all, the remainder of the evidence does point pretty clearly to Straker. But should we be comfortable with Sherlock's solution?

Other questions can be raised about it. Holmes's theory asks us to imagine something that, on the face of it, seems a bit implausible. Holmes suggests that Straker, a highly experienced horseman, had gone to the moor because Silver Blaze was too spirited to permit the trainer to make the incision without the horse's protest. Nevertheless, on the moor, where he has nothing to tie the horse to, Straker supposedly lit a match while holding a candle. Wouldn't an experienced horseman expect a reaction from a nervous racehorse to a nearby flash of light?

Another question concerns loose ends. Presumably Straker's motive was monetary gain. But since he was well known as the trainer, could he have wagered against his own horse and then collected the winnings without being recognized? Such a question could lead Holmes to look for an accomplice, but Holmes doesn't pursue this angle.

Of course, were we able to put such questions to him, Holmes may be able to answer satisfactorily. And even if his account is not in the end flawless, we still have much to learn from him.

1.3.4 Holmes's Strategy

One of those lessons is not to remain content with answers that we haven't tested. Holmes himself devotes the majority of his energy to asking himself questions, many small questions that break the mystery into manageable parts.

Rather than possessing a mysterious power to ask just the right questions, Holmes is guided by his attitude toward solving the mystery: he looks continually for evidence that may prove his hypotheses wrong—disconfirming evidence. Holmes remains unsatisfied with simply explaining the bits of evidence and answering challenges to that explanation. He actively questions in order to disprove hypotheses.

How does he proceed? First, he follows the leads of his previous questioning. Notice how all the questioning we have examined interlocks; his questioning is never haphazard, never disconnected. Second, he relies on his accumulated background knowledge (e.g., the flavor of opium, how to cut a horse's tendon subcutaneously) to suggest hypotheses and avenues to test them. And third, he thinks carefully about what sorts of facts may be relevant to investigate the mystery.

Holmes's investigation progresses so much further than Gregory's because Holmes comes to see the mystery as a very different type of problem than Gregory does: Holmes eventually sees the mystery as a death

"NEVER MIND INSPIRATION. I NEED BACKGROUND MATERIAL ON ATOMIC PHYSICS."

© 1997 by Sidney Harris

Inspiration is delightful—when it happens—but you can't count on it. Besides, as Holmes demonstrates, little progress can be made in thinking without appropriate background information.

and disappearance rather than a murder and abduction. Thinking of the mystery as a murder and abduction narrows the potential solutions Gregory can consider. For example, if Straker were murdered, then Gregory must look for a murderer, someone who intentionally killed Straker. But, of course, no one murdered him. And once Holmes stops assuming that Straker was murdered, he is able to see all sorts of facts as potentially relevant to the solution of the mystery (the match, the lame sheep, the milliner's bill), facts that seem unimportant to Gregory.

What is relevant to solving a problem depends very much on what kind of problem it is. For example, had the story been concerned with the medical phenomena surrounding Straker's death (we could imagine a fanciful story of this type written for readers of a medical journal), the issue might have been the nature of events causing death following such a blow to the head. If so, questions concerning the nature of the nervous system, the flow of oxygen to the brain—i.e., events within Straker's body following the blow to his head—become most important, whereas such details, though factual, lack significance for the story as Doyle actually tells it. It makes every bit of difference in solving a problem, answering a question, or addressing an issue that you understand what is relevant to that problem, question, or issue. It is Holmes's reassessment of what is involved in the mystery that enables him to find his way to a solution.

Holmes discovers very few new facts in the course of his investigation. Instead, he reconsiders the significance of the facts he already possesses in light of the questions he poses to himself. Moreover, he discovers new facts (e.g., the lame sheep) only because his questions and answers have enabled him to see where he might look for a new fact.

Finally, Holmes accepts no solution to the mystery until he satisfies himself that he cannot produce any more developments that will upset it.

1.3.5 Strategies in Brief

1. *The Critical Attitude:* Holmes takes an aggressive approach toward finding out which of his ideas will hold water. He actively tests hypotheses by trying to disprove them, not simply by finding evidence to support them. He tests them, and generates new hypotheses, by asking and answering questions. And he doesn't give up until he can produce no further developments that can upset his case.
2. *Background Knowledge:* Holmes relies on his wide-ranging knowledge to check for possible problems in his line of reasoning and to suggest new hypotheses.
3. *Defining What Is at Issue:* Holmes reflects not only on the facts of the case but also on the nature of the mystery. Rather than simply trying to amass more facts, he considers what is relevant to solving the mystery, and weighs whether he is asking the right questions in the first place.

1.4   The Rhetorical Situation

Holmes tells us at the end of the story that the puzzle of the curried mutton "was the first link in my chain of reasoning," and from that clue we are able to piece together his order of questioning—but we, the readers, must do that, for Holmes does not lay it out neatly for us. Instead he divulges what information he wishes when he wishes to divulge it. For instance, when he allows Silver Blaze to remain at King's Pyland to the dismay of Watson, who fears that Colonel Ross will not show any mercy, Holmes says, "The matter does not rest with Colonel Ross. I . . . tell as much or as little as I choose." We may ask, then, how he decides what he wishes to tell, to whom and at what moment he wishes to tell it, and in what regard we, his readers, hold him as a result of his decisions. These are the very questions any writer (or speaker) must ask:

1. How do I discover what I want to say?
2. How do I want to affect my audience?
3. How can I present my ideas so that my audience considers them?
4. How do I want my readers to regard me?

These questions broaden our awareness of Holmes's task: he must consider not only the data, or clues, in the case, but also how he will present his findings to others involved in the case—what we may call the "rhetorical situation." Holmes seeks the best conclusion, the one that best accounts for the evidence, as does any good reasoner and writer. But he does not lay out his reasoning either as he develops it (we must reconstruct his process) or in the tight fashion of a case thoroughly worked out. What guides him?

We can answer by shifting our context. Along with Holmes we have thus far considered our task to solve a mystery, although, prodded by Holmes, we have shifted our definition of what mystery needs to be solved. However, there exists a mind behind Holmes's: Arthur Conan Doyle's. Doyle is the writer who invented the story, and his purpose is different from Holmes's and ours as we follow Holmes. Doyle wished to entertain readers, to hold them in suspense, to tantalize them with details they could mold into their own theories. Doyle determines what Holmes will divulge and when, according to a plan that differs from Holmes's. Let us consider these four questions from Doyle's point of view.

1.4.1 How Do I Consider What I Want to Say?

Most writers begin by considering the nature of their subject: what is known about it, the importance of the issues, whether a dilemma can be solved, the viability of different positions, and its context. Doyle presents the case as significant: it involves a human death and the disappearance of not just any horse but a marvel. In other words, it matters. Moreover, it is not easily resolved; reasonable people may see the matter differently. Yet it can be resolved, and the story argues for a particular resolution.

Doyle lays the story out using a common strategy. First, he shows us the major issue and that it matters: Watson says, "There was but one problem before the public which could challenge his powers of analysis, and that was the singular disappearance of the favourite for the Wessex Cup, and the tragic murder of its trainer." And he quickly establishes Holmes's ability to address the problem with his display of ingenuity in determining the speed of the train. Second, in Holmes's scenario Doyle gives us the primary case in opposition to the one for which the story will argue, and Watson confirms that the Inspector's theory is much as Holmes predicted. Holmes raises some objections to this hypothesis, which the Inspector counters. Third, Doyle devotes the bulk of the story to detailing Holmes's finesse in figuring out the mystery, using Watson to let us know when Holmes has an insight that he does not immediately reveal.

1.4.2 How Do I Want to Affect My Audience?

Doyle's purpose in writing the mystery is to delight his readers with both the challenge of the mystery and Holmes's ingenuity.

1.4.3 How Can I Present My Ideas So That My Readers Consider Them?

Doyle must consider three different aspects of his readers' response to his story: their attitude toward the subject, their knowledge of its particulars, and the way they will use it. He can assume that most of his readers enjoy the suspense of a mystery story; that is, most of his readers look favorably on his task. He does not need to overcome any serious resistance in order to engage his readers. And since the story is fiction, he is in full control of what his readers know about the case. Since his readers come to the story for entertainment, he arranges the details to provide it. He lays the story out with our needs continuously in mind. He begins with what we need to know first: the major issue and that it is worth our time. He continues with what we need next: the status of thinking on the issue, current hypotheses, and the methods and questions of those who have already considered the matter. Then he divulges enough information for us to form our own hypotheses but keeps us in suspense. He chooses this method not because it is the single best method of organization, but because it is what we expect *when reading a mystery*.

1.4.4 How Do I Want My Readers to Regard Me?

Because "Silver Blaze" is fiction, Doyle's readers respond to him obliquely, through the voices of his fictionalized characters and the skill with which he creates the story. In part, they respond to the style in which he writes, a matter that will be taken up in Chapter 9. And in part, they respond to his "ethical appeal."

Writers can appeal to three different responses in readers. Clearly the most common is the "rational appeal." Doyle relies almost exclusively on this appeal, and our text focuses primarily on it as well. It is an appeal to the thinking mind—both the critical and the intuitive. Second, writers may wish to rouse readers' emotions, making an "emotional appeal," to underscore the rational appeal or to stimulate the readers to action. Doyle chooses largely to avoid emotional appeal in this story, instead confronting the readers at every moment with Holmes's skill as a reasoner. (Indeed, the emotional appeal can be abused, for instance when it leads us to discount our reasoned response rather than enhance it.) Third, writers appeal with their very presence, felt in the style of the writing and in the presentation of material, creating an "ethical appeal." We can speak of high ethical appeal when we are inclined to listen to a writer or low ethical appeal when we feel moved to discount what the writer is saying.

Most of us would agree that Doyle achieves a fairly high ethical appeal. We're willing to listen to his story and accept Holmes's solution to the mystery. We know of Doyle even before we read "Silver Blaze," through his reputation as a master of the mystery story, but previous reputation counts much less than the way writers present themselves in the writing at hand. Why do we listen to Doyle? We appreciate his skill in crafting a story that includes all the important clues without making the case seem too easy and without holding any necessary clues until the very end, frustrating our ability to form hypotheses along with Holmes. In addition, we respond to his characterization of Holmes. Holmes studies the case thoroughly; he does his homework. He reasons well. We never catch Holmes in sloppy thinking, nor do we ever feel he misleads us. Moreover, Holmes is respectful. He shows respect not only for the case itself but also for everyone involved in it: Gregory and his hypotheses, Watson and us as we follow the master. Holmes approaches the case and Doyle the mystery story in such a way that predisposes us to be convinced.

Thus, the rhetorical plan underlying Doyle's strategies encompasses all four questions. "Silver Blaze" is a mystery story, and that context controls what information is relevant to the story as well as its presentation. Doyle's purpose is to entertain readers and challenge their ability to solve a mystery. His audience, he may well assume, consists primarily of readers who delight in the difficulty of Holmes's task and reasoning and who will therefore be favorably predisposed to consider Holmes's hypotheses. And he creates his hero, Holmes, in such a way that we readers admire him tremendously—and may want to emulate his reasoning.

1.5 A Hint of What's to Come

In this first chapter we have looked at "Silver Blaze" from two angles: as a model of the reasoner's art, displayed in the skill and character of Holmes, and as a piece of writing in which Doyle makes a variety of decisions in order to succeed. In what follows, we shall pursue in greater detail the threads introduced here, explaining and practicing the skills manifested by both reasoner and writer. A major theme of this book is that writing and reasoning are closely connected activities; we stand to learn much by using each to enhance the other. The following chapters pursue in a variety of contexts important connections between the arts of the writer and the reasoner.

2

Defining a Topic for Thinking and Writing

2.1 Specifying the Issue

When you set out to write, you may find a variety of demands surrounding your selection of a topic. You may be writing for a class, a publication, or for yourself. You may have been assigned a topic, or you may be free to design it yourself within certain confines (e.g., the aims of a course, the nature of a publication). Perhaps you are writing simply to expand your own understanding. In most cases, whether you have decided to pursue a topic because it interests you or because you have been asked to do so by someone else, you need to do some planning before you will be ready to write.

Clearly you will need to know something about your topic if you are going to write intelligently about it to someone who will listen to you. You will have to learn about your subject matter through some kind of investigation (observation, library research, laboratory experimentation, interview, reflection, and any other means of obtaining information and developing your thought on a topic). But before you are ready even to investigate, you need to do some preliminary thinking about your topic, about who will read your paper, and about the particular constraints of the assignment.

What goes into specifying a topic for thought or writing before you can investigate it fruitfully? Topics you may wish to reflect on and write about may be either quite general or quite specific, ranging from the simple "Write a paper on abortion" to "Explain and defend a utilitarian position on the ethics of abortions for women in the second and third trimesters of pregnancy, when those women's lives are not threatened by the pregnancy, and when they have not become pregnant as a result of rape or incest." There is little doubt that you would need to specify further the topic if working on the first of these assignments, but even in the latter case you have work to do before you undertake any research.

To see what needs to be done, assume that you attend a university that holds an essay contest every year with cash prizes for the best entries, and you decide to enter the contest because you can use the cash.

Besides, the contest rules ask you to write about birth, a topic about which you have some interest. You set out to complete the essay by the deadline. Where can you start?

You could go to the library and look up *birth* and some related terms, but which ones? *Babies, fetuses, obstetrics, pregnancy, abortion, gynecology, birth trauma, natural childbirth, amniocentesis,* and *Dr. Spock* all come immediately to mind; how many others are lurking on other computer screens? A typical university library has probably hundreds of entries accessible through this short list of terms. The project begins to look like a rather massive and oppressive undertaking. Maybe that $100 prize isn't worth it after all. You look again at the contest rules: nothing more is said about the nature of the topic you are to write on—just "birth." Clearly birth is a pretty wide-ranging topic. In fact, you must specify your topic further *before* you can hope to undertake useful research.

2.1.1 Two Strategies: Mystery and Conflict

Most writers begin by thinking about the information they have on a topic, just as you will want to, but simply cataloguing information will not necessarily lead you closer to a topic, just as Inspector Gregory's survey of information did not lead him to discover how Straker died or Silver Blaze disappeared. Instead, at this point you need to determine what kind of issues birth involves. Clearly there are many possible issues to address under the heading *birth*. One way to begin clarifying your topic is to list some questions that intrigue you about birth. You then have a list of topics ready for further development.

2.1.1a Mystery   Does something on this list strike you as particularly mysterious about birth? You may find it mysterious, for example, that someone can form a deep emotional attachment to a fetus—that is, to someone who does not interact socially with you, someone whom you cannot even see. Focusing on what seems fundamentally puzzling to you can help make your writing more authentic: it may reflect your own search for answers to a serious question. At the same time, your writing can become a significant tool in your own efforts to deepen your understanding when you are seriously engaged with a question.

2.1.1b Conflict   Does anything on the list pose a conflict about birth? That is, do some questions allow reasonable people to disagree? If so, the topic is ripe for persuasive writing. However, you must guard against superficial conflicts. The mere fact that you can find someone who disagrees with you won't, by itself, make the conflict a serious one worth investing your time as a writer. To avoid pseudoconflict, pose the question as a dilemma: Do you (and other reasonable people) want to have both options but find it impossible to have them both simultaneously?

For example, you may be intrigued by the question of who should have the responsibility and right to make decisions about the prenatal care of fetuses. On the one hand, you believe the mother ought to be responsible for choices that affect her fetus and herself. You think mothers should be informed about prenatal care but not coerced into a single course of action. On the other hand, recognizing the serious effects certain drugs and smoking can have on fetuses, you also see the value in requiring expectant mothers to modify their behavior while pregnant. Obviously, you cannot have both of these options at the same time.

Or you may be concerned with the relative safety for mother and baby of various birth traditions and technologies. You may believe that the fetus and mother will both fare better the fewer the drugs and the less intrusive the medical procedures at birth. You are especially wary of unnecessary cesarean sections. But you also recognize that some fetuses do become stressed and that some medical procedures, including cesarean sections, do in fact make birth safer for fetus and mother.

Both of these dilemmas encourage you to identify the most important issues. You cannot rest comfortably with arguing the "right" decision over a "wrong" decision, for you can see from the outset that any answer will be to some degree imperfect. Yet you cannot ignore the questions entirely, because some decision must be made, again and again, as women carry and give birth to babies. Questions that you can state as dilemmas provide you with topics worthy of your time to reflect and write as well as topics worthy of your readers' time to read and consider.

2.2 Placing Your Topic in Context

Once you have selected from among such competing interests, you still need to give your topic a somewhat sharper definition. You may have noticed that the sample questions fall (roughly) into different frameworks: some are questions of a medical nature (safety of birth traditions), while others are primarily ethical (control of birth decisions), and still others are biological or psychological in orientation (emotional attachment to the fetus). Once you identify your topic as psychological or ethical or medical in nature, you have already done some work on identifying the broader framework in which your topic falls.

Understanding what that framework is, and what it implies, can help you further define the topic. When you read the Sherlock Holmes story, you understand that he is a detective and that the issues he is concerned with generally fall into the framework of suspenseful mysteries; you understand that often such mysteries concern some danger to a person that Holmes must remove through employing "the science of deduction," as his creator, Sir Arthur Conan Doyle, calls it. Just by understanding the nature of the enterprise in which Holmes is engaged, you know quite a bit about the story before you even begin.

Analogously, if you decide to pursue the question of who should have the right and responsibility to determine prenatal care, you know your question is an ethical one, and recognizing this context will help you to understand what kind of investigation to conduct into your topic. For example, it may help you to realize that, although powerful traditions may place much of the responsibility for such decisions in the hands of the medical experts, it does not follow that this tradition is the ethically correct one. "That is the way things have always been done here" is not a convincing reason in ethics.

Of course, the fact that a topic falls within one framework does not preclude any other perspective from having some bearing on it: you could not go very far in answering ethical questions about birth, for example, without factual information, often including medical, psychological, and historical information. So you have to be careful not to be narrow-minded in identifying the scope of an issue. Nonetheless, identifying such a framework can help you know how to focus your investigation. Even though other factual information is relevant to sorting out ethical questions about birth, not all is: knowing that the framework is primarily ethical helps you to know what additional information would be worth having and what can be ignored. This is what we mean by saying that an issue must be situated within a "context."

The context of a topic is like the walls of a room: some things are in the room and other things are outside the room, depending on the configuration of the walls. Whatever is found outside the space defined by those walls is "irrelevant," inappropriate to the context, and therefore should be ignored. The walls define what is within and what is without the scope of our concern.

For example, in "Silver Blaze" Holmes is concerned with solving a mystery. At first he thinks the mystery is a murder and abduction. Thinking of it that way immediately makes certain things relevant. Where there is a murder there must be a murderer, and that means someone who intentionally brings about the death of the victim. Hence the intentions and motivation of those involved become relevant. Of course, if Straker's death were accidental, no such intention need be involved. Holmes' success in solving the mystery results from his redefinition of the issue in such a way that a new context is specified: new things become relevant and other things become irrelevant. The configuration of the walls changes.

One of the important lessons of Holmes's shift is that understanding the context of an issue is not the same as taking a position on it. In other

© 1997 by Sidney Harris

The temptation to allow irrelevant issues distract us can be quite powerful!

words, knowing what is involved in the problem you are trying to solve is not the same thing as having a solution. Rival solutions to the same problem must have much in common: the same things are relevant to the problem in both cases. (That is what enables us to talk to each other when we disagree.) In that sense, Holmes and Gregory do not really have rival hypotheses because they are not addressing the same issue. To make his solution stick, Holmes has to argue that the problem Gregory is trying to solve is not the problem that needs to be addressed. Understanding an issue, then, is not a matter of knowing what view to take on it. Rather, it is a matter of knowing what is relevant and what is irrelevant to thinking about it.

2.2.1 Beginning with the Framework

Perhaps you don't yet have a particular question about birth that you would like to answer in writing your prizewinning essay. What then? You might start by trying to identify a framework within which to think of your topic. That is, you can begin by thinking of broad categories in which your topic might fall: birth as a medical, psychological, ethical, religious, or biological issue. Then you can try to spell out what some of the biological, ethical, or religious issues are and select one that interests you.

To proceed, you can identify some of the major categories within such frameworks without worrying at the outset about specific applications to your topic. For example, you might begin by listing some typical categories one thinking about medical issues might consider. Here are just two:

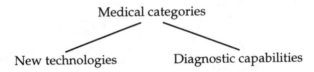

By asking how birth fits into such categories, you may begin to see some fruitful issues emerging. The following chart shows how thinking about the general medical category of diagnostic capability can lead you to more specific questions to investigate. As the tree descends to the second level, you begin to see specific diagnostic capabilities emerge.

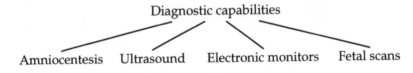

For each of these categories several obvious factual questions can be raised that might lead you to a topic. For example,

What is this test used to diagnose?
What are its risks for the fetus?
What are the risks for the mother?
Who should have such diagnosis and who should not?

These questions are fairly obvious; you can raise all of them before you do any preliminary research. Once you select a lead and do a bit more investigating, you can sharpen the series of questions to apply more concretely to your topic, eliminating those that are less fertile and discovering some new ones.

2.2.2 Moving from One Framework to Another

Alternatively, you can see how such categories can lead to interesting questions within another framework. Suppose, for example, that you want to consider birth from an ethical standpoint. Even though the questions just raised are factual, it isn't hard to see how they might lead to a host of ethical questions. For example, consider one of the diagnostic tools mentioned, amniocentesis. The following tree shows some of its possible uses:

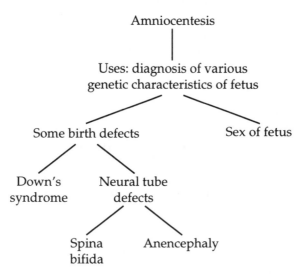

As you look at the tree, you can see that amniocentesis provides information both about conditions that are threatening to the fetus's well-being and those that are nonthreatening. If you also ask why you want such information, you get such answers as these:

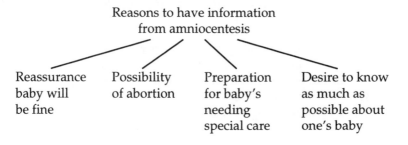

Looking at the data displayed in these trees, you can ask some important ethical questions about amniocentesis. Here are just two that might arise at this point:

1. At present, since no intervention exists to correct or alter the conditions discovered by amniocentesis, women can opt only to abort or to continue the pregnancy. Obviously the larger question of whether abortion is ethical will be pressing here. But you can raise another question without settling that large issue: should amniocentesis be recommended and performed when the pregnant woman herself rejects the possibility of abortion?
2. Other questions you can raise concern the use of information about nonthreatening conditions. For example, is it a good thing to know the sex of one's baby before it is born? Should one abort to select for the sex of one's baby?

Situating a topic in a wider framework, and then exploring its context, leads you to see the kind of issue you are approaching and to begin asking questions. The context also helps you to know what evidence counts in answering those questions and what alternative views may be held on the issue.

Now you may be ready to investigate your subject through library research, interviewing, or some other form of investigation. Most productive of all will be research that enlarges your awareness of the variety of positions possible on your topic. Before you proceed too far, however, consider the rest of the rhetorical situation: how you want to affect your readers, how you want those readers to respond to your paper, how those readers are likely to use your investigation and what they may object to in it, and the way in which you, the writer, wish your readers to regard you.

Exercises 2.1–2.2

I. Specify an issue about birth worth investigating, and put it in a context that helps you to discover what is relevant and what is irrelevant to thinking about it. Answer the following questions to guide you in this process.

A. Ask two questions about birth that you find truly mysterious (that is, questions you cannot answer but would like to). Explain why these questions seem mysterious to you.
B. Where do you see the possibility of significant conflict concerning birth? Pose the issue as a dilemma.

C. Consider each of the following categories within the medical framework and apply them as best you can to birth, first by listing some specifics you know about, then by raising some factual questions about these specifics.

1. New technologies
2. Intervention and prevention
3. Alternatives to traditional medical approaches
4. Changing conceptions of doctors, patients
5. Malpractice suits and insurance

D. Show how the questions you raised in Question C can lead you to raise other questions within another framework, such as an ethical, religious, or historical one.
E. Explain briefly what is relevant and what is irrelevant to investigating three of the issues you developed in response to the preceding four questions.

II. Identify two different dilemmas suggested by the following data. Then write a two-page editorial convincing your readers that the dilemmas are important enough to warrant investigation. Do *not* try to resolve the dilemmas; simply argue that they exist.

A. On TV crime occurs about ten times as often as it does in real life.
B. In Saturday morning cartoons violent episodes occur every two minutes.
C. Thousands of studies have found a link between violence on TV and aggressive or violent behavior in children and adolescents.
D. Studies show that children and adults who watch TV a lot view the world as a more violent place than people who watch less TV.
E. Some studies indicate a relationship between poor school performance and heavy TV watching.
F. Obviously, when children watch many hours of TV, they are removed from the active pursuits of reading or playing with other children.
G. A definite link exists between TV viewing and childhood obesity.
H. Thirty percent of the commercials aired during children's programming advertise food, much of it cereal loaded with sugar.
I. On TV you have to be thin to be popular, to be loved, or to get a job.
J. On TV men outnumber women about 3 to 1. Whites outnum-

ber minorities disproportionately. Elderly people are rarely shown on TV, nor are sick, retarded, handicapped, or fat people.

K. Lawyers, doctors, athletes, detectives, and entertainers are represented far more often than other occupations.

L. Some studies suggest that shows highlighting powerful superheroes foster aggressive behavior in children.

M. Children who tend toward aggressive behavior are affected much more than less aggressive children. Apparently the more passive child is able to process the aggression without adopting it.

N. Young children who watch a lot of TV display less imagination, and in their play the aggressive overpower the more passive.

O. TV news can be violent and upsetting to young children.

P. "PG" in film rating stands for "parental guidance"; PG films often include questionable language and violence.

III. Define at least one dilemma suggested by the following data. Decide who must recognize the importance of this dilemma in order to make sound decisions, and write a letter to that person explaining the ramifications of the dilemma you have identified.

A. Politicians have started to advocate mandatory pre-kindergarten classes for 4-year-olds and all-day, academically oriented kindergartens for 5-year-olds. The mayor has promised that by fall every 4-year-old in the city will be enrolled in some kind of pre-kindergarten program.

B. Some kindergartens require entrance tests, give report cards, and have graduation requirements.

C. Louise Bates Ames, associate director of an early childhood education research organization, says, "It's all this super-baby nonsense—pushing children to do things that they aren't ready for. What many parents don't understand is that 4-year-olds aren't ready for academic work, and the average 5-year-old isn't ready for all-day school."

D. For the past several decades most American educators viewed preschool and kindergarten as a low-pressure, non-academic experience in which children would acquire schoolroom skills, such as sitting quietly and answering questions in complete sentences.

E. In the mid-1960s most early childhood educators believed that 3- and 4-year-olds should be involved in some type of preparation for kindergarten and helped launch Head Start, a preschool program for the economically disadvantaged, and similar programs.

F. In 1983 slightly more that 38 percent of preschoolers were enrolled in some kind of early childhood education program, double the number in 1970.

G. A good prekindergarten program, according to early childhood educators, has several goals. It should help the child with simple tasks, such as holding a pencil correctly and drawing a recognizable figure. It should reduce fear of speaking in groups and encourage expression in complete sentences. Math games should teach children to count, and reading programs should help children to recognize their own names, the letters of the alphabet, and the sounds of letters.

H. A study of a Head Start program in Michigan, spanning sixteen years, supported the perception that preschool classes can give children a boost toward success in their academic careers. More Head Start graduates completed high school, entered college, and held higher-paying jobs than their peers who did not attend this preschool program.

I. Ames says that successful students are produced because "parents become involved in their children's academic careers. Encouraging this involvement isn't necessary for middle-class parents because they are already involved." She says it is therefore a mistake to apply programs designed for economically disadvantaged children to children from middle-class backgrounds.

J. Larry Dougherty, assistant superintendent of the Greenwich, Connecticutt school district, says, "The screening process is not used as a gatekeeper. It is a way to find the appropriate program for the student. Screening also gives teachers a sense of how kids cope with school environment."

K. Carol Goren, one of the designers of the Santa Monica-Malibu United School District's kindergarten program in California, says, "Many of the children who are coming to school today already have spent a full day at school and even longer in a day-care situation. These kids are ready for a full school day."

L. The more academic kindergartens still contain the traditional game playing, painting, and listening to the teacher read a story. The academic features have been added for those children who are prepared.

M. Parents of children not prepared are often advised to send their children to a preschool in preparation for kindergarten.

N. Ames says, "Our data show that one-third of children in kindergarten weren't physically or psychologically ready to be in school. A lot of children who are labeled as being learning disabled are actually just a grade ahead of where they should be."

IV. Define two dilemmas raised by the following data and place each in an appropriate context. Then decide which of the data are relevant and which irrelevant to investigate each dilemma.

Details of a Play:
A. It occurred in the New York Yankee Stadium during the July 24, 1983 game between the Yankees and the Kansas City Royals.
B. George Brett, a Kansas City third baseman, hit a ball out of the park in fair territory, 450–500 feet.
C. Billy Martin, manager of the Yankees, complained to home-plate umpire Tim McClelland that Brett's bat had pine tar above the 18-inch mark.
D. There is a rule against pine tar, normally used on the lower 18 inches of the bat to enhance the grip, from going above 18 inches. The rule grew out of the practice of pounding nails into the bat illegally to drive balls further and then covering the nails with pine tar. There is no prescribed punishment for breaking this rule.
E. Umpire McClelland ruled Brett out, disqualifying the run.
F. Brett ran at McClelland and was restrained.
G. Brett's bat had the same pine tar during earlier plays.
H. American League president Lee McPhail ruled the following Tuesday that the hit was a home run after all, requiring the run to count and the remainder of the game to be replayed.
I. The spirit of the rule was not violated (Brett had pounded no nails into the bat), but the letter had been.

2.3 Purpose

Just as defining the context of your subject helps you to decide what is worth pursuing and what you can ignore, so defining the purpose of writing helps you to know what information to include, what to omit, and, most important, where to begin. If you decided to write about why amniocentesis should not be used as a diagnostic tool for all women, you may be tempted simply to list all the reasons you can think of: reason No. 1, reason No. 2, . . . reason No. n. If you cannot include all the reasons you discover, however, how can you decide which reasons to exclude? How can you decide which to expand most fully, which to curtail, which to put first? You need a method better than flipping a coin or deciding simply to explain those reasons you best understand. You can take most of the guessing out of these decisions if you don't ponder your information isolated from your reason for presenting it to others. In order to shape your imagination you must focus on your readers and how you want your writing to affect them.

As a writer, you want to communicate something to your readers. Doyle, for example, wanted to delight and challenge his readers with a mystery. That's a start. He knew what the finished product should look like generally, about how long it would be (a short story, not a novel), and something about the ordering of details. However, a purpose stated so generally does not, by itself, give much guidance. Doyle needed to conceive of his purpose more specifically, perhaps as an attempt to tantalize his readers by leading them to expect one kind of investigation (for a murderer) and then surprising them with another, all without withholding any necessary clues. Such a specifically stated purpose offers considerable guidance: what information to include, how to sequence it, what to emphasize. That's the kind of "purpose" you want to articulate for your own writing.

How do you find your purpose? There's no one way. You may wish to begin by defining your purpose broadly, thinking of the genre (mystery story, letter of application, explanatory essay, lab report) and the general response you want to elicit from your reader (delight and challenge, get the grant, be thought an imaginative thinker or careful researcher). Other broad purposes include:

- persuading someone to change his or her mind
- getting a wedge in, getting your reader to keep an open mind about your point of view
- providing your reader with needed information so that she can make a decision
- instructing someone in the best way to do something
- letting your readers know there are options available other than those they are narrowly focusing upon
- explaining something difficult
- justifying something morally
- convincing readers a problem exists in a situation

You can no doubt think of many more general purposes, most of which stimulate persuasive writing. Each of these helps you to recognize the large scope of a piece of writing, but conceived only in broad terms, a purpose will not help you know what to include or where to begin your presentation. Thinking only "I want to get the grant" will not help you determine the content, organization, or tone of the letter.

Second, you can think about purpose by considering the expectations of your readers. Doyle's fans have some fairly well-established expectations when they read a mystery, as does someone reading grant applications. You must decide how to meet—or alter—those expectations. Consider a simple example. Suppose you are asked in an essay exam to compare home ownership with renting. If you are taking a class in economic history, you may need to explain the changes that have occurred in the relationship between owners and tenants, with the result that you will need to consider historical details to convince your reader that you have a reasonable explanation of how the particular relationships between landlords and tenants have evolved into the current situation. But if you are responding to this question in a real estate class, you may choose to argue that home ownership, contrary to conventional wisdom, is not more financially advantageous than renting today. As a result, the historical information may not be at all necessary, and it may even get in the way of convincing your readers that they should accept your unconventional point of view.

Ultimately, however, you must express your purpose quite specifically; the more specifically, in fact, that you can identify your purpose, the more useful it will be. You may need to do some open-ended thinking before you can articulate your purpose in anything but broad terms (Chapter 3 offers a number of strategies to help you) because you cannot articulate a specific purpose without quite a bit of information and clarification. You will probably be unable to state a specific purpose early in your thinking. Rather, you will develop it as a result of the way you specify your issue, place it in context, consider your broad purpose, and your readers. Once you can articulate it, however, you will find the writing surprisingly easy.

Consider these two statements of purpose for the essay question in the economic history class:

1. To show what I know about the history of an important economic relation.
2. To show that I understand the Marxist interpretation of the changing relations between classes as exemplified in the landlord-tenant relation and to convince my instructor that this interpretation explains the present situation better than the others we have studied.

The first purpose would probably fit just about any question on such an exam. It doesn't help you know how to write the essay. The second statement is much more helpful because it focuses the question on narrower issues that you can address. Of the wealth of material available to you, you know where to start and where your essay will lead.

2.4 Audience

You have considered your audience, those who will read your writing, in a rudimentary way as you contemplated purpose. In order to decide how to affect your audience, you identified the readers and considered their expectations. You were responding in a very general way to audience, assuming, for example, that all mystery buffs share some of the same expectations about mysteries, just as all readers of applications, lab reports, or essay exams look for some of the same features when reading these kinds of writing. Knowing more exactly how the particular readers of your writing are likely to respond to it will aid you immeasurably in deciding what information and approach you might pursue and how to mold your information and arguments to achieve your purpose.

Ignoring your readers—assuming they will simply follow your arguments however you present them—can be quite hazardous. You yourself have no doubt at one time or another been put off by a writer, perhaps because he assumed you would respond favorably to his broadside attack on a proposal close to your heart or because he belabored what to you is obvious. Of course, a different reader may not take offense at all; she may share the writer's disapproval of the proposal or need to hear all that detail you learned long ago. You must make the best judgments you can about your readers before you put pen to paper or you risk insulting or boring them—or producing any number of other unintended effects.

Your readers, for instance, may derive meaning you hadn't intended or fail to derive the meaning you thought you expressed. The dismay at not communicating the right meaning is known to every student who writes an essay exam the teacher claims does not include all the information the student thought it possessed. Or consider this letter:

Smith and Smith Brokers, Inc.
Office Boy Position

Dear Sir:

   I am writing to you in response to the ad you placed in the *L.A. Times* regarding the position of office boy. I am presently a freshman majoring in pre-law. I am on the debate squad here at the University. I am also involved in other activities such as radio broadcasting and doing the public address system at the basketball games. While doing all of these things I have maintained a B+ grade point average. I have been very busy these past two semesters and would like to remain so during the summer.

(Cont.)

Basically, I am applying for the job of office boy for two reasons. Essentially, I would like to learn about the intricacies of the stock market, (1) so I can better manage my own investments, and (2) because I need a second career option open to me should I lose interest in law. Working at Smith and Smith would enable me to accomplish both of these goals. Needless to say, I am very, very interested in the stock market.

As a freshmen on the top debate program in the country I have learned what hard work really is. My capacities on the squad here resemble those of an office boy in some respects. For instance, I must do several hours of research on our debate topic every week. I also do a lot of the squad's typing and busy work. Most of this work is for the senior debaters. As an indication of my hard work and dedication, I must submit the fact that I did more research this past summer than any freshmen has in the history of this prestigious program. This summer I also had to categorize and file some 20,000 pieces of evidence. I have always thrived on this sort of hard work.

I should hope my lack of experience does not serve as an inherent barrier to my getting this position. Although I have not taken any courses relating to the market, I do possess a fair amount of knowledge about stocks. My father was a broker before he became an investment advisor. I have derived most of my knowledge from my father. Owning stock has also increased my knowledge of the market. I really enjoy analyzing the Mansfield Stock Charts whenever I get the opportunity to do so. I also read my father's market letter as well as letters from his firm as often as possible.

I sincerely hope my lack of experience is overshadowed by my evidence of personal interests and qualities. I am, indeed, greatly interested in working for your firm and, correspondingly, learning a lot about the market.

Sincerely,
Ari Gantz

This writer was pleased with the case he made for himself as a candidate and expected to get the job. He had, after all, shown that he was an active student, and he had given evidence that he was industrious and not opposed to routine chores. He was quite surprised when others were not as impressed as he was. Other readers were quite put off by his two reasons for wanting the job; they thought he was only concerned with his personal ambitions and not with the company or the job. Besides, they asked, why should a company hire someone who just wanted to explore a second, fall-back career? They also didn't know how to respond to the list of personal data in the first paragraph, and they were suspicious of his reliance on his father. They read "personal interests and qualities" in the last paragraph quite differently than the writer intended; they saw the interests as self-serving and the overriding quality as arrogance. Readers often derive meaning that surprises, and annoys, writers. This writer does have a case to make. Considering his readers will help him make it in such a way that they can hear it.

Some writers say, "Yes, of course there's a reader" but, not knowing what to do with that information, proceed as if none existed. Others, attempting to make the piece relevant to "everyone" (today and, perhaps, in 50 years), purposely ignore readers. Still others claim that their writing is "objective" and think that considering a reader as a human being who responds in idiosyncratic ways may detract from their "objectivity." Perhaps they think of readers on the model of computers: information is inserted and then retrieved intact. But even here, new programmers and users are often dismayed when a computer fails to make some obvious assumption the user made, or fails to understand the information as the writer thought it should be understood. Rather than there being no audience, they find a rather uncompromising one to contend with!

In addition to irritating your readers unnecessarily if you ignore them, or simply failing to communicate, you also lose a powerful aid to your writing. Consider some further consequences of ignoring the reader. First, it is difficult to shape a piece of writing separated from its intended reader. How much detail should you include on any given piece of the argument? Which subissues can you ignore, which not? If you consider what your reader needs to know for you to accomplish your purpose, you can answer these questions, but ignoring the reader makes them difficult to consider. Some writers look for mechanical answers, such as to cover everything mentioned in the thesis and nothing else; others elaborate those issues they know most about and ignore the rest. Still others elaborate the more difficult ones. But the question of difficulty cannot be divorced from the person: what makes them more difficult and to whom? You end up selecting the issues difficult to you, the writer. You end up writing for your own benefit, perhaps to understand the material. That is often a beneficial exercise, but you want to avoid confusing it with making a case to others.

It is impossible to divorce a piece of writing from the writer and reader, for the one shapes the understanding in the first place (even so-called objective description is still selected, arranged, and molded by someone's understanding of it), and the other derives the meaning. Readers remember the meaning *they* derive, and if what they derive differs from what the writer intended, then the writer has not communicated successfully. However much the writer may like to complain of an ineffective reader—and we all feel that way some of the time—ultimately it is the writer's responsibility to guard against misapprehension, for it is the writer who wishes to communicate an idea. And that is the central point: the writer's goal is not simply to put words on paper, to "express herself," but to use those words to communicate an idea, an interpretation, a plan of action, a request.

2.4.1 Analyzing Your Audience

How can you analyze your reader, especially if you don't know her well or if many different people will read your writing? Even if you feel you are creating a fictional reader—and the more specifically you envision your audience the more likely you are to fictionalize it—you must proceed. You can begin by considering your reader's motive for reading your piece, her familiarity with your topic and its issues, and her attitude toward both your topic and your approach to it.

2.4.1a Audience Concern 1: Why Is My Reader Reading My Paper?
How will your reader use your writing? Is your reader seeking information and arguments in order to make a decision? What kind of a decision? Is he looking for entertainment? Does he need to confront some difficult question, hoping you may lead him to some insight? Is he looking for new interpretation of a text, or is he interested in knowing how well you understand the accepted interpretation? Knowing how your reader (or readers) will use your writing aids you immeasurably in deciding what kind of detail to include and how much.

For example, if your reader needs to make a decision based on the information and arguments you present, he will become frustrated reading a daily log of your research; he will expect you to synthesize your findings and present alternative cases, with your evaluation of them, on how to proceed. But a lab researcher who wants to evaluate your experimental procedures will look for that daily log. Likewise, if your history teacher reads an essay exam to discover how well you have mastered the material covered in class, she may not be able to reward a novel interpretation of the subject matter without evidence that you have indeed mastered the requisite topics. Your school's current affairs magazine, though, will likely reject such a summary, however polished, in favor of a new and persuasive interpretation. (So, for that matter, might your history teacher if instead of an exam she had assigned an essay in which you were to demonstrate your ability to apply the methods of analysis you had studied in class.)

Consider how a counselor writing a report on her work with a client might analyze the ways in which her readers will use her report. She may consider what she needs to tell another counselor taking over the client about the progress of the sessions to date, deciding how much detail she needs to include about the sessions she has conducted. She may also consider how her supervisor will use it to check on her work and how it may be used in a court of law, where some aspect of the client's future may depend on what she says. Each reader will use this report differently. Knowing the different potential readers and their different uses, this writer can accommodate their needs in her writing—omitting personal comments that would be inappropriate if read in court but including enough information about the day-to-day activities to make it comprehensible to the new counselor.

A writer who does not consider her audience may inadvertently say something she does not mean to say (such as a personal comment to the new counselor that might hurt the client in court) or leave out information critical to her readers' understanding of the case. A report or essay is not "good" in and of itself; it is good in so far as it satisfies its purpose.

2.4.1b Audience Concern 2: How Familiar Is My Reader with My Topic?

Do you need to describe the situation that gives rise to your topic, or are your readers sufficiently familiar with it that you need merely remind them of its salient features or point out the connections between certain, well-known features? For instance, if you write a review of a new play, you may have to summarize it briefly if your readers are unfamiliar with its plot, but if you review the new production of *Hamlet*, you may be able to omit such a summary. One student, in asking for an appointment to present his company's line of electronic components to a distributor, needed to know how much his reader, the CEO, knew of his product. He learned that the CEO knew a great deal about passive components but very little about the writer's line or distributing program. Therefore, this student knew that he could safely avoid discussing passive components in general but that he must be quite specific in describing his company's particular line.

Complications arise, of course, as the number of readers increases. If you write a proposal for your company to expand into the west end of town, you must address several different audiences whose familiarity with your project and research varies. You write first of all to your supervisor, who has been following your research closely and eagerly awaits your case for expansion. But after she endorses the proposal, she must submit it to several other officers with only limited information on the project, and the report will eventually be filed for future reference, to be read by those completely unfamiliar with your work or the reasons why you initially undertook the study.

© 1997 by Sidney Harris
If you ignore the needs of your audience, even the most brilliant idea may fall flat.

Your justification for writing, in fact, is the one thing few, if any, of your readers will understand at the outset. Yet in order to appreciate your case, they must understand why your topic is important. Students often assume the teacher is familiar with the background of the topic—even more so than the student—for he made the assignment and directed the reading and discussion leading up to it. But although the teacher may be more familiar with the topic in general, he will not know why you chose your particular approach to the assignment. Even in a classroom assignment, the context you see for responding to a question may differ from that envisioned by the teacher, and a teacher looking for one thing in a paper may not be able to hear something else without your supplying a different context. Omitting the rationale for a particular approach is one of the major reasons readers "miss" what an essay has to say.

2.4.1c Audience Concern 3: What Does My Reader Think of My Topic? How Will She Respond to My Approach?   Is your audience interested in your topic? If not, you may need to spend some time explaining its importance before the reader is willing to listen to your ideas about it. On the other hand, an already interested audience may not need much help seeing the importance of your discussion, and spending much time get-

ting these readers into the issue may mean some won't bother attending to your brilliant ideas when they finally hear them.

In any case, you must probe beyond your reader's initial interest in your issue. More important, how will he react toward the conclusion you wish to argue in your writing? Is he predisposed to disagree with you, or is he already on your side? The two situations call for different treatments. On the one hand, if you can figure out where your reader might resist your conclusion, you can address his concerns directly. Is he open to being persuaded by good reasons on this issue? Does he harbor strong feelings about other things you should know about? On the other hand, if your reader already agrees with you, you don't need to convince him of your view. Such a paper would be pointless. Perhaps you want to expand his understanding of the details of the case or help him see why those who disagree with your shared view have yet to come around. Knowing the audience's attitudes can help you refine your purpose in writing.

2.4.2 Some Problems with Respect to Audience

2.4.2a Multiple Audiences   How can you address several different readers who will use your writing differently and bring to it vastly different understanding and attitudes?

You cannot accommodate everyone at once. While you fill in the background for one audience, you bore another, and when you address the more knowledgeable audience, you lose the less knowledgeable one. The key is to know who the *primary* audience is and write to that audience consistently, but in such a way that other readers can accommodate themselves to that audience. Readers can—and do—role play.

For example, if you write a letter to the editor responding to an editorial, you are writing to both the editors and the readers of that publication. Probably you will be more concerned about influencing the readers than the editor, but you need to remember that the editor (or staff) will decide which letters to print. The editor is therefore a secondary audience, one who may limit the kind of response you can make, but you still mold your response to the publication's readers.

2.4.2b When You Don't Know Much About Your Audience   What if you don't know much of anything about your readers? Where do you start?

You can begin by looking over other writing that interests them. You could prepare to write your letter responding to the editorial by reviewing other, previously published editorials to get an idea of the range of opinion and approaches selected for publication. If you address the readers of a magazine, you can review it. What kinds of articles does it publish? Can you estimate the educational background of the typical reader?

Does the publication have any particular political bent? Is it politically oriented at all? Is it addressed to readers who are knowledgeable about your issue? Are there any particular issues frequently represented there? What kind of advertising does it carry? How do readers represent themselves in personal ads if there are any? Even if you know no one who reads, say, the *Nation* or *Reader's Digest*, you can begin to describe some relevant features of your audience by reading the publications carefully.

Likewise, if you are struggling to write a class assignment designed to help you think and write like a member of a discipline's community of writers, you can familiarize yourself with the major publications read by members of the field. Ask your teacher to suggest a few that will provide you with the range of articles considered significant by the discipline at large. You can discover quite a bit about the expectations, conventions, and tastes of your readers by skimming the tables of contents and some articles.

2.4.2c Writing Primarily to Teachers   Writing to teachers can present special difficulties. Unlike the writing you do on the job or as a volunteer or citizen, which you address to an audience less well informed than you are, the writing you present to teachers covers subjects you are learning and they have studied for years. It is an artificial situation. But, then, you do not really write *to* your teacher (except when you write a note asking for an appointment or an extension on an asignment). You write to someone else, perhaps an audience given in an assignment or scholars in the field, and the teacher, like a coach, helps you refine your thinking and writing. You are seldom asked to alter your teacher's opinion to receive a passing grade; that might prove too demanding. Rather you are asked to accomplish some other goal. That goal will vary from discipline to discipline, course to course, and assignment to assignment. But you can still use the guidelines listed above to analyze the special relationship between student-writer and teacher-reader.

First you must be clear about the intended audience (even if this audience never actually sees the paper). If no audience is stated in the assignment, you must determine an appropriate one. That may be a matter of deciding which professional journal's guidelines you will follow, defining a particular person or committee (your congresswoman, the local school board), or deciding on a genre (business letter, lab report, review). You may find it helpful to ask, "Who most needs to hear what I have to say?" But do not simply ignore your readers, even if they are not stated overtly in an assignment. They exist, and they exert an influence on your writing.

Once you have defined your intended audience, you can analyze it according to the guidelines given above. Pay special attention to the way your intended audience will use your writing, clarifying in particular the constraints given in the assignment. Consider the reasons your teacher, a secondary reader, made the assignment and be sure to accommodate them. Just because your teacher-reader knows the major issues and arguments on your topic does not mean you can gloss over them; your intended audience may not know them, and one of your teacher's reasons for reading your paper may be to see how well you understand those issues and arguments.

Second, take full advantage of your teacher's coaching your writing. His comments may help you discover where you have misconceived an issue, where to research further, how to argue more cogently, how to follow a discipline's format for presenting information and conclusions. Use those comments to strengthen your writing so that when you do write to peers or those less knowledgeable on a subject, you can do so confidently.

At this point, consider audience analysis primarily a tool to help you discover what you need to say. By investigating your readers' use of your writing, their familiarity with your subject, and their attitude toward your ideas, you can discover which issues you need to attend to in order to gain your readers' ears. That does not mean you need to change your view if you have arrived at it by carefully investigating your topic; rather, it means you consider the ways you can present your view so that your readers, who impose their own standards, assumptions, and expectations on your writing, can, at least for the moment, appreciate the way you see things. If you find you have difficulty writing to a particular audience, that you are blocked rather than generating ideas, try envisioning a different audience to begin. Some writers find it helpful to imagine someone they feel comfortable writing to nodding or frowning just beyond the paper or screen. You can always revise later to make your writing appropriate to the real audience. Especially as you revise, you can reconsider your readers as a means of organizing your arguments and giving clues to direct them to the fullest understanding of what you have to say.

2.5 Persona

At the same time as your readers respond to what you say and how you say it, they respond to you, the writer. How do you want your readers to regard you? What kind of "persona" do you wish to present?

You may come across to your readers in any number of ways: as well-informed on your topic, inquisitive, open- or closed-minded, reflective or biased, confident or lacking in confidence, rational or irrational, emotional or unemotional, committed or uncommitted, careful or careless, a person of good will and integrity or someone devious. You must decide how you want your readers to perceive you and why.

How can you control the persona, your image, as it comes through your writing? You have two major resources: your style (the subject of Chapter 9) and your "ethical appeal." Ethical appeal (the term is Aristotle's) refers to your very presence in your writing, and you are there however much you might like to hide. If your readers are inclined to listen to you, you have achieved high ethical appeal; if they discount what you say, you have low ethical appeal. You cannot simply insert something here or there to achieve high ethical appeal. Rather, the totality of a piece of writing—the conception and articulation of your ideas and the manner in which you present them—produces either high or low ethical appeal.

Consider some examples. Sherlock Holmes achieves high ethical appeal: that is, you are probably willing to consider his case and even admire this clever thinker. You may have been inclined to listen to Holmes even before you read this story because you knew of his reputation, but reputation counts for less than the way he establishes himself in the writing at hand. (He could weaken that reputation, and, disappointed, you could discount him entirely.) He understands not only the subject at hand but also enough about related issues to ask leading questions and produce a good case. He studies the situation assiduously, he reasons well, and he is respectful. He is never sloppy, either in collecting data or building them into a case, and he never misleads his audience. He neither overstates his case nor insults others also trying to piece one together. He maintains his integrity at all times.

Unlike Holmes, the would-be office boy fails to inspire his readers to consider him seriously, even though much of what he says is valuable. His readers resist his claims because they do not trust him, because they do not believe he has their interests in mind. He overstates his case; he tries too hard. His tone is all wrong.

Consider another example of failed ethical appeal, a marriage proposal from Jane Austen's *Pride and Prejudice*:

> My reasons for marrying are, first, that I think it a right thing for every clergyman in easy circumstances (like myself) to set the example of matrimony in his parish. Secondly, that I am convinced it will add very greatly to my happiness; and thirdly—which perhaps I ought to have mentioned earlier—that it is the particular advice and recommendation of the very noble lady whom I have the honour of calling patroness. Twice has she condescended to give me her opinion (unasked too!) on this subject; and it was but the very Saturday night before I left Hunsford—between our pools at quadrille, while Mrs. Jenkinson was arranging Miss de Bourgh's footstool, that she said, "Mr. Collins, you must marry. A clergyman like you must marry.—Chuse properly, chuse a gentle woman for *my* sake; and for your *own*, let her be an active, useful sort of person, not brought up high, but able to make a small

income go a good way. This is my advice. Find such a woman as soon as you can, bring her to Hunsford, and I will visit her." Allow me, by the way, to observe, my fair cousin, that I do not reckon the notice and kindness of Lady Catherine de Bourgh as among the least of the advantages in my power to offer. You will find her manners beyond anything I can describe; and your wit and vivacity, I think, must be acceptable to her, especially when tempered with the silence and respect which her rank will inevitably excite. Thus much for my general intention in favour of matrimony; it remains to be told why my views were directed to Longbourn instead of my own neighborhood, where I assure you there are many amiable young women. But the fact is that being, as I am, to inherit this estate after the death of your honoured father (who, however, may live many years longer), I could not satisfy myself without resolving to chuse a wife from among his daughters, that the loss to them might be as little as possible, when the melancholy event takes place—which, however, as I have already said, may not be for several years. This has been my motive, my fair cousin, and I flatter myself it will not sink me in your esteem. And now nothing remains for me but to assure you in the most animated language of the violence of my affection. To fortune I am perfectly indifferent, and shall make no demand of that nature on your father, since I am well aware that it could not be complied with; and that one thousand pounds in the 4 per cents, which will not be yours till after your mother's decease, is all that you may ever be entitled to. On that head, therefore I shall be uniformly silent; and you may assure yourself that no ungenerous reproach shall ever pass my lips when we are married.

(Austen 100–2)

Mr. Collins fails to achieve high ethical appeal (and the hand of his "fair cousin," Elizabeth Bennet) not only because of his tone but also because he chooses the wrong arguments. He has two arguments: in the first he offers three reasons why he should marry, and in the second he gives (essentially) one reason why he should choose his wife from among Elizabeth and her sisters. You can display these arguments in order to see them more clearly. (Chapter 4 will introduce diagramming in detail; these will simply help you visualize Mr. Collins's case.)

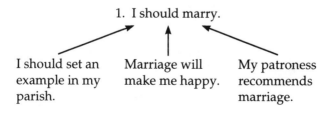

1. I should marry.

| I should set an example in my parish. | Marriage will make me happy. | My patroness recommends marriage. |

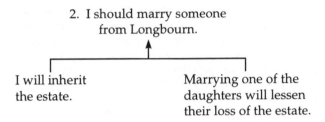

2. I should marry someone
from Longbourn.

I will inherit
the estate.

Marrying one of the
daughters will lessen
their loss of the estate.

Mr. Collins makes a case more appropriately delivered to himself, arguing that he ought to marry and, if so, to whom. He does make a case for why Elizabeth should marry him, if a reasoned case is appropriate at all! She might well expect some emotional appeal, for a marriage proposal is certainly one occasion in which emotion is appropriate. He is disrespectful, however elegant his language, and he misleads, however naively. How can Elizabeth believe that he feels any affection for her when he fails to follow through on his claim that he will assure her in "animated language" of the "violence" of his affection? And how can she believe that he is indifferent to money when he carries on for eight lines in quite some detail about how much he will gain from his marriage to her? Clearly he has spent more time pondering finances than affection.

You achieve ethical appeal by the totality of your writing, including features to which you may be blind. Here is a list of those overriding considerations that incline readers to accept what you have to say:

1. You know the subject matter; you have done your homework.
2. You reason well. You make the best case you can, neither claiming more than your evidence warrants nor misleading your reader by unfounded appeals or omissions. You are careful to present information accurately.
3. You are respectful—of the subject, your reader, and those with whom you disagree. You present your case with integrity.
4. Your tone is appropriate for the occasion, the subject, and the reader.

And here are some of the ways reasoners and writers (perhaps inadvertently) lower their ethical appeal.

1. If your reader discovers that you have ignored information or some line of reasoning, or if you have missed an important article in your research, she may question your work overall. A reader may reason that since you have ignored this evidence, you have not done your homework very thoroughly and may have ignored other important information.

2. If your reader feels misled by specious reasoning or by some feature of the writing that distracts her from an argument, she will distrust you. If she catches you making a mistake, however small or however minor to your overall case, she may well discount the whole thing; what other mistakes might you have made that she has not detected?

3. If you rail against the ill-conceived and stupid ideas of those who disagree with you, your reader may question your integrity. If your presentation seems poorly set out or organized or developed, your reader may think it unworthy of her time. If you did not spend the time to develop a case, why should she spend the time to unravel it? If you make careless manuscript errors— spelling, punctuation, ill-chosen words—your reader will think you cared insufficiently for the subject, the essay itself, or her. Readers are quite unforgiving if they detect sloppiness of any sort.

4. If your tone is inappropriate or your style obtuse, you may put your reader off, perhaps to the point that she will simply refuse to read what you have written.

Consider one final example, a letter written by a student who tried to enhance her ethical appeal. To a large degree she has succeeded.

UR Covered Insurance Co.
8686 Altercation Road
Riverside, CA 92405
ATTN: Harry Heartless, Claims Adjuster

Dear Mr. Heartless:

As you are aware, I was recently involved in an accident with your insured, Rick Reckless. I appreciate your prompt claims assistance; however, there is one additional issue that needs to be discussed. It is the matter of $984.00, which is the amount required to paint the car entirely.

I fully understand that your normal policy is to paint only those parts that are damaged, and if this were a minor "fender-bender" I would certainly agree. However, as you know, my car suffered major damage to both the front and back, and because of the force with which I was hit, even the side panels are buckled and will have to be repaired and painted. Because the color is a metallic silver, there is no way that it can be matched. Since the undamaged parts are the roof and the two

(Cont.)

---

doors, I'm sure you will realize that my car will look like a patchwork quilt unless it is repainted completely.

I can assure you that I would not feel so strongly about this if I were at fault in any way. However, as you are well aware, I was a totally innocent bystander, rear-ended by your insured who was issued a citation for drunk driving. There was no way in which I could have avoided the accident. Why, then, should I be required to pay $984.00 to have my car restored to the same condition it was before the accident?

I feel that I have been more than reasonable about this. I did not ask your company to pay for a rental car even though it would have been more convenient than using the car my teenager normally drives. I did not suddenly develop neck or back pains as I understand some people do in an accident of this type. I have acted entirely in good faith, asking only that my car be repaired and returned to me looking just as it did before your insured ran into it. I hope that you will agree that this is not too much to ask under the circumstances.

I am confident that your good judgment will enable us to settle this matter to our mutual satisfaction. Please let me hear from you as soon as possible.

Sincerely yours,
Felicity Fairness

Try to point out this writer's attempts, both direct and indirect, to achieve high ethical appeal. Do you think Mr. Heartless will pay the extra $984.00?

2.6 Putting It All Together

Considering the entire rhetorical situation, you must attend to four elements: the *context* of the topic; the *purpose(s)* for writing; the expectations, uses, knowledge, and attitudes of the *audience*; and the *persona* of the writer.

The Rhetorical Situation

1. *Context:* What kind of writing is this to be? What is relevant to the issue?
2. *Purpose:* How do I want to affect my readers?

3. *Audience:* Who are my readers, or alternatively, who needs to hear what I have to say? How will my readers use my paper? What do they know about my topic? What do they think of my subject, and how might they object to my approach?
4. *Persona:* How do I want my readers to regard me, the writer? How can my language and my presentation of my material affect the way I come across to my readers?

Exercises 2.3–2.6

I. You have been assigned to write a short article on nutrition to be included in the monthly PTA newsletter. No further instructions were given. You realize you must first decide what is at issue, determine your context, understand what kinds of positions may be taken on this issue—and you must make the issue seem important to the parents, your readers. Complete the following preparations:

A. State your subject as a mystery or dilemma.
B. What is your context? What issues are therefore relevant, what irrelevant?
C. Describe your audience. How will readers use your article? What do they know about the dilemma you stated in A? What is their attitude toward your approach?
D. Describe one position on this issue that differs from your own. How will you deal with this position in your article?
E. What, briefly, may be your purpose for this article?
F. What persona will you *avoid* using for this article?
G. How will you establish good ethical appeal?

II. Write a three- to four-page *proposal* for a major persuasive paper. Writing a proposal is not the same as writing the paper, or even a mini version of the paper. Your task in the proposal is to convince your instructor that your project is worth your time to investigate and write up, and that it is possible to complete with the resources (both source material and time) available to you this semester.

A. *The Subject*

Choose a subject you really want to write about, one that is important enough to you that you can make your readers see its importance as well. The paper you propose to write must be persuasive: it must attempt to exert an influence on your readers, to make them see your subject from your point of view. Do not propose an essay that intends merely to inform.

B. *The Proposal*

1. Identify the issue you will address in your paper. Try to express the issue as a dilemma, a conflict between two (or more) contending options you wish to have but must instead choose between. Remember that you are not going to argue an obviously good choice over an obviously bad one. Rather you must choose among several "good" options or discover whether an option really is good or not. Then identify your context and suggest what you know to be relevant regardless of how you resolve the dilemma.

2. What is your purpose in writing this paper? How do you want to affect your readers and why is that your aim?

3. Identify the readers who most need to hear what you have to say. Will you present your ideas to an individual, a committee, or several independent readers? If you were to publish this essay, where might you submit it? Analyze the ways in which your readers will use your essay, their knowledge of your subject, and their attitude toward your approach. (Provide a separate audience analysis of your classmates if they will read your paper.)

4. Consider how you want your readers to regard you. How will you establish good ethical appeal? Do you have the resources necessary to achieve a convincing persona?

3

Invention

You have already been inventing—generating ideas—as you defined important issues to discuss and considered context, your readers, your persona, your purpose. And you have no doubt been using a variety of strategies to get started on a project, strategies you have practiced and honed over years of thinking and writing about subjects as diverse as whom to vote for in an election, what subjects to study, what to wear to an important lunch, whether to take on the extra responsibilities of a new job.

You may wish to examine your own repertoire of strategies. Jot down at random some answers to this question: What do I do when I write, or stare at blank paper wishing to write? Consider what you do as you begin, get stuck in the middle, or refine your writing. Don't censor anything at this point or be too concerned initially about whether you are naming a "generating" strategy. Here is a list generated by a reasoning and writing class:

- just start writing
- find a quiet place
- list ideas
- outline
- read
- just think
- read my work out loud
- find my favorite pen and pour a glass of juice

- ask someone else to look at my draft
- review my purpose
- jump to a different section of the paper
- talk to someone about my topic
- take a shower
- reread what I've written
- leave (clean closets, jog, etc.)
- look up some of my terms to make sure I understand them

To this list you would of course add "consider the context and audience!"

You can see that you already have a number of strategies and that your strategies may differ radically from someone else's. For instance, you may not want to talk about your ideas with anyone until you have them fairly well established, whereas someone else may begin by talking to others. An outline, helpful to some writers, may terrify you and block your thinking; you may prefer just to start writing and see what happens. This chapter will demonstrate a number of strategies that can help you to

"Well—and I'm not just saying this because you're my husband—it stinks."

Drawing by Mankoff; © 1994 The New Yorker Magazine, Inc.
Asking someone else to look at your draft can help, but it has risks!

generate ideas and arguments. Some, like brainstorming, are familiar; others will be new. Some can be used for any writing assignment; others are more limited. We suggest you try each one several times until you are comfortable enough with it to see how it can help you.

Suppose you have the following assignment. Consider the information and your task. Then you can practice some generating strategies to get started.

3.1 The Case of the Spelunkers

I. The Case: Five members of a spelunking (cave exploration) club were on an expedition when a landslide trapped them in an underground cave. Though deeply buried, they tried to transmit their distress on a radio they carried with them. After being buried for six days, they established radio contact with a rescue party, which began efforts to dig them out. Four days later the rescuers informed the spelunkers that they could not reasonably anticipate rescue any earlier than another twenty days since the equipment needed to dig them out was in bad repair and spare parts could not be flown in any sooner than that.

The trapped explorers described their deteriorating physical condition and the diminishing food and water supplies to the medical experts at the other end of the transmitter. When asked, the physicians informed them that it was highly unlikely that they could survive the remaining twenty days given their current condition and supplies. When pressed by the spelunkers for an opinion, the physicians reluctantly agreed that four of them could survive the twenty days if they consumed the flesh of the fifth. Later the spelunkers requested a legal opinion on such an action from the attorney general's office, but the attorney general's office declined to respond. No one else at the other end of the transmitter was willing or capable of giving an authoritative legal opinion on the matter.

It was Dezi l'Abinnac who had first suggested the idea of a lottery to decide which of their number they might consume. After much discussion of the mathematical problems involved, they agreed on a fair method of determining the issue, using the dice one member of the group was carrying.

Before the dice were cast, Dezi declared that he was withdrawing from the arrangement and wanted to wait longer before resorting to this action. The others accused him of a breach of faith and proceeded to cast the dice. When he declined to take his turn, the others cast for him and asked him whether he had any objections to the fairness or the manner of the throw. He stated that he had none. The throw went against him, and he was eventually put to death and consumed by his companions.

The remaining spelunkers were eventually rescued and brought to trial. All four were charged under a law that states, "Whosoever shall deliberately take the life of another person shall be punished by death." Though the standard sorts of exceptions that can prevent the imposition of the penalty for murder (such as self-defense or criminal insanity) are recognized in their jurisdiction, the judge, in giving his instructions to the jury, cautioned that such excuses and justifications need to be used with the utmost care, suggesting that he thought they did not apply to the present case.

(Adapted from Fuller)

II. Your Task: You are a member of the jury, and the case now rests in your hands. After a number of days of deliberation, the jury has made little progress. About half the jury seems to favor conviction, while the other half opposes it. When the foreman requests assistance from the judge in breaking the deadlock, the judge suggests that each side write out its arguments and present them the next day in written form to the other side, in the hope of settling the issue. He especially recommends that the authors speak plainly and avoid the pretense that they know anything special about the law. He explains that a jury's job is to bring the common sense and good judgment of reasonable people in applying the law as presented by a judge in his instructions. No further knowledge of legal niceties is needed, he says. Your side has selected you to write out its view of the matter because you have presented the position so coherently in the jury room. So you now have to write out the arguments for your position to present them to the jury. Should the spelunkers be convicted or not?

3.2 Freewriting

Writing is itself generative. E. M. Forster said, "How do I know what I think until I see what I say?" The act of writing sentences, rather than a list of key words (most often names of things), helps you to see where ideas lead and how they relate to each other. Do not think of your early efforts at writing as a draft of the paper; that puts so many constraints on you—organization, mechanics—that you may not be able to focus single-mindedly on your ideas. Instead, know that you will revise, that you will probably throw this writing out altogether, that at this stage writing is a generating strategy. One powerful way to help you use writing to generate ideas is called "freewriting."

Freewriting forces you not to censor. The rules are, in one sense, quite simple: you write for ten minutes without stopping. If you suddenly have nothing to say, you may repeat your last word or sentence until your ideas begin again, but you may not let your pen remain motionless. And that is the key to the whole process: focusing your attention—and pen—on new ideas without stopping when your mind temporarily goes blank.

You can use freewriting at any stage of writing: to think about context, your audience, what you already know about your topic, a potential mystery or dilemma, or, later on, to clarify a tricky section or renew your imagination. The name "freewriting" comes from the freedom you have in associating ideas, allowing tangents and seeming irrelevancies to intrude. And it is this material that may trigger an original insight. You cannot become embroiled in editing your writing (crossing out, emending, fixing a sentence) because you are consumed by filling the blank space ahead, and that allows your mind and ideas to expand.

Typically, a freewrite seems easy at first; you simply write down what you know. At this stage the writing itself is often smooth and clear. But then you run out of things to say. (If you write for the entire ten minutes without running out of things to say, you can set a longer time limit or narrow the focus of the freewrite. Freewrites are most useful when they force you to break out of the material that seems easy to write.) Once you have uncluttered your mind of the obvious sentences about your topic, it is free to invent new material. But that usually does not happen easily or immediately. Often, at this stage, the writing is garbled. Sentences begin

© Edward Koren

Freewriting helps break down barriers we erect when we censor our writing at too early a stage.

and then trail off; words and sentences repeat. But then, suddenly, something new and entirely unexpected may appear, something you had not even considered, or at least considered important—and it may be quite exciting. And just as suddenly the freewrite takes on an energy it lacked, an energy you may be able to capture and infuse into your paper. All in ten minutes!

Of course not all freewrites turn out like this. You may write for ten minutes and not get that far. But they do have terrific potential for stimulating your imagination. If one does not help you, try another, starting out on a different tack. Here is a freewrite written in class by a student who had read the information about the case of the spelunkers and was given the following instruction: What issues need to be considered in reaching a verdict in this case? Notice that the student was not burdened at the very outset by having to make a decision. She was able to concentrate her thinking on what was relevant to the case, whatever her ultimate verdict may be.

"Spelunkers," by Gillian Thackeray

The central issue is the value of human life. Is the value of many lives more important than the value of one life? Is the verdict of murder under I don't know what I'm writing is murder contingent upon the circumstances? As far as I can remember a murder has to be committed with intent. It is, I believe the intentional taking of a human life. What can there be which is intentional and taking of a human life which is not murder? Could this be a question of temporary insanity or self defense?

Since one person refused to take part in a process of elimination that the majority were in favor of and since it was his suggestion in the first place, could this be considered proper execution? Society seems to believe that some taking of life is all right under some circumstances, like capital punishment. Since these people were insulated and nobody from the outside world would offer any opinion did they form their own society which would make its own laws or were they still subject to the laws of the state in which they were in? It seems that isolated as they were one might think of them as having their own jurisdiction.

What about the issue of cannibalism? It is illegal, is it not? Depends, I suppose, if they could make their own laws. It's quite probable that they would not be able to. How does law come about? Common law is based on precedents. Are there any? What about the case of the people in the Andes? And are there any statutes on the book which would come to bear

Time was called, ten minutes. Notice how many different issues came out in this freewrite: the value of life, the right to life, the relationship of intent and sanity to the act, exceptions to protecting one's right to life, the effect of laws on an isolated society, cannibalism, and effects of precedents on this case. Not only did Gillian raise these issues, but she also explored them. As soon as she raised the issue of right to life, she looked for exceptions, testing her first idea of its sanctity, discovering exceptions that some people accept. Also, she discovered that the question of whether cannibalism is illegal depends on whether the spelunkers were bound by the laws of their state or whether they were sufficiently isolated to form their own society and laws.

These discoveries did not all come smoothly (even though this is quite a clean freewrite). By the third sentence, Gillian was already questioning whether she knew what she was writing about; and that sentence, once it picks up the topic again, shifts the focus away from the value of life, which she had been exploring, to the relationship between an act and the circumstances in which it is committed; and the next sentence launches on yet a different tangent, intent. That's the nature of freewrites. Writing is recursive: as soon as you write one idea, it may lead you to another or affect the way you think about another. That in turn makes writing—especially freewriting—such a powerful generating strategy.

3.3 Unpacking Code Words

As one student suggested in the initial brainstorming exercise, reconsidering some major terms, or abstractions, can help you generate more ideas. Sometimes you use such words as *important* or *interesting* not just as ambiguous judgments, but to try genuinely to say something. When asked just what you mean, you may find that your explanations include ideas even you were not initially aware of. That's exciting. That's generating new ideas. Look at your writing—a freewriting, a list of ideas, a draft—and try to find code words, or have a classmate search them out for you. Then list, as precisely as you can, all the meanings packed into the word. Do not substitute another abstraction for the code word; you will end up with just a different code word. Instead, name all the concrete information that lies buried in the word. Gillian could unpack *isolated* and discover more than she had initially thought:

isolated

- isolated from family and friends (and their support)
- isolated from all community except the other spelunkers
- forced company of other spelunkers
- isolated from community's opinion (no one would give a legal opinion of their plan)
- can't go to work
- can't honor obligations, appointments
- can't do anything to speed up their recovery
- limited food and no chance of getting more soon
- fear of imminent death
- no natural light
- fuel running out too?

- If the spelunkers are really that isolated, can the laws be applied to them in the same way they are applied to people living in our society?

Look what can happen as you unpack a code word. You may discover a possible lead, one you had not anticipated, and a direction for further thinking.

That is what you pursue, after all, when you generate ideas: new leads to consider. That is ultimately how you discover what you really think, what is best to say about an issue, what is true.

3.4 Brainstorming

You may have been tempted to begin your exploration of the spelunkers' difficulties by "brainstorming," by listing ideas about the case as they came to you. Brainstorming is one of the most widely used—and successful—strategies for invention. It is, of course, what you did in the exercise that opened this chapter. Like freewriting, brainstorming can be useful at many stages of writing. Again like freewriting, brainstorming is most effective if you do not censor ideas. Write them all down. One may not seem especially fruitful at first but may turn out to be the seed of an original and powerful idea; if not, you can always discard it later. For instance, included in the brainstorming list at the beginning of this chapter are two entries that may at first seem frivolous, if not entirely irrelevant: "leave (clean closets, jog, etc.)" and "take a shower." You may be embarrassed to admit to doing them or not see how they can be generating strategies. But they ought not to cause you embarrassment. As you write, your mind sometimes becomes focused narrowly on what you have just written, keeping you from seeing new angles on a subject. Leaving, thinking of something else, often helps you to remove those blinders so that you see your subject fresh again. Psychologists call it "incubation."

After unpacking the code word *isolated*, Gillian considers the possibility that the spelunkers are innocent because, isolated as they were when they made their decision, they formed their own society and had ultimate jurisdiction over it. Is this a good position? She brainstorms awhile:

- They were concerned with the law, since they asked for an opinion before casting the dice.
- They thought they were bound by the community's laws (since they asked for an opinion)?
- Does it matter what they thought?
- Since no outsider would offer counsel or opinion, the outside world had given up its jurisdiction.

What other reasons are there to say the spelunkers are innocent?

- It is justifiable to sacrifice one human to ensure the survival of many.
- They were not thinking rationally (but they sure seemed to think the situation out; they didn't act on impulse).
- Since they killed Dezi in order to survive, it was self-defense and not murder.
- By suggesting the method determining who should die, Dezi himself authorized the killing.

Who's bringing these charges, anyway?

- Were they really isolated, since they had the radio?

Notice what happened here. Some ideas themselves raised other ideas; you can see the progression in the first three notes. But brainstorming is very seldom tidy. You put your ideas down as they come so as not to lose them. You can cluster the ideas later, for instance putting the question about the radio up with the others concerning whether the spelunkers could be held to the community's laws. Some ideas lead you back to the data (or, for some assignments, the library). You will eventually discard others.

As Gillian thought about her hypothesis, she kept challenging her notions. That is itself a powerful generating tool. In fact, she decided, after considering her freewrite, that the spelunkers really were culpable. She wrote a working hypothesis: "The spelunkers should be convicted because every human being has not only the right to live but also the obligation to uphold the right of other individuals to live."

3.5 Generating Backward from the Opposition

Developing the best case you can that runs counter to your own position helps you to generate ideas in a number of ways. You may actually change your mind, especially if you arrived at your initial position before carefully considering sufficient information and argument. Even if you do not accept the opposition's case, you will likely gain respect for it. Before you examine a position that runs counter to your own, you might find it easy to ridicule. "How could anyone think such a thing?" you may ask. By discovering how a reasonable person could arrive at a position that differs from yours, and especially by developing such a position yourself, you learn new ways of addressing the issues. At the very least, when you attempt to persuade a person who holds a position contrary to your own, you are able to do so in a knowledgeable and respectful way.

Carefully constructing the opposition's case can aid a writer in more pragmatic ways as well. Once you discover what the arguments are, you are able to respond to them. You know what information to verify; you know what kind of inferences to consider. You are in a better position to recognize and respond to objections to specific parts of your own case, and you may even discover new reasons for holding your own view. But you will not be able to make use of this powerful generating tool unless you generate your opposition's *best* case.

It will not help you to generate a weak case that runs counter to your own. Although you may temporarily feel justified in holding your view, you will not have gained any new insight into it, and it is to gain new insight that you use generating strategies. Try to write the best case you can that runs counter to your own. That may involve developing more than one line of argument arriving at a conclusion you may not agree with. Try to write the case in such a way that your opposition would agree that it is a good case. That is what Gillian tried to do when she wrote the following case.

The Case of the Spelunkers: Why They Should Not Be Convicted

The spelunkers should not be convicted of murder for the killing of Dezi l'Abinnac for some very strong reasons.

The first and foremost reason is that the only people or court that has jurisdiction over the spelunkers is the spelunkers themselves. The spelunkers had requested an opinion of the legality of the action of killing a member of the group from the attorney general's office. The attorney general's office had declined to respond and by this action gave up jurisdiction over the spelunkers. To be sure, while ignorance of the law is no excuse, one must *be able* to determine what the law is before one can be held accountable to it. Thus the spelunkers had requested legal counsel from the most authoritative source in the land and had been given no answer. In the absence of law, they were at liberty to make their own law, based on majority vote. This is exactly what they did, and since they abided by their own law, they did nothing illegal. They cannot be convicted of murder.

The other issue that comes to bear is that Dezi l'Abinnac had tacitly agreed to his own execution by determining the method by which the group would select the person to be killed. This is not mitigated by the fact that he later withdrew his support because he did not object to the method in principle but merely favored the idea of delaying the final decision. Thus, not even the member of the group who was executed was against the idea. It was a unanimous decision. The only way the spelunkers can be held accountable for their actions by an outside court of law is if they give up their own jurisdiction.

This case makes use of what Gillian considers the best ideas from her freewrite and subsequent brainstorming. Many of the ideas are fleshed out and the initial questions answered. For instance, she claims (implicitly) that the spelunkers were isolated from the law even though they had radio contact and even though they seemed to accept outside jurisdiction by their questioning the attorney general's office because they received no answer from that office or help in making their decision.

Gillian's opposition case is certainly not frivolous. Determining the best case, however, may be difficult. Gillian chose not to pursue her earlier idea that sacrificing one human being to ensure the survival of many is justifiable or her suggestion that the killing was done in self-defense. Indeed, trying out all arguments may be impractical. But potential problems may yet exist. If you ignore a line of reasoning that your readers consider significant, they may wonder whether you know of it, whether you have considered it. They may not be fully able to listen to your ideas, thinking that, had you been aware of theirs, you would have been persuaded by them—a matter of ethical appeal. You may find some help in deciding which arguments to pursue by reading what others have written on your subject or by talking to others interested in it.

3.6 Dialogue

Writing a dialogue, a conversation with yourself or between two people, can help you generate ideas at any stage of writing: deciding what is relevant to your topic, what position you may take, how others may respond to a given position. Writing a dialogue leads you to respond to ideas, and respond to responses, and thereby helps you to pursue ideas further than you may by using some other generating techniques. This is an especially useful generating strategy for developing arguments because it not only helps you to think through lines of reasoning, but also helps you avoid jumping from one argument to another rather than responding to or really using the arguments you have already raised.

Here is a dialogue that helped Gillian develop her final case in favor of convicting the spelunkers.

Gillian: Killing Dezi l'Abinnac was both morally and legally wrong.

Friend: Let's look at it legally first. What is the definition of murder?

G: Taking a life deliberately.

F: But there are circumstances under which taking a life is permitted, like war, capital punishment, and self-defense.

G: None of those conditions applies here. This was not an attempt to preserve a way of life, protect one's family, or maintain ideas, the reasons we condone killing in war. Nor was this an attempt to rid society of someone who is a threat to the lives of others or to discourage such threats from others, the justification for capital punishment. And Dezi did not pose a threat to the lives of the other spelunkers, at least not directly, so self-defense does not seem appropriate.

F: But they did kill Dezi in order to survive. That sounds close to self-defense.

G: But not in the strict sense. He was not an immediate threat to them, and he was no more a threat to them than they were to him. He simply happened to come up with a smaller roll of the dice than the others. He was chosen arbitrarily. He was sacrificed.

F: OK. Perhaps this killing doesn't fit any of the categories of acceptable killing I mentioned, but maybe there are others. What about the survivors of the plane wreck in the Andes? They ate others killed in the crash.

G: But I don't think they killed anyone they ate. [Check this point.] We have to compare this situation to one in which people are starving to death. Would we condone selective killing so the majority could survive in Ethiopia? Or, closer to home, would we find it acceptable to kill some people for others to survive if a disaster cut off our food supply and prevented travel—like an earthquake, a hurricane, or even nuclear disaster? That seems barbaric.

F: So we're talking about the moral issues now?

G: Yes.

F: If we were to pit the strong against the weak, that would be wrong.

G: Even if we could develop an arbitrary method to determine who is sacrificed, would it be less barbaric? It seems to me that our laws have been developed to preserve the individual. We believe that every person has the right to life, liberty, and the pursuit of happiness. Dezi l'Abinnac was denied that right.

F: He would have been denied that right even if they had not killed him since they would most likely have all died.

G: But it's a matter of intention. Had one of the spelunkers killed him in a delirious state because of lack of nourishment, I could have more easily understood it. But they chose to kill someone. They deliberately chose to kill, and that, to me, is murder.

F: But is delirium the only expression of an abnormal state of mind? I think the spelunkers, under considerable stress from lack of food, isolation, and fear, were in fact suffering from temporary insanity. They had no hope of survival; none of the information given them was encouraging. Think of how moody someone with a cold or the flu is. With their deteriorating physical condition it's not surprising they were willing to consider a desperate move. Just because they seemed reasonable—thought out a solution—doesn't mean they were able to judge the wisdom of that solution.

G: You may have a point there, but cave explorers are used to mental and physical strain. Even if the strain at the end was excessive, early on could they not have doubted the bad news you mention, that the rescue could not "reasonably" be expected, that the physicians thought it "highly unlikely" they could survive?

F: Perhaps, but the doctor's agreeing that killing one could save the rest implied that the situation was hopeless, and they could reasonably assume that the attorney general's refusing to say their idea was wrong was an implicit approval. They all agreed that they would be saving the lives of four of them.

G: But I can't get past the barbarity of it, however much strain they were under. They deliberately took someone's life.

Gillian may not use all this information overtly in her paper. Some lines of argument she may discard as not offering serious challenges to her view; questions may be implicit. But the dialogue format does help her discover and respond to issues and identify those features of her own case that seem most compelling.

3.7 After Generating: Forming Hypotheses

At some point generating, like searching for yet one more article in the library, can become simply a means of putting off the paper itself. One way to avoid this sort of procrastination is to form a hypothesis.

If you were to list independent data, the so-called "facts" of a situation, you would simply have described that situation. Such description has its place, of course—in newspaper reporting, for instance—and it requires skill to write well. But most of the time your readers will want to know what the description leads to and why they are reading it. Finding answers to such questions is the subject of most of this text, and we have been forming hypotheses in response to sample questions along the way. A hypothesis is a possible answer to a question, one that can be tested, supported, modified, refuted, kept, or thrown out.

Two hypotheses in this chapter illustrate the point. Gillian hypothesized early on that the spelunkers were innocent because they formed their own community and had ultimate jurisdiction over it. She then investigated what it meant to form a community and to have jurisdiction over it. Her investigation led her to discard that hypothesis as less compelling than another one, that the spelunkers should be convicted because every human being has not only the right to live but also the responsibility to uphold others' right to live. In both instances, she was able to use the terms of the hypotheses themselves to generate arguments and mold them into a coherent presentation.

Exercise 3.1

Here is a case with which to practice these generating strategies, following Gillian's model.

The Case of Roswell Gilbert   Roswell Gilbert lived with his wife, Emily, in a seaside condominium in Fort Lauderdale, Florida. They had been married 51 years. Roswell, a 76-year-old retired engineer, had been caring for Emily, who at 73 had Alzheimer's disease and osteoporosis. Her mind wandered; her spinal column was gradually collapsing. He sat at her bedside day after day, feeding her, bathing her, talking to her. He remembered the times they danced together, discussed the news over dinner, traveled to Spain. He remembered how he loved her. But illness had changed her. There came a time when she screamed, or just stared. He saw panic in her face. Seldom did she recognize him. She would ask, "Who are you?" At times he hoped for a cure, or at least relief; perhaps, he would think, a new doctor could help. But she continued to worsen. She required larger doses of painkillers, and she seemed more frantic. For a month Roswell considered killing his wife to spare her from living as "a suffering animal." Finally, as she sat on their couch, he shot her through the head with a Luger.

There had been some precedents—parents or siblings or children pulling the plug from life-support systems, husbands or wives or friends aiding a suicide. Two years before, another Fort Lauderdale man, 70 years old, shot his 62-year-old wife in the stairwell of a hospital; she, like Emily Gilbert, suffered from Alzheimer's disease. Four years before, in San Antonio, a 69-year-old man shot his 72-year-old brother to death in a nursing home. Just that year, a Miami man had shot his 3-year-old daughter twice in the heart while she lay comatose after a freak accident.

Roswell Gilbert was accused of murder; a jury convicted him, and he was sentenced to 25 years in prison with no chance of parole. He would then be 101 years old. The governor was asked to grant clemency. When questioned, most people in Florida favored letting him go free.

(Adapted from "Florida Governor" and "Mercy Death")

Your Task   You are a member of the governor's Clemency Advisory Committee, which has been discussing the matter for some time now without coming up with a position. The committee believes that clarifying the issues may help, and because you have expressed yourself so cogently in the past, it has asked you to write a paper arguing your position on the matter. (Another member of the committee will write the opposite position.) Explain to the committee members the position you think they should recommend to the governor and your reasons for holding that view.

3.8 Beginning to Put Your Case Together: A Checklist

The following checklist offers seven questions to explore as you construct a case. Many of the details encompassed by these questions will be expanded later as we discuss clarifying and evaluating arguments. In Chapter 8 we will return to the checklist to discuss some of the ways arguments can go wrong. But for now, considering the questions may help you begin to formulate your arguments.

1. **Have you defined the context clearly?** In order to get started, as you have now seen, you need to determine what your topic is and what it is not. Your understanding of your topic may change, and frequently it will when you do more research and make new discoveries, but to get a project under way, you have to make at least provisional decisions that guide where you look for information and what you can safely ignore. In other words, you begin by determining what you must know in order to come to reasonable decisions about your topic. A clear conception of your topic helps you avoid being distracted by irrelevancies, and it helps remind you not to ignore important aspects of that topic.
2. **Have you considered important views on your topic?** While original thought is valuable, it's pointless to reinvent the wheel unnecessarily. You will discover ideas for arguments by paying attention to the conversation about your topic that already exists. Familiarize yourself with that conversation. In particular,

   A. Find out whether those you are listening to have any special expertise on your topic. There may be information available that you need to use, and you need it from reliable sources.
   B. Is there a public debate about your topic? What can you learn from the discussion, even if the participants are not experts? How do others understand the issues surrounding your topic, and which arguments seem persuasive to them?
   C. Are there opinions about your topic that you should consider more fully? In particular, you need to pay attention to people who may disagree with you because they may have something important for you to consider in formulating your view and arguments.

3. **Have you clearly specified your position?**   Determine what position you are arguing. State your conclusion as carefully as you can, distinguishing it from related claims.
4. **Have you selected acceptable evidence?**   Are your reasons obviously true or plausible? Are they matters of common knowledge? If not, can their truth be defended?
5. **Do your premises together provide sufficient grounds for your conclusion?**   In addition to being true, do your reasons provide solid support for your conclusion? Should someone who accepts them as true therefore also accept your conclusion as true or likely to be true? Which evidence seems strongest? Which seems important but not entirely convincing? Can you qualify your argument to reflect limited support without undermining your purpose in proposing the argument?
6. **Have you considered your audience?**   Consider the audience to whom you want to present your argument: what do they already know about your topic and the particular argument you are advancing? Can you presume they are familiar with its details, or do you need to spell everything out? Are they likely to agree with your conclusion, or do you have to be careful how you present your points to avoid their displeasure? Are you leaving some things unsaid in order to hide them from criticism?
7. **Are your ideas expressed clearly and accurately?**   Go back and tune up the language—is it clear? Precise enough? More precise than you need? Do you present data and viewpoints (especially points you disagree with) accurately and fairly? Would someone who disagreed with you have any reasonable complaints about the language you select to characterize the issues or their views?

3.9 What's Next?

Part II explores many of the details mentioned in this list more fully. In particular, Chapter 4 introduces ways you can identify arguments and understand their parts; Chapter 5 takes up issues of clarity and the language in which arguments are expressed; Chapters 6 and 7 discuss methods of evaluating arguments; and Chapter 8 focuses on common errors people make in reasoning. Part III returns to writing, this time taking up the work of turning drafts into writing that is truly ready for the public.

PART II

Discovering the Best Arguments

4

Identifying Arguments and Their Structures

4.1 Identifying Arguments

In the first three chapters we considered the background of reasoning and writing: the questions that give rise to argumentation, the importance of thinking carefully about what is relevant to an issue before successful reasoning about it can occur, methods for generating leads, and the rhetorical situation in which writing occurs. Now we turn our attention to arguments themselves: constructing our own and reconstructing others', and then evaluating them. We will begin by looking at short passages of writing, first to discover whether they contain an argument and then to clarify exactly what the passage argues for and how it supports its claim.

4.1.1 What Is an Argument?

In "Silver Blaze" both Inspector Gregory and Sherlock Holmes propose theories to account for the same data. They arrive at their theories by moving from the data to the theory. Reasoning in general can be characterized this way: as a motion from one thought (or claim or assertion) to another. But reasoning does not involve just any kind of motion from one claim to another. A reasoner moves to his or her main point by giving *support* for it, moving from reasons to a conclusion. We say that the reasoner "argues" for his or her conclusion and that the entire group of assertions, including both the reasons and the conclusion they are offered to support, is an "argument." An argument is the product of reasoning and involves two elements: the point being argued for (the conclusion) and the reasons given in support of it (the premises).

It is important to bear clearly in mind the distinction between an argument, in the sense intended here, and a dispute, disagreement, or quarrel. As a matter of ordinary English we do use the word *argument* to refer to disagreements of various kinds. But as we use the term here, an argument—what you produce when you offer reasons to support a conclusion—does not require any disagreement with anyone. It is possible to produce an argument for completely uncontroversial claims. In fact, you can produce our kind of argument all by yourself, and you will do so often in trying to figure things out. So when we speak of an argument, we do not refer to disagreements or disputes.

4.1.2 Identifying Arguments

In many cases distinguishing arguments from passages that do not involve argumentation presents little difficulty. Either the context of a passage or the writer may make it perfectly clear that reasons are offered in support of a conclusion. But in other cases, when you are not so sure that an argument is present, you need to know how to find out. As in solving other problems, success depends upon asking yourself the right questions.

Because an argument offers some statements in support of a conclusion, that particular statement, the conclusion, plays a prominent role in any argument. So you can first ask:

1. Is there one statement that appears to be the most important point of the passage?

If there is one such statement, then you can ask:

2. Are the other statements offered in support of or as reasons for that statement?

If you answer "yes" to both questions, then the passage is an argument. Consider the following example:

> There are certainly some circumstances in which it would be permissible to perform an abortion. Suppose the mother's life is endangered by the presence of the fetus. It is permissible to kill a human being in self-defense. And sometimes abortion is just such a case of self-defense.

Ask each question in turn. (1) In this passage, one statement does indeed have a special prominence: Abortion is at least sometimes permissible. (2) The other statements do function to establish this point by offering reasons to support it. You can answer "yes" to both questions, so you can safely conclude that this passage contains an argument.

It is important to recognize that *a statement is a premise or a conclusion only in the context of an argument:* no statement is *inherently* a premise or conclusion. A statement is a premise if it is offered as support for the conclusion, and a statement is a conclusion if it is the point for which support is offered. The same statement can serve in one argument as a premise and in another as a conclusion. In fact, in some arguments a statement plays both roles at the same time.

Consider the statement, "Abortion is at least sometimes permissible." In the preceding argument it functions as a conclusion. But in another argument (or in a continuation of the same argument) it may offer support for a further claim, that Mary, whose life is threatened by her pregnancy, should be able to have an abortion. In this case it is a premise.

Knowing that a statement can be a premise or conclusion *only* in the context of an argument can help you distinguish arguments from nonarguments. If you have good reason to think a statement is either a premise or a conclusion, then you also have good reason to think an argument is being offered.

4.1.3 Linguistic Cues Help Identify Arguments

Linguistic cues can help sort out the roles statements play. Certain words and phrases indicate that a statement plays the role of premise or conclusion. Learning to recognize these indicator phrases also helps you determine which statements in a passage are premises and which conclusions.

4.1.3a Premise Indicators   The following words and phrases suggest a premise (there are more, but these are probably the most common ones). In each case the statement *following* the indicator is the premise:

- for the reason that . . .
- as a consequence of . . .
- seeing that . . .
- may be inferred from . . .
- for . . . (when not used as a preposition)
- since . . . (when not synonymous with *after*)
- as shown by . . .
- because . . .
- follows from . . .

4.1.3b Conclusion Indicators   The following words and phrases suggest a conclusion. In each case the statement *following* the indicator is the conclusion:

- therefore . . .
- thus . . .
- consequently . . .
- it follows that . . .
- so . . . (has some exceptions)
- then . . . (not when preceded by *if*, and not when used temporarily)
- implies that . . .
- entails that . . .
- hence . . .

Exercise 4.1

Read each passage to determine whether there is an argument. If there is, underline the conclusion and place each premise in brackets. Circle any premise or conclusion indicators.

1. If Nixon were really guilty of all those crimes, then Congress would have impeached him. But they didn't. So he must have been innocent.

2. Observers of working conditions in Asia, Africa, and Latin America argue that today's Western shoppers are the final link in a trade chain that relies on exploited child labor to produce cheap products—a form of slavery that is no less odious because it goes largely unseen.

(Hammond 20)

3. You can believe what he says about finances. After all, he's a famous financial advisor, isn't he?

4. The schipperkee must not be a dog, for it has no tail. Everyone knows that dogs have tails.

5. If our town permits pot-bellied pigs as pets, lots of adult pigs will be turned in to the animal shelter since many people adopt them without knowing about their needs and behavior. In fact, most people are ill-equipped to deal with them. In addition, the costs of animal control have skyrocketed in recent years, and pigs, given their need for lots of space, would add an unnecessary burden to the shelter budget. All in all, it would be best to prohibit pigs as pets.

6. Then, in 1855, someone discovered a tablet in southern Mesopotamia that was inscribed in an unknown language. Scholars assumed it was the oldest language in the world. No one was optimistic about the prospects of its decipherment; it had no affinities with any language known to man.

(Potok 21)

7. Some hunting spiders locate mates by finding and following the draglines laid down by mature females of the same species. Experiments have demonstrated that male web spiders can often tell by touching the web whether it contains a mature female. Male orb weavers and other web spiders with poor vision announce their approach by plucking the strands of the female's web. Others stroke and tap the female cautiously. Spiders with

good vision, such as wolf spiders and the brightly colored
jumping spiders, dance and wave their legs before their mates.
A nursery web spider presents his mate with a fly before mating.
(Levi and Levi 10)

8. In a traditional country home, where the old ways are still
respected, a little ceremony takes place before each meal. The
father of the house takes a little rice, forms it into a ball with his
fingers, and places it outside on the land so that birds and
insects may share the earth's bounty with his family. It is a
charming act but one that is also deeply significant.
(Bhumitchitr 17)

9. I say that the pious is to do what I am doing now, to prosecute
the wrongdoer, be it about murder or temple robbery or anything
else, whether the wrongdoer is your father or your mother or
anyone else; not to prosecute is impious. And observe, Socrates,
that I can quote the law as a great proof that this is so. I have
already said to others that such actions are right. . . . These
people themselves believe that Zeus is the best and most just of
the gods, yet they agree that he bound his father because he
unjustly swallowed his sons, and that he in turn castrated his
father for similar reasons.
(Plato, *Euthyphro* 5e–6a)

10. You have heard that it was said, "You shall not commit adultery."
But I say to you that everyone who looks at a woman lustfully
has already committed adultery with her in his heart. If your
right eye causes you to sin, pluck it out and throw it away; it is
better that you lose one of your members than that your whole
body be thrown into hell. And if your right hand causes you to
sin, cut it off and throw it away; it is better that you lose one of your
members than that your whole body be thrown into hell.
(Matthew 5:27–30)

11. If a person is not to stifle his human feelings, he must practice
kindness towards animals, for he who is cruel to animals becomes hard also in his dealings with men.
(Kant 240)

12. Many years later, as he faced the firing squad, Colonel Aureliano
Buendia was to remember that distant afternoon when his father
took him to discover ice. At that time Macondo was a village of
twenty adobe houses, built on the bank of a river of clear water
that ran along a bed of polished stones, which were white and

enormous, like prehistoric eggs. The world was so recent that many things lacked names, and in order to indicate them it was necessary to point.

(Marquez 11)

13. As different schools later elaborated the Buddha's original teaching, quite diverse, even contrary, teachings and practices arose, each claiming to be the correct expression of the Buddha's insight, with the implication that the other schools were mistaken. The three main branches of this divergence are known as the Hinayana (the Lesser Path), the Mahayana (the Greater Path), and the Vajrayana (the Path of the Thunderbolt). But Sangharakshita (a Buddhist thinker) saw from the very outset the underlying unity of Buddhism. He saw it in the following way: he recognized the implication for this problem of the entirely transcendental nature of the Buddha's Enlightenment—transcendent, that is, over all our normal ways of knowing, accessible only to the "eye of Wisdom." Words and concepts, as the Zen saying has it, can only be "fingers pointing at the moon"—they can only indicate a higher truth that they cannot capture. If Enlightenment is, by its very nature, beyond all thinking, then no one expression of it can claim to be exhaustive. Thus the various schools of Buddhism can be seen as expressive of different roads to the same goal.

(Adapted from Subhuti 28–29)

14. No-fault divorce has abolished marriage today, but there is nothing inevitable or immutable about this state of affairs. The divorce rate can be brought under control by mere mortals. All we need to do is limit the circumstances under which marriages may be dissolved to mutual agreement or grounds (such as adultery, desertion, and criminal physical abuse) that clearly involve a wrong by one party against the other and that by their very nature constitute a violation of the marriage vows as they are traditionally understood. If we make it harder to leave a marriage, more people will decide they can make a go of it in their marriage after all.

(Adapted from Plunkett 54)

15. Insurance policies aimed specifically at those between 50 and 80 promise security, easy approval, low rates, and a policy that cannot be canceled if premiums are paid. So far so good. But many persons seeking these plans only think they have a problem getting insurance. Frequently someone with a questionable medical history and insurability problems can buy significant coverage for less than these plans cost. What's more, unlike these

plans, the coverage often offers benefits payable from the first
day, on the full amount of the policy.

(Lipson 286–87)

16. For most humans, especially those in modern urban and subur-
    ban communities, the most direct form of contact with nonhu-
    man animals is at mealtime: we eat them. This simple fact is the
    key to our attitudes to other animals, and also the key to what
    each of us can do about changing these attitudes. The use and
    abuse of animals raised for food far exceeds, in sheer numbers of
    animals affected, any other kind of mistreatment. Hundreds of
    millions of cattle, pigs, and sheep are raised and slaughtered in
    the United States alone each year; and for poultry the figure is a
    staggering three *billion*. (That means that about 5,000 birds—
    mostly chickens—will have been slaughtered in the time it takes
    you to read this page.) It is here, on our dinner table and in our
    neighborhood supermarket or butcher's shop, that we are
    brought into direct touch with the most extensive exploitation of
    other species that has ever existed.

(Singer 96)

17. There are writers, a few of them, who stir an immediate personal
    response. You need only read a few of their pages and you know
    right off that an unspoken, subterranean kinship will blossom.
    Usually it's not the writer's opinions or subjects that grip you,
    it's the tone of voice, perhaps a lilt of wry sincerity or a murmur
    of reflectiveness. For me, the Italian-Jewish memoirist and
    novelist Primo Levi is such a writer. I stand at some distance
    from his culture and even more from his experience—he is a
    survivor of Auschwitz—yet when I read his books I feel a sense
    of exhilarating closeness. I want to start holding imaginary
    conversations, as if Primo Levi and I were friends who had
    known each other for years.

(Howe 3)

18. You choose a lover according to how you want to be loved, and
    you choose a sex partner according to how you wish to be laid.
    There is no guarantee whatever that the person you love and the
    person you find most sexually desirable are one and the same.
    There are just certain things a lover may be unable to give you,
    and it may be good sex.

(Vannoy 24)

19. I should like to call attention to a strange distortion of the facts
    of which men otherwise sensible are found guilty. They call
    masturbation a substitute for the normal sex act. Ah, what might

not be written about the word "normal" sex act! But here I am dealing only with the idea of "substitute." . . In one form or another onanism (masturbation) accompanies a man throughout his life, while normal sex activity only begins at a particular age, and often ceases at a time when onanism takes on a childish form of conscious playing with the sexual organs. How can the one process be regarded as a substitute for another which only starts fifteen to twenty years later?

(Groddeck 45)

4.2 Displaying the Structure of Arguments

In an argument of any complexity there may be more than one conclusion and a number of premises leading to each of these conclusions. Before you can evaluate an argument, you need to be clear how the various premises and conclusions relate to each other. A pictorial device may help you keep such relations straight. After some practice, you should be able to diagram the structure of fairly complex arguments.

4.2.1 Diagramming Complete Statements

An argument, remember, is a set of statements, some of which are offered in support of one member of the set, and generally all of the statements are claimed to be true.[1] Your diagrams, therefore, should consist of complete statements.

Constructing diagrams based upon complete statements, however, raises two potential problems: first, some arguments include premises or conclusions that are not complete statements, and second, some statements themselves include parts that look like statements but do not function as statements in a particular passage. Let's consider each problem in turn.

4.2.2 Diagramming Incomplete Statements

Suppose you were to diagram the following argument:

There are a number of reasons, each sufficient on its own, why we ought to avoid wearing furs. The animals from which they come have to be

---

[1] Sometimes we consider arguments when we are uncertain of the truth—or even certain of the falsity—of the statements, but the simplest case to begin with is one in which the arguer asserts all of the statements to be true.

killed for us to obtain them; trapping and ranching are both cruel practices; so wearing an animal's skin for unnecessary, luxurious purposes
is highly reproachable.

For the most part, this argument is pretty clear. But notice that the premise
"trapping and ranching are both cruel" contains two claims, each of which
may be true or false, and each of which provides support on its own for
the conclusion that we ought not wear furs. This statement can be broken
into two statements:

Trapping is a cruel practice.

Ranching is a cruel practice.

By separating these claims, you clarify the different elements of the argument so that you may evaluate it. It may turn out that you wish to defend
the claim that trapping is cruel but not that ranching is cruel. Had you not
split the original statement into two claims, you would have difficulty
evaluating its truth. Considering two separate premises helps you to see
the actual strength of the argument.

4.2.3 Diagramming Complex Statements

Other statements consist of parts that may look like separate claims but
do not function separately. Splitting these into separate statements invites trouble. For example, consider an argument like this one:

If your hen has no chance to have sex with a rooster, then her eggs will
be unfertilized. Since you want fertilized eggs, you'd better introduce
your hen to a rooster.

You may be tempted to think that the first sentence can be broken into two
separate statements in order to diagram the argument more fully:

Your hen has no chance to have sex with a rooster.

and

Her eggs will be unfertilized.

But these statements are not parts of this argument: if they were, then
each of them would be presented as true. Clearly this argument claims
the opposite: it is an argument *for* introducing your hen to a rooster (a
conclusion inconsistent with the claim that your hen has no chance to
have sex with a rooster) in the hope of *having fertilized eggs* (something

one does not have if the second part were true). The argument itself makes sense, but not if either part of the "if . . . then . . ." (called a *conditional*) statement is true.

Notice that in this case the entire conditional statement is true, even though neither of the sentences from which it is constructed is. This is not unusual. For instance, it is true that "if there were a cure available for AIDS, then unprotected sexual intercourse wouldn't be as risky as it is today," even though there is no known cure for AIDS. Conditional statements can be true even when their parts are not, except in one case: where the if-clause (known as the *antecedent*) is true and the then-clause (known as the *consequent*) is false. So you cannot infer that a conditional statement is false from the fact that a component of a conditional statement is false, nor can you infer that the components of a conditional statement are both true from the truth of the entire conditional statement!

Be careful, then, not to separate "if . . . then . . ." statements when you identify the parts of an argument. A conditional statement functions as a single claim. Its meaning derives directly—and only—from the relationship it expresses between its two parts. It can do its work in an argument, and be true, even though its parts, when taken separately, are not themselves true.

Also beware of separating "either . . . or . . ." statements or those joined by just "or." Often "or" separates parts of a statement that appear to stand on their own, but the "or" structure prevents us from reading them separately. Consider this argument:

> Either the Internal Revenue Service does its job, or it doesn't. If it does its job, it's a threat to freedom, since it deprives us of our property and also makes government less accountable. If it doesn't, it's a threat to justice, because it increases inequalities. So the IRS is either a threat to freedom or a threat to justice. In either case, it should be done away with.

A number of statements here employ "or," but one example should make the point clear. The first statement tells us that the Internal Revenue Service either does or doesn't do its job. That is (trivially) true, and the argument uses the claim. However, the argument does not actually depend on the truth of either part of the claim; for this argument it does not matter which one of these options turns out to be true. In fact, they cannot both be true: they are *contradictory*. If you were to separate the two parts of the first statement, you would suggest that the argument rests on contradictory statements, and whatever flaws the argument may ultimately have, contradicting itself is not one of them. It is a mistake to divide the first statement into two simpler statements.

Some other statements that derive their meaning, and truth, from the relationship between their parts rather than from the parts independently use the following constructions: *unless* ("Nixon would not have resigned unless the threat of impeachment were strong"), *whenever* ("Whenever a person goes to the movies, he is transported into a fantasy world"), *only if* ("Only if you stay up all night will you be able to complete the assignment"), and *just in case* ("A statement is a premise just in case it is being offered as reason for something else").

Unfortunately, you cannot rely on a mechanical rule to determine whether you ought to break a statement into its parts. You have to remain sensitive to the sense of the passage, deciding whether it asserts the parts of its complex statements as well as the whole complex.

4.2.4 Types of Argument Structure

Premises may lead to conclusions in one of three ways. A simple argument often works according to single structure in various combinations.

4.2.4a Serial Arguments   Serial arguments move from a single premise to a conclusion and then from that conclusion to another conclusion. Consider the following argument adapted from Bernard Rollin's *Animal Rights and Human Morality* (49):

> The taking of animal life for food is unjustifiable, for we can live well without taking animal life, and consequently our mere gustatory predilection for meat does not override an animal's right to its life.

The first line of this argument is the conclusion, and the next two provide premises for it. Notice the indicator word *consequently*; it indicates that the last statement, "our mere gustatory predilection for meat does not override an animal's right to its life," is supported by the other premise (which is signaled by the premise indicator *for*). We can depict this relation in a tree diagram as follows (note that we will always place the conclusion at the top of our diagram and use an arrow to indicate the direction from premise to conclusion):

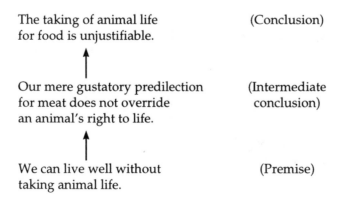

The taking of animal life for food is unjustifiable.	(Conclusion)
↑	
Our mere gustatory predilection for meat does not override an animal's right to life.	(Intermediate conclusion)
↑	
We can live well without taking animal life.	(Premise)

In serial arguments a single statement plays the role of both a conclusion and a premise (called an *intermediate conclusion*). It's important not to be misled by indicators; you can use either a premise indicator or a conclusion indicator to flag an intermediate conclusion. In some places, you will find them both used together—sometimes in a seemingly odd conjunction of indicator words, such as *since, therefore.*

4.2.4b Convergent Arguments   In convergent arguments two or more reasons independently support a conclusion. The argument cited previously about wearing furs suggests that it should be treated as convergent; it begins, "There are a number of reasons, each sufficient on its own, why we ought to avoid wearing furs." You might diagram that argument as follows:

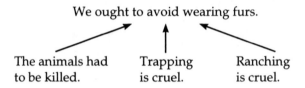

We ought to avoid wearing furs.

The animals had   Trapping   Ranching
to be killed.   is cruel.   is cruel.

The separate arrow from each premise to the conclusion indicates a separate line of reasoning to that conclusion.

4.2.4c Linked Arguments   Linked arguments also offer more than one premise for a conclusion, but these premises provide a *joint* reason. In conjunction with each other they support the conclusion; by themselves they do not (or at least not as strongly). A simple example of a linked argument is this:

> If your car is out of gas, then it won't run. And it is out of gas. So don't expect it to run.

You can diagram this argument as follows:

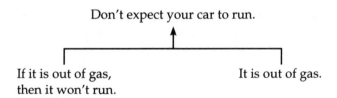

Don't expect your car to run.

If it is out of gas,   It is out of gas.
then it won't run.

The two lines join the separate premises to form *one arrow*, indicating that they lead jointly to the conclusion. This device distinguishes linked from convergent arguments. You can test the accuracy of your diagram by reading from the bottom, from the initial premises, to the top, substituting the word *therefore* for each arrow.

4.2.4d Which Kind Is It Really? A Note of Caution   You will find most arguments clearly serial, linked, or convergent. Occasionally, however, you may have difficulty determining whether an argument is linked or convergent, even after you have carefully considered the distinction between the two forms. Don't worry too much about that. The point of diagramming is to display your understanding of the relationship between premises and conclusions so that you can assess the argument. If two different ways of depicting the argument seem justified, try each one. Select the one that presents you with the stronger argument since you want to understand the argument at its best. If both interpretations represent an equally strong argument, the choice doesn't matter.

4.2.5 Diagramming Arguments with Several Structures

The argument about the Internal Revenue Service (Section 4.2.3) combines several structures to form a slightly more complex argument diagram:

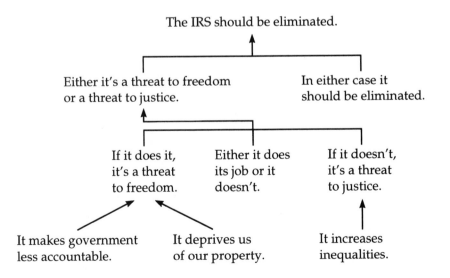

Notice how the diagram clearly depicts the various relationships between premises and conclusions, helping you to understand its structure. Notice also how the arrows, read as *therefore*, help you to test the accuracy of your representation.

Exercise 4.2

1. Diagram each of the passages containing arguments in Exercise 4.1.
2. Make up an argument of your own for each of the three structures, and then make up a fourth argument that combines at least two types of structure. Diagram all your arguments, of course!
3. Select a letter to the editor of a newspaper and diagram the argument you find there.

Sometimes we consider arguments when we are uncertain of the truth—or even certain of the falsity—of the statements, but the simplest case to begin with is one in which the arguer asserts all of the statements to be true.

5

Reconstructing Arguments

Before you can evaluate an argument, you must understand it fully, and that entails not only discovering which premises support which conclusions but also carefully scrutinizing each of those parts. When you clarify the meaning of an argument, you "reconstruct" it. You have already begun reconstructing arguments by diagraming them. Diagrams display the structure of an argument—that is, which premises provide reasons for which conclusions. To continue reconstructing an argument you must clarify its language and supply any unstated parts.

5.1 Clarifying Meaning

Sometimes you must clarify the meaning of terms, phrases, or sentences before you can understand arguments posed by others or, for that matter, your own arguments. Clarifying the meaning of a statement can lead you to recognize an important criticism of an argument and to rework your own argument.

5.1.1 Paraphrasing

You can clarify an argument by paraphrasing either all or part of it. A paraphrase expresses the original meaning in your own words; it should be about the same length and as detailed as the original. (In this way a paraphrase differs from a summary, which is a shorter, less-detailed version of the original.)

Paraphrasing enables you to test your understanding of an argument. Writing out an argument in your own words, or your own argument in different words, can reveal exactly where you find it difficult or obscure. You may be astonished at your difficulty articulating a passage that seems clear to you in the original version. In addition, by paraphrasing an argument, you can clarify it so that you are able to evaluate it. You may discover, for example, how little is said in some pretentious-sounding passage or separate what is said explicitly from implicit attitudes expressed by the language's tone.

When you paraphrase, you have two important responsibilities. First, you should be fair and charitable. Your paraphrase should reflect the best possible interpretation of an argument, the one that is most likely to be accurate or true. If you can interpret an argument in more than one way, give it the best reading. That is, give it the interpretation that is most likely to be true or plausible. If you do not paraphrase it charitably, your ultimate evaluation will be less than effective, since it will not have considered the strongest version of the argument. (You may even be attacking a "straw man," an irrelevant argument. See Section 8.2.2b for more on the straw-man fallacy.)

Providing a charitable reading does not mean that you must ignore errors. In particular, you need to pay attention to constraints other than truth when deciding which reading to give a sentence. What might be the most plausible reading of someone's words in terms of truth may not be the reading most likely to help support the conclusion of the argument in question. So you have to balance these elements to determine the best overall reading of someone's words.

Your second responsibility is to make the paraphrased argument as clear as possible. Although an argument may be obscure in a number of ways, two in particular lead to confusing or deceptive argumentation: ambiguity and vagueness.

5.1.2 Ambiguity

Ambiguity occurs for a number of reasons. One source of ambiguity is the many words in English, called *homonyms*, that carry more than one meaning. Such words as *audit, comb, fire,* and *tragedy* provide simple examples:

1. a. She *audited* the course in feminist theories.
   b. The IRS *audited* his tax return.

2. a. They *combed* the hillside but were unable to find the diamond.
   b. They *combed* each other's hair.

3. a. After *firing* up the kiln, we cannot open it until it cools sufficiently.
   b. "Downsizing" is a euphemism for *firing* workers.

4. a. A number of Shakespeare's finest plays are *tragedies*.
   b. The earthquake in Sakhalin Island was a *tragedy*.

© 1997 by Sidney Harris

Ambiguity can occur not only because words and phrases have more than one meaning, but also because entire sentences are sometimes put together in ways that lend themselves to multiple interpretations. "He didn't die because he ate fish" is a sentence that can be understood in two ways (did he die, or not?), but every word in it is unambiguous. However, just because an expression *can* have a variety of meanings does not, by itself, make a statement ambiguous.

> An expression is ambiguous when, in context,
> it remains open to more than one interpretation.

Because the context makes each of the previous examples 1–4 clear, none can be considered an example of ambiguous language. Yet sometimes the possibility of multiple interpretations is not ruled out by context. Subtle ambiguities can make a very serious difference to reasoning.

Philosopher Dan Magurshak demonstrated this point in relation to conclusions that others have drawn from the claim that the Holocaust is incomprehensible. Many people do speak of the destruction of European Jewry as an especially incomprehensible event. After all, how can the coordinated, mass destruction of an entire people be comprehended? How can we understand the intentional murder of millions by a state that supposedly represented the epitome of civilization? How can we make sense of civilized adults burning babies alive?

> [I]ncomprehensibility, at the very least, means the impossibility of understanding fully and adequately the "jointly sufficient," or the necessary, conditions for the Holocaust's occurrence. It means that even after ideally exhaustive historical, psychological, and sociological analyses, the researchers would still have failed to penetrate the essence of this event. It also implies that, since control and prevention of such outrages presuppose some understanding of their essential components, a generation whose scholars remember the past may, because of its incomprehensibility, still be doomed to repeat it. Indeed, some would-be investigators might even conclude that, since [the Holocaust] is inexplicable, scholarly "remembrance," except for honoring the dead, is rather fruitless.
>
> (Magurshak 421-22)

As Magurshak explains, drawing such conclusions may result from using the term *incomprehensibility* in different ways. For example, *incomprehensibility* may mean that no answer can be given to the question why such events occur. Or it may mean that such events are emotionally overwhelming—think about the live babies being thrown into the flames. These are different ideas. What is emotionally overwhelming may nonetheless be capable of explanation (just as the aesthetic wonder that sometimes overwhelms people as they view a sunset does not imply that sunsets are theoretically impenetrable by science). One would be mistaken to draw the conclusion that further study would be fruitless because the Holocaust is incomprehensible in the sense of being emotionally overwhelming, because the fruit of further study might well derive from comprehension in the sense of explanation. Despite the overwhelming emotions one may understandably experience in reflecting on the Holocaust, further study may well help to understand how states commit systematic murder, how it is possible for others to stand by and do little or nothing as it happens, and therefore whether and how such events may be avoidable. These are surely desirable goals. Thus, the quoted passage above exploits the ambiguity of *incomprehensibility* to arrive illegitimately at its conclusion. This kind of exploitation of ambiguity is an example of *equivocation*—we will discuss it more fully when we return to fallacies in Section 8.7.2.

When you discover ambiguity in an argument, you will want to understand it and if possible eliminate it, "disambiguating" the argument.

If the argument is your own, and you know the intended meaning, simply clarify the passage by recasting the sentence or developing the context. If you are reconstructing someone else's argument, clarify the ambiguous statement in your paraphrase by choosing the reading that contributes best to the argument. You can avoid ambiguity by rewriting the ambiguous passage or by placing it in a context that clarifies it:

1. You can *replace* the troublesome expression with one that is less likely to cause confusion. For example, the statement "Smitty, a fireman, let us down," may be ambiguous. You can clarify it by saying, "Smitty disappointed us" or "Smitty lowered us to the ground."
2. If you want to retain the expression (be sure you have good cause if you do), you can clarify it by *expanding* it. You may say, for instance, "Smitty let us down with a rope" or "Smitty let us down when he failed to claim what is rightfully his."
3. You can clarify the *context*. For example, if you say, "Smitty let us down," in the course of discussing his failure to perform his job as well as you had expected, the context determines how the sentence is to be interpreted.

5.1.3 Vagueness

A term or expression is potentially vague when it fails to clarify borderline cases. For example, some people are clearly wealthy and some clearly poor, but many people do not fit neatly into either of these categories. They are borderline cases. Note that we consider them borderline cases not because we lack information about their finances—we may know their assets and liabilities exactly and still be unable to decide whether they are wealthy or poor. The potential vagueness is a feature of the terms—or concepts—themselves.

But just as not all potentially ambiguous statements are ambiguous in all contexts, just because an expression can be vague does not, by itself, mean that it is always, or even usually, vague.

> An expression is vague if its context demands greater precision than the expression provides.

A term is vague (that is, its use becomes problematic) when it leaves borderline cases fuzzy in a context that requires them to be clear. For instance, the terms *wealthy* and *poor* present no problem in many contexts. However, they are not precise enough to set tax rates. To avoid endless and unsolvable disputes about tax liability, tax law must define borderline cases exactly. That is why tax tables mention not wealth but income amounts rounded to the nearest dollar. The vagueness is largely eliminated since (a) there are clear conventions for rounding to the nearest dollar, (b) taxable assets are defined in law, and (c) tax laws specify the amount of tax liability for every possible combination of assets. (Of course, tax laws are quite complex, so there can still be areas of vagueness even after this considerably more precise set of terms is used.)

You can determine whether a term is vague by asking if, in context, it leaves these doubts:

1. Is there doubt about whether the term applies to this case?
2. Does it make a substantial difference whether or not the term applies to this case?
3. Does the doubt arise from something other than a need to collect more facts about the case?

If you can answer "yes" to all three questions, the term is indeed vague in the context where you find it.

Once you have identified a term as vague, what can you do about it? Just as you can eliminate ambiguity by replacing the troubling expression with a clear one, so you can eliminate vague terms by substituting more precise ones (such as substituting precise dollar amounts for the vague term *wealthy* in the example above). However, you may not be able to replace a vague term until you know where to draw the line in borderline cases. To decide, you will need to define the vague term.

But where do you find your definition? Different kinds of definitions yield different results because they serve different purposes. Some definitions can be found by looking in standard dictionaries. These, called *lexical definitions*, report common usage of a term. They are appropriate when you need to understand how a word is ordinarily used. Such definitions are far from arbitrary; they can be correct or incorrect, depending on whether or not they accurately reflect the common usage of a term.

Some dictionaries also report uncommon uses of terms. Technical dictionaries are full of them. These, called *technical definitions*, may be special uses of terms found in everyday language (for example, *valid* and *sound* are understood in special ways by logicians) or definitions of terms unfamiliar outside a specialized field (such as referring to an argument with a particular form as *modus tollens*).

Other definitions, called *stipulative definitions*, cannot be found in either ordinary or specialized dictionaries because they don't exist until someone creates them. A researcher may introduce a new term as part of a theory and then, of course, specify its meaning. Terms like *neutrino*, *x-ray*, and *endorphin* most likely were introduced this way. Or someone may adopt a term already in common use that expresses an idea close to that needed for a theory and then narrow its meaning to clarify it in the context of the theory. Our definition of *argument*, for instance, is consistent with, but narrower than, some of the ordinary uses of the term. Mathematicians have used *argument* in yet another sense when talking about the *argument of a function*.

When you eliminate a vague term by definition, you must provide a stipulative definition. You must decide how the borderline cases are to be addressed. Unlike lexical definitions, stipulative definitions are neither correct nor incorrect, accurate nor inaccurate. Nevertheless, they can be more or less successful. When you define a vague term to clarify it, you do so to serve a purpose: to clarify a border. You—and others—can always evaluate how well the definition serves its purpose. (Consider, for example, how well the dollar amounts used in tax law, and the continuing debate about those amounts, help to clarify wealth.)

When you eliminate vagueness through definition, keep the following in mind:

1. What is the purpose for which the term in question proves too vague?
2. What are the consequences of defining the term in a particular way, and can you accept them? Are there better ways of making the term more precise?

Answering these questions will both guide you in defining vague terms and keep you from defining terms unnecessarily. You may want to define terms early in a discussion simply because they are potentially vague. Beware of this urge. You can divert your attention from the critical issues in an argument by focusing unnecessarily or too early on definitions or, worse, produce a smokescreen against seriously considering a view. It is possible to get on quite well in many discussions without defining crucial terms. Define only those terms that are actually vague, that threaten your understanding, and not those that are merely potentially vague.

Exercise 5.1

I. Paraphrase the following passages to clarify their meaning.

A. Cancer is, after all, a matter of attitude. If you have given up trying to synthesize your energy potential, you are already on the road to energy distortion, and that causes cancer. Keep synthesizing and avoid cancer.

(Alpha Sprout)

B. Journalists say that when a dog bites a man that is not news, but when a man bites a dog that is news. This is the essence of the language instinct: language conveys news. The stream of words called "sentences" are not just memory prods, reminding you of man and man's best friend and letting you fill in the rest; they tell you who in fact did what to whom. . . . When scientists see some apparent trick in nature, like bats homing in on insects in pitch blackness or salmon returning to breed in their natal stream, they look for the engineering principles behind it. For bats, the trick turned out to be sonar; for salmon it was locking in to a faint scent trail. What is the trick behind the ability of *Homo sapiens* to convey that man bites dog?

(Pinker 83)

II. Some of the following sentences are ambiguous. Provide at least two reasonable paraphrases of the sentences you think are ambiguous, pinpointing the source of the ambiguity if possible. If the sentence is not ambiguous, provide a single paraphrase of it.

A. All that glitters is not gold.

B. Criticism of antidrug laws is often misinterpreted as approval of drug use.

C. Though Johnny Carson hosted *The Tonight Show* for more than two decades, David Letterman hosted more shocking shows than did Carson.

D. Don't they teach you to be polite in school?

E. He's religious.

F. Hansen claims its sodas are "natural."

G. Stiff Opposition Expected to Casketless Funeral Plan

(Newspaper headline qtd. in Pinker 79)

H. Sam always tells the truth.

I. She didn't marry because she was a widow.

J. Visiting faculty can often be a source of inspiration.

K. Unanimity [among scientific experts] is often the result of a political decision: dissenters are suppressed or remain silent to preserve the reputation of science as a source of trustworthy and almost infallible knowledge.

(Feyerabend 88)

L. Dear Abby: Do you think a man would rent a motel room

and ask a lady to go there to "cuddle"? This is no joke.—The Lady

> Dear Lady: Only if he couldn't do anything else.

(Los Angeles Times, March 2, 1988)

M. What's a Grammy Worth?

(Los Angeles Times headline, March 2, 1988)

N. Blessed is he who considers the poor.

(Psalms 41:2)

O. Classified ad: "We can locate almost anyone! Real fast! Results guaranteed. Mr. Keen—'tracer of missing persons'"

(Los Angeles Times, March 2, 1988)

P. Human beings are unique among the primates in the intensity and variety of their sexual activity.

(Wilson 145)

Q. Embarrassed officials of the Acme roofing company are concerned about continuing reports that their own roof, despite all their efforts, continues to drip water every time it rains. The word is that they are trying to plug the leak.

III. Eliminate the ambiguity in each of the following sentences by using all three methods discussed on p. 103:

A. Where did you get infected?
B. Ginny ran the marathon.
C. When I looked up the meaning of *obfuscation*, I found confusion.
D. I can't recommend her too highly.
E. I saw the space shuttle flying past Cape Canaveral.
F. I almost had a car repossessed.

IV. Explain how potentially vague terms in the following passages actually interfere with your understanding of the issue.

A. Every now and then a proposal is made to detain without opportunity for bail people who have been arrested and charged with committing serious crimes and who are considered to be "dangerous." Explain what difficulties such a proposal creates. Do you think the difficulties are insurmountable?
B. Imagine you are an administrator at a university. The Board of Trustees, recognizing that the decrease in the number of students

this year forces them to restrict the offerings of the institution, has just instructed you to eliminate the "dead weight" from the school. You must now make some proposals to the appropriate faculty committee for discussion. What will your proposals be, and how do you justify their selection?

C. Identify three vague terms in any source you wish (e.g., from a textbook, newspaper, or magazine). Explain why you think they are vague as used. How can their vagueness best be eliminated?

5.2 Supplying Missing Parts

Once you have clarified an argument, you can ask whether its presentation omits any pertinent information. Not uncommonly, writers and speakers leave premises and even conclusions unstated. Nonetheless, these premises and conclusions must be assumed if an argument is to succeed. Identifying them is an important part of reconstructing arguments.

5.2.1 Assumptions

An *assumption*, a statement presented as true without support or demonstration, can be either explicit or implicit in an argument. When it is explicit, we will call it a *mere assertion*, when implicit, a *missing premise*.

5.2.1a Mere Assertions   When a point is made without any visible support, without any evidence, we say it is *merely asserted*. Consider this argument:

P1: Socrates was a citizen of Athens.
P2: Only men could be citizens of Athens.
P3: So Socrates must have been a man.
P4: All men are seduceable.
———————————————————————
C: Thus, Socrates was seduceable.

Although P3 is supported by P1 and P2, no evidence is offered for P1, P2, and P4. P1, P2, and P4 are "assumed" by the argument whereas P3 is not. You need to identify such assertions in order to see the structure of an argument, in order to ascertain which statements are supported by which other statements. We depict mere assertions in a tree diagram as branches with no branching beneath them.

But an argument may also assume other information, information that is crucial to its success but is not stated overtly. Such assumptions are referred to variously as *implicit, tacit, unstated,* or *missing* premises.

5.2.1b Missing Premises   Why omit something that is actually part of an argument? The writer may think the point too obvious to mention, assuming that readers will readily supply the missing information. A Burger King ad made such an assumption:

> The bigger the burger, the better the burger.
>
> The burgers are bigger at Burger King.

The conclusion, that burgers are better at Burger King, can safely be omitted; listeners can be counted on to supply it accurately. More deviously, an author may seek to hide a claim that might reveal a weakness in the argument. Or, commonly, the arguer is not fully aware that the argument requires the missing information.

Supplying missing premises (and conclusions) is not a matter of mind reading or even trying to discover what the arguer believes (since she herself may be unaware that her argument relies upon them). Sometimes, as a matter of scholarship, you may wish to hunt down an author's beliefs and discover their connection to a particular argument, but that is not your most common concern in looking for missing premises. In seeking missing premises, you want to understand an argument sufficiently to judge whether you should be convinced by it. Therefore, you look for claims implicit in the argument as stated.

Why focus extensively on what is implicit in an argument? You may discover assumptions of which the author is unaware. You can identify missing premises in your own argument as well as in others'. And the writer's beliefs may not be the only (or even the best) way to get from the given premises to the conclusion. If you want to assess the value of an argument, you must consider it at its best. Therefore, let the argument, not the arguer, motivate you as you identify missing premises.

5.2.2 Finding Missing Premises

How do you know what is implicit in an argument? Ask yourself whether the premises offered to support a conclusion are sufficient to infer it. That is, consider each inference, each arrow in your diagram.

Consider this argument (adopted from Valasquez 151–53):

> In a system with free markets and private property, producers are motivated to provide what consumers want at the lowest price. Hence, producers will always try to use resources as efficiently as possible.

Clearly this argument assumes that efficient use of resources helps producers keep prices down. (This argument makes a number of assumptions, but focus on this one.) How do you know this is the assumption? You know that this claim (or something like it) is implicit in the argument because you know that if this additional claim is not true, the given premise ("In a system with free markets and private property, producers are motivated to provide what consumers want at the lowest price") would not provide strong enough support for the conclusion. Since an argument is intended to provide adequate support for its conclusion, you may suppose that it is committed to whatever is necessary to provide that support.

Thus, you know that an argument has omitted a premise when you can say that the argument as presented does not provide sufficient support for its conclusion. In such cases the argument makes a "leap." The aim of supplying missing premises is to articulate what has been leapt over. Once you see what has been omitted, you will be able to determine whether the leap is justified or not.

Four criteria should guide you in identifying missing premises (adapted from Hitchcock). The first follows directly from the primary purpose in identifying missing premises, to strengthen a weak argument:

5.2.2a Added Premises Should Be Powerful Enough to Sustain the Inference   Consider this example (adapted from Velasquez 23–25):

> As a loyal agent, a manager should serve the employer as the employer would want to be served. Therefore, a manager should single-mindedly act to serve the self-interest of his or her employer.

An assumption links the duty to serve an employer *as the employer would want to be served* to serving the employer *in whatever ways will advance the employer's self-interest*. Which of the following serves best as the missing link?

1. Managers want to serve the best interests of their employers.
2. An employer wants to be served in whatever ways advance his or her self-interest.

Consider the first suggestion. Does the addition of this premise make the argument strong enough? Unfortunately not, since what managers *want* for their employers may differ from the *duties* they have to their employers. Adding this premise does not increase support for the conclusion.

The second suggestion is better; adding it to the argument supplies some needed strength. But even with this additional premise, the stated argument is not sufficiently strong to support the conclusion. The conclusion claims that managers should promote the self-interests of their employers single-mindedly. Nothing has yet been said to support this single-mindedness. You need to supply an additional premise that connects this single-mindedness with the conclusion. You know a missing premise exists, remember, when it is needed to get from the stated premises to the conclusion.

Consider these two possibilities:

3. The only duty a manager has in acting as manager is to serve the employer as the employer would want to be served.
4. A manager should place the duty to serve his or her employer as the employer would want to be served above most other duties.

The second choice may seem more plausible than the first, but the first is what the argument requires. By "single-mindedly" pursuing the interests of the employer, the manager must place this duty above others. The second option does not restrict the manager to this extent; it is not sufficiently restrictive. So the argument needs the first claim.

You can write out, and then diagram, the resulting argument as follows:

P1: As a loyal agent, a manager should serve the employer as the employer would want to be served.

MP1: An employer wants to be served in whatever ways advance his or her self-interest.

MP2: The only duty a manager has in acting as manager is to serve the employer as the employer would want to be served.

C: Therefore, a manager should single-mindedly act to serve the self-interests of his or her employer.

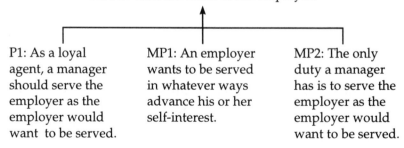

C: A manager should single-mindedly act to serve the self-interests of his or her employer.

P1: As a loyal agent, a manager should serve the employer as the employer would want to be served.

MP1: An employer wants to be served in whatever ways advance his or her self-interest.

MP2: The only duty a manager has is to serve the employer as the employer would want to be served.

Notice that MP1 and MP2 are linked (not convergent) with the premise that assumes them. Because missing premises are added to strengthen an inference, they act as *part* of a reason for a conclusion, and thus they should always be added as links.

5.2.2b Added Premises Should Be as Weak as Possible   Although added premises should be powerful enough to strengthen the inference sufficiently, they should be as weak as possible (without undermining the first criterion). That is, the less they claim about the world, the more likely they are to be true. Notice the difference between the weaker first statement in each of the following pairs and the more powerful second statement:

1. A. Many men are sexist.
   B. All men are sexist.
2. A. No one wants to take an unnecessary risk of acquiring AIDS.
   B. No one wants to take any risk of acquiring AIDS.
3. A. His hair is dark.
   B. His hair is jet-black.

If you claim the B statements as true, you are also committed to claiming the A statements as true, but not the reverse. If there is just one nonsexist man, 1B will be false whereas 1A may still be true. Because the stronger B statements make greater claims than the weaker A statements, they can go wrong more easily.

Since you reconstruct an argument to give it its best reading, you want to avoid burdening it with a claim any stronger than necessary for the premises to support the conclusion. If a statement you identify as a missing premise turns out to be false, whereas a weaker premise you might have added is not, you have set up the reconstructed argument for unfair criticism.

Consider this argument:

P1: This metal was heated.
_____
C: Therefore, this metal expanded.

What connects P1 to C? One possible link is this premise:

MP1: Everything expands when heated.

MP1 certainly strengthens the inference from P1 to C sufficiently, fulfilling the first criterion. But we should hope this is not the best candidate, since it is clearly false. The argument may yet succeed with a different premise:

MP2: Metals expand when heated.

MP2 is weaker than MP1 but will still do the job, so it is preferable. Suppose you reconstruct the argument with MP1 identified as missing premise and then (correctly) point out that MP1 is false. Although you may accurately criticize the reconstructed argument, you would not be attending to the original one.

5.2.2c *The Supplied Premise Should Not Work Independently of Existing Premises*   If it does, you have not supplied what is missing from an argument but instead substituted a different argument for the original. Suppose someone argues:

> P1: The fire began in two separate locations at the same time.
> ---
> C: The fire was caused by arson.

Consider this as the missing premise:

> MP1: Hubert saw someone set the fire, and he is a reliable witness.

It would be nice to have a reliable eyewitness—this would certainly add strength to the overall case one could make that arson had occurred. But notice that the addition of MP1 strengthens the argument independently of P1 rather than by working in conjunction with it. The resulting argument would not link P1 to MP1, but would constitute a convergent argument. A better candidate for a missing premise to link P1 to C would be:

> MP2: It is unlikely that a fire would start in two locations at the same time unless it had been intentionally set.

MP2 is preferable because it helps us see why P1 leads to C.

5.2.2d *Supplied Premises Should Not Be Trivial*   Identifying a missing premise makes explicit something that is implicit in an argument. Be careful to avoid adding something trivial, something that does not help you understand the intricacies of an argument. For instance, you may propose this as a missing premise in the argument about expanding metal:

> MP3: If this metal was heated, then it expanded.

Notice that adding this premise does strengthen the inference adequately. But the resulting strength is trivial: the added premise simply states that if the original premise is true, then so is the conclusion. It does not help you to see *why* that is so, the task of supplying a missing link between them. This added premise (MP3) trivializes the process of identifying missing premises.

Exercise 5.2

I. Determine which statement is the best missing premise for each argument and explain what is wrong with the others.

A. He's a redhead.

Therefore, he's probably short-tempered.

  a. Redheads are short-tempered.
  b. Some redheads are short-tempered.
  c. Most male redheads are short-tempered.
  d. Most redheads are short-tempered.

B. Applicants for U.S. citizenship must pass a test for proficiency in English.

Therefore, foreign-language ballots are largely unnecessary.

  a. English-language ballots are not written in language more difficult than that required on the citizenship literacy tests.
  b. If people can't be bothered to take the time to learn enough English to read a ballot, they should not expect to be able to vote.
  c. Foreign-language ballots falsely imply that Hispanics and Asians cannot read any English.

II. Write out the missing premises for each of the following arguments:

A. A check of bilingual ballot users in New York in 1991 disclosed that 75 percent were used by United States citizens who would not have voted if there were no ballot available in their native language.

Foreign-language ballots help make our country more democratic.

B. Increasing the number of male teachers would provide more diverse models for children to identify with.

Increasing the number of male teachers would be beneficial.

C. He's a homosexual.

So he shouldn't be appointed to a position that requires clearance for classified documents.

D. To lead a happy life, people must be able to look forward to something after death.

Atheists must lead unhappy lives.

E. Laws are supposed to protect everyone equally.

So the laws should be available in public libraries in language that ordinary people can understand.

F. Owning life insurance is the best way to furnish money for funeral expenses, money to help the family out of its debts, and money to pay off mortgages and send children through college.

So every father should own life insurance.

G. If the state may tax dissemination of ideas, it may set the tax rate.

Thus, a tax on disseminating ideas would infringe the right of free speech.

H. Suppose a vegetarian became ill, and a doctor prescribed a beef tea. Vegetarianism builds the spirit and not the body.

Therefore, he would not be a vegetarian any longer.

(Adapted from Gandhi 323)

III. Consider the argument of the following letter. What is Morgan's conclusion? What assumptions are needed for him to reach that conclusion from these premises?

> I don't think that he [President Clinton] knows that there were about 4,800 American citizens living then in Hiroshima in 1941, who intended to return home but could not. They were under suspicion and some treated as spies by the Japanese. By 1945, most were still there. In the U.S. today, we have upwards of 700 American citizens who are atomic bomb survivors. We can't undo the past, but please let us not go out of our way to bless our past mistakes.
>
> (Morgan A11)

IV. The following question and response appeared in Marilyn Vos Savant's Parade magazine column, "Ask Marilyn":

> Q: In which of the following two ways do I help my country more: buying a $20,000 American-made car or donating $20,000 to an American charity?
>
> A: If we multiply your gesture many times among many people all over the country, then buying all those cars (or any other goods or services) will be better for the economy. But if you're interested in maximizing the impact of your particular contribution, donating the dollars to charity would make them stretch further, because the transaction escapes the taxes that fuel the government bureaucracy. When you buy a car, the transaction is laden with taxes. First, you have to earn at least $25,000 to pay some $5000 in various income taxes and still have $20,000 left over for the car. Then, when you buy the car, you may pay around $1300 in local sales taxes. The auto dealer will then have to pay tax on

his profit after paying the automaker for the car. And the automaker will have to pay tax on its profit, etc.—all the way down to the assembly line. In other words, the same dollars are taxed again and again, with comparatively little of it going to the employers and employees of the American auto industry.

(Vos Savant 12)

A. What ambiguity did Vos Savant detect in the question? Was she right that the original question was ambiguous in that way?

B. What is the most reasonable interpretation of "helping my country"? Is this expression vague or ambiguous?

C. Determine which of the following options most accurately reflect assumptions made in Vos Savant's response:

1. The reasons she offered to show that one's personal spending of $20,000 on an American-made automobile would not have as great an impact on the economy as her spending the same $20,000 on charity depend upon the assumption that:

   a. Money paid in taxes is no longer part of the economy.
   b. Employers and employees in the auto industry do not make enough money.
   c. Money paid for a product that does not reach the employees and employers in that industry does not help our country (e.g., because tax money sometimes goes toward foreign aid).
   d. Although money paid in taxes may remain within our economy (after all, taxes are spent on public works projects, welfare, defense, etc.), it is not likely to create jobs or incentives to produce more.
   e. (Your own suggested missing premise)

2. The estimate that $25,000 in income is required to purchase a car depends on which assumption?

   a. People who buy cars usually do not take out automobile loans.
   b. You can't get an automobile loan unless you have at least enough after-tax income to pay for the car.
   c. Most people purchasing cars are not able to escape paying taxes (e.g., by having enough deductible business expenses to adjust income to a nontaxed level), and a rate of about 20 percent is the minimum income tax.

5.3 Case Study: Sample Analysis and Reconstruction

As you reconstruct an argument, you must make judgments, and when you do, others may reasonably disagree with you. Keep in mind that your aim in reconstructing arguments is to understand the argument as fully as possible—and in the best possible light.

Consider the following report from the *Los Angeles Times* (October 8, 1984) about the first presidential debate of 1984:

> On the thorny issue of abortion, President Reagan took the position that "until and unless someone can establish that an unborn child is not a human being, then that child is already protected by the Constitution, which guarantees life, liberty and the pursuit of happiness to all of us."

In order to reconstruct Reagan's argument you first need to clarify some statements:

1. As the argument is presented, the conclusion is not stated, but it is fairly obvious. You may be tempted to express it in such terms as "Abortion is not justified." At a minimum, Reagan argues that we should do something to ensure what he takes to be the implicit constitutional prohibition of abortion, so a good candidate for a conclusion may be "Additional prohibition of abortion is needed." This expression of the conclusion satisfies the purpose of the argument without committing Reagan to more than necessary to accomplish that purpose.

2. In addition, it is clear that the force of "until" in the first statement is that "no one has yet" established that an unborn child is not a human being. Otherwise his argument would not provide reasons for or against abortion, but only tell us what we need to find out in order to solve the problem.

3. Given this reading of "until," Reagan's argument appears to move from what *has not* been established to what *cannot* be established. It seems to read, "No one has yet established that the unborn are not human, so no one can establish it." That is an obviously bad argument: what has not yet happened may still be possible. Is there an interpretation not so obviously flawed? In fact, nothing important seems to hang on putting the issue in terms of what *can* be established: a weaker claim about what has happened appears to be sufficient for his argument. So we may restate his claim as "Unless someone has established. . . ."

4. Reagan's choice of words, using *child* rather than the more clinical *fetus* or *embryo* (depending on the stage of pregnancy), may look prejudicial to those who favor the permissibility of

abortion. Indeed, referring to the fetus as a child may produce certain emotional reactions that referring to it as a fetus would not produce, since we associate "child" with those already born (and sometimes even distinguish infants from children). Changing the terminology should reveal whether the argument relies illegitimately on such an association. Replace "child" with "fetus" to see to what extent Reagan relies on these emotional associations.

5. You may also question Reagan's use of the word "us" when he states that the Constitution guarantees certain rights to "all of us." Who does Reagan mean by "us"? Is this pronoun's referent ambiguous?

In this context, "us" may include human beings, human beings who have been born, or American citizens. You may think the guarantee covers only American citizens because the Constitution gives protection of a special sort to citizens. For example, the 14th Amendment (where the protection of life, liberty, and property [1] appears) refers specifically to American citizens. It begins by defining citizenship: "All persons born or naturalized in the United States, and subject to the jurisdiction thereof, are citizens of the United States." It goes on to prohibit the states from abridging the privileges or immunities of citizens. Such focus in the 14th Amendment supports the conjecture that "us" refers to American citizens. However, notice that this reading implies that the protections in question are provided specifically to citizens—i.e., those human beings who have either been born or naturalized in the United States, a status that no fetus has attained. If so, Reagan's premise is clearly false: the Constitution does not already protect the fetus, even if it is a human being.

But you can disambiguate "us" more plausibly. The section of the 14th Amendment providing the guarantees to which Reagan refers shifts terms. The first two sentences of the amendment define citizenship and the protection of the privileges and immunities of citizens. The second sentence then shifts from "citizens" to "any person": "Nor shall any State deprive any person of life, liberty, or property without due process of law; nor deny to any person within its jurisdiction the equal protection of the laws." This passage holds that there are certain protections accorded citizens and other protections accorded all persons, apparently meaning citizens and noncitizens alike. You may conclude, then, that "us" refers

---

[1] Reagan seems to confuse the 14th Amendment's protection of property with the Declaration of Independence's mention of the "pursuit of happiness." Notice that the confusion isn't important, since the relevant issue concerns the right to life, not that of property or happiness, and this is present in both the Constitution and the Declaration of Independence. Thus a charitable reader can overcome the problem by eliminating reference to either property or happiness.

to human beings in Reagan's premise. Since the resulting premise will not suffer from being *obviously* false, and since it is a plausible interpretation of the words in the context of the amendment, it is a better interpretation of what Reagan must have meant by "us."

Our reconstruction of Reagan's argument to this point looks like this:

P1: No one has established that a fetus is not a human being.
P2: Unless someone has established that a fetus is not a human being, the fetus is already protected by the Constitution.
P3: The Constitution guarantees the right to life to all human beings.

C: Additional prohibition of abortion is necessary.

Once you have clarified the statements you find explicit in the argument, you can ask whether it harbors any significant assumptions. To see whether it does, you can diagram the argument as you now have it:

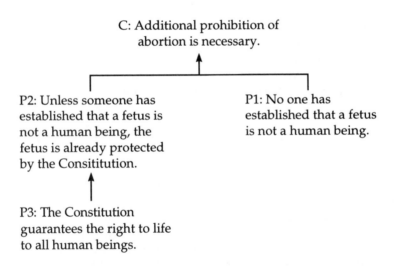

The constitutional guarantee (P3) is relevant to the conclusion because it suggests that if the fetus is a human being, it is subject to these protections. That is, P3 leads to P2. In turn, P2 shows that prohibition of abortion is called for only if no one has established that the fetus is not a human being, which P1 asserts. So P1 and P2 are linked in leading to C.

Consider each inference in turn, beginning at the bottom of the diagram. Can P3 lead to P2? Unless we *should* presume the humanity of the fetus until proven otherwise, P3 does not provide sufficient support for P2. You can clarify the argument by linking this missing premise to P3 to arrive at P2:

MP1: We should presume that the fetus is a human being unless it has been established otherwise.

Now consider the inference from P2 and P1 to C. C is supported by P1 and P2 together (they are linked) because they in turn imply the intermediate conclusion:

IC1: Fetuses are already protected by the Constitution.

You now have another inference to consider. Is IC1 sufficient to arrive at C? Notice that the argument calls for prohibition of abortion over and above that which now exists. Why is that necessary? Why not rely on the court's authority to enforce the constitutional protection of the fetus, claimed in IC1? The argument clearly relies on another assumption:

MP2: The present constitutional guarantee cannot be relied on to protect the fetus.

Without this assumption it is not clear, given the premises, why Reagan prefers prohibiting abortion to some other solution, such as making a case to the Supreme Court to enforce this guarantee.

Are IC1 and MP2, then, taken together, sufficient to arrive at C? Not quite. MP2 grounds the need for additional protection, but it still assumes that

MP3: When a constitutional guarantee of a right cannot be relied upon, additional means of guaranteeing that right are necessary.

So the argument, appropriately diagrammed, looks like the diagram at the top of the following page.

Reconstructing the argument reveals it to be considerably more complex than it first appeared. And only by articulating all the parts of the argument can you evaluate it. (Often, in fact, it is the unstated assumptions, the missing premises, that prove most fruitful to evaluate.) For example, you can ask whether those premises which lack supporting premises are true. Consider MP1. How can MP1 be defended? What is it about the fetus that could justify us to presume "humanity" and to expect those in favor of abortion to bear the burden of proof? Is this a reasonable expectation?

Or look carefully at MP2. Why has the (alleged) present constitutional guarantee not been enforced by the Supreme Court? Your answer may in turn cause you to question whether the Constitution already does cover the fetus. But, then, if IC1 is wrong, either one of the premises supporting it (P1 or P2) must be false or the inference from them to IC1 is weak.

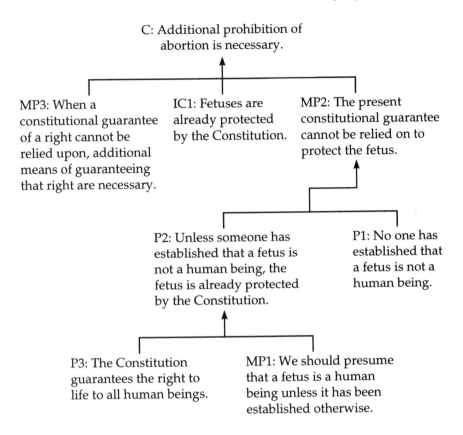

C: Additional prohibition of abortion is necessary.

MP3: When a constitutional guarantee of a right cannot be relied upon, additional means of guaranteeing that right are necessary.

IC1: Fetuses are already protected by the Constitution.

MP2: The present constitutional guarantee cannot be relied on to protect the fetus.

P2: Unless someone has established that a fetus is not a human being, the fetus is already protected by the Constitution.

P1: No one has established that a fetus is not a human being.

P3: The Constitution guarantees the right to life to all human beings.

MP1: We should presume that a fetus is a human being unless it has been established otherwise.

Questioning P1 and P2 may lead you to compare the Constitution's use of the word *person* and the use of *human being* in this argument. Is *human being,* a term we did not question in our reconstruction, ambiguous (that is, should we question it)? Perhaps it admits of more than one interpretation: (1) biological membership in the species *Homo sapiens* and (2) the moral or legal possessor of certain rights, the possessor of what some call the status of "personhood." Has Reagan traded on the potential ambiguity of *human being* here?

The preliminary work of reconstructing an argument clarifies what it means and articulates those parts of it not stated explicitly, all in an effort to bring to the fore potential issues for discussion and critical assessment while at the same time being "charitable" to the author. Since you want to assess the arguments at their best, you set aside any initial objections that you may see easy ways to overcome so that you can focus on more serious questions later. Those more serious questions arise from careful reconstruction.

Reconstructing an argument prepares you to evaluate it. Will Reagan's argument bear up under scrutiny? The next chapters will give you some tools to help you form an opinion of it and other arguments.

Exercise 5.3

I. Decide which parts of the following passages are arguments. Describe the function of those sections that contain no argumentation and reconstruct the arguments.

A. "Unmarried Couple Convicted of Lewd Behavior in Bed" (from an ACLU newsletter):

> A Wisconsin judge has upheld the 1978 conviction of an unmarried couple who were fined $75.00 each for engaging in lewd and lascivious behavior by sleeping together.
>
> The couple were staying overnight in a Wauwatosa, Wisconsin home they were hired to paint when police investigated and surprised them in bed.
>
> Wisconsin Civil Liberties Union cooperating attorneys James Reiher and Harvey Goldstein argued on appeal that the local ordinance violates a person's right to privacy because the state has no right to regulate sexual conduct between consenting adults.
>
> Circuit Judge Lawrence Gram disagreed. In upholding the couple's conviction, he said, "I guess we really go back to some of the most fundamental law of all—the law of Moses, the Ten Commandments. Law has been concerned with this area [sexual behavior] for a long time.
>
> "If you can't legislate morality, then we shouldn't be saying 'thou shalt not kill' and 'thou shalt not steal.'" There's an interrelationship between the law and moral behavior.

B. From Richard M. Nixon's "Checkers Speech," September 23, 1952 (excerpted from "Nixon" A22):

> My fellow Americans: I come before you tonight as a candidate for the Vice Presidency and as a man whose honesty and integrity has been questioned.
>
> The usual political thing to do when charges are made against you is to either ignore them or deny them without giving any details.
>
> I believe we've had enough of that in the United States, particularly with the recent administration in Washington, D.C. To me the office of the Vice Presidency of the United States is a great office, and I feel that the people have got to have confidence in the integrity of the men who run for that office and who might obtain it.
>
> I have a theory, too, that the best and only answer to a smear or an honest misunderstanding of the facts is to tell the truth. And that's why I'm here tonight. I want to tell you my side of the case.
>
> I am sure that you have read the charge and you have heard it that I, Senator Nixon, took $18,000 from a group of my supporters.

Now was it wrong? And let me say that it was wrong—I'm saying, incidentally, that it was wrong and not just illegal. Because it wasn't a question of whether it was legal or illegal; that isn't enough. The question is was it morally wrong?

I say that it was morally wrong if any of that $18,000 went to Senator Nixon for my personal use. I say that it was morally wrong if it was secretly given and secretly handled. And I say that it was morally wrong if any of the contributors got any special favors for the contributions that they made.

And now to answer those questions let me say this:

Not one cent of the $18,000 or any other money of that type ever went to me for my personal use. Every penny of it was used to pay for political expenses that I did not think should be charged to the taxpayers of the United States.

It was not a secret fund. As a matter of fact, when I was on *Meet the Press*—some of you may have seen it last Sunday—Peter Edson came up to me after the program, and he said, "Dick, what about this fund we hear about?" And I said, well, there's no secret about it. Go out and see Dana Smith, who was the administrator of the fund. And I gave him his address, and I said that you will find that the purpose of the fund was to defray political expenses that I did not feel should be charged to the government.

And third, let me point out, and I want to make this particularly clear, that no contributor to any of my campaigns has ever received any consideration that he would not receive as an ordinary constituent.

I just don't believe in that, and I can say that never, while I have been in the Senate of the U.S., as far as the people who contributed to this fund are concerned, have I made a telephone call for them to an agency in their behalf. And the record will show that, the records which are in the hands of the administration.

6

Evaluating Arguments I: Deductive Reasoning

6.1 Evaluating Arguments

You have come to identify an argument and understand it independently of judging it to be strong or weak. Indeed, only after identifying an argument and reconstructing it accurately are you ready to evaluate it; that is, to decide whether it is a good argument. Nevertheless, you evaluate arguments all the time, so most of the tools in the next two chapters will be familiar, even if you haven't thought of them before as reasoning tools.

What is a good argument? That depends first of all on its purpose. You may try to explain something puzzling, or to convince others to do something or to consider an idea you believe to be true, or to reveal an error in an assumption of some other argument. Different goals place different demands on an argument, and even when broad goals remain the same, the rigor of the standards you apply to determine success may differ. To establish a mathematical theorem, for instance, you may expect a knock-down proof that allows no exceptions, whereas to decide how best to distribute money available for equipment, a university had better not wait for knock-down proofs or the money will never get to those who need it. Nevertheless, arguments can be better or worse.

Generally (though not universally) an argument aims to establish its conclusion as true. To evaluate whether an argument succeeds in establishing the truth of its conclusion, you evaluate both the truth of its individual statements and its form. An analogy may help. If you want to build a house, you need both materials and plans. The materials can be wood or stone or plaster; what you choose depends a great deal on the plan. The plan is the set of instructions that tells you how the materials should be combined to become a house, where beams go, how high ceilings should be, the angle of the roof, and so on. Each of these parts, the materials and the plans, can be good or bad independently. The materials may be flawed (the wood termite-ridden) or the plan inadequate (the roof may collapse no matter how strong the wood because its weight hasn't been adequately distributed). Clearly a successful house depends on *both* good materials and good plans, each appropriately matched to the other.

Arguments, like houses, consist of materials and a plan for joining them. And they may suffer a weakness in either of the dimensions independently: either in material or plan. Like a strong house, a strong argument depends on the joint quality of both elements. Let's see how this analogy works.

The "materials" of the argument (its wood and mortar) are the statements that compose it. You can evaluate the statements used as premises and conclusions independently of their role in the argument. That is, you can judge whether the premises are true, plausible, or believable without considering their role as premises in the argument.

An argument's "plan" is its structure, the underlying logical relation between premises and conclusion or, more loosely, the way statements function together to lead to a conclusion. The premises in a successful argument lead in a legitimate way to the conclusion whether or not they are true, or they may fail to lead to the conclusion even when they are true or plausible. Therefore, you can speak of the amount of support that premises provide a conclusion without referring to whether those premises are true.

To summarize, an argument is successful overall when two conditions have been met:

1. The premises are true (or believable).
2. The premises support the conclusion.

Since you can distinguish these elements—whether the premises are true, and how much support they offer the conclusion—you can study each separately, as long as you remember that the best arguments satisfy *both* conditions. Determining whether premises are true forces you to rely on your background information and research (something we can only point to here); the next two chapters will aid you in evaluating the strength of arguments by analyzing their structures.

6.2 Deductive Versus Inductive Reasoning

Traditionally, people have distinguished between deductive and inductive reasoning, but you must take care in making such a distinction to avoid some common mistakes.

6.2.1 General Versus Specific

More than 2,300 years ago the Greek philosopher Aristotle, probably the first to study logic systematically, held that all deductive reasoning is a matter of inferring something more specific from something in general.

For example, you might argue as follows:

> All people are mortal.
> Socrates was a person.
> _____
> So Socrates was mortal.

In this argument a general claim about people leads deductively to a more specific claim about an individual person.

Correspondingly, inductive reasoning is held to be just the reverse, proceeding from something specific to something more general:

> Socrates was mortal.
> Aristotle was mortal.
> Plato was mortal.
> _____
> So most ancient Greek philosophers were mortal.

This distinction between deduction and induction has survived because, up to a point, it works. Deductive reasoning seems to reveal what is implicit in the premises, and certainly exhibiting particular cases that fall within the scope of more general cases reveals what is implicit in them. Similarly, reasoning that expands beyond the claims in the premises requires only inductive strength, and moving from specific cases to more general claims seems to expand beyond those cases.

However, this distinction will not help you to understand many arguments because much reasoning fails to fit these patterns. Consider this argument:

> Newt Gingrich is a conservative.
> Newt Gingrich is speaker of the House of Representatives.
> _____
> So anyone who knows the speaker of the House of Representatives knows someone who is a conservative.

The premises mention only a specific individual, while the conclusion is quite general, including anyone who knows the speaker of the House. If you consider only the distinction between general and specific statements, you would have to classify this as an inductive argument. Yet this argument, as you will soon see, is deductively successful.

Similarly, some arguments expand beyond the claims of their premises without moving from specific statements to more general claims. Consider this example:

> Every rainy day in the past my dog has preferred to stay indoors.
> Every rainy day in the future my dog will prefer to stay indoors.

Nothing in this argument need be described as a move from the more specific to the more general (if she's an old dog, there are probably more days referred to in the premise than the conclusion!), yet clearly the conclusion invites you to go beyond what is asserted in the premise.

Other arguments move from specific claims to specific claims with no mention of anything general, and still others from general to general with no mention of anything specific. Some of these are best defined as deductive and others as inductive. As a result, distinguishing between inductive and deductive argumentation according to the generality of statements proves ultimately unsatisfactory.

6.2.2 Standards Rather Than Kinds

Identifying two distinct classes of arguments turns out to be very difficult. As a result, logicians today generally distinguish between deductive and inductive *standards* of reasoning rather than between deductive and inductive *arguments*. That is, they do not consider there to be two distinguishable classes of arguments but rather two standards according to which all arguments can be evaluated. The context of an argument determines which standard applies.

Some contexts require arguments in which the premises provide the strongest possible support for the conclusion: they guarantee it. Such arguments are successful only when the premises provide complete support for the conclusion. Arguments that meet this high standard are called *deductively valid.*

In other cases, the premises need provide only some degree of support. They make the conclusion more probable, more reasonable, or more believable, even though some doubt may linger after you grant the premises. Such arguments are said to be *inductively strong.* Inductive strength comes in degrees. Unlike deductively valid arguments, all of which provide the same amount of support for their conclusions (complete!), one inductively strong argument may be stronger than another.

6.3 Deductive Validity

What does it mean for an argument to provide complete support for its conclusion? Consider the following argument:

A. If water is H_2O, then it contains oxygen.
   Water is H_2O.
   _____
   So water contains oxygen.

The premises in this argument support the conclusion completely; *if you accept the premises, you must accept the conclusion.* This argument is structurally successful. The premises also happen to be true. However, because you consider the truth of the premises separately from questioning how much they support the conclusion, this argument would provide the same degree of support even if its premises turned out to be false. That is the case in example B. Notice that even though both premises in example B are false, they provide the same level of support for their conclusion as the premises in A do for theirs:

B. If water is H_7O, then it has 19 parts hydrogen.
   Water is H_7O.
   _____
   So water has 19 parts hydrogen.

If water were H_7O, it would be made of 7 parts hydrogen, not 19, so the first premise is false. The second premise is also false. But notice that the premises do support their conclusion. If these premises *were* true, the conclusion would also *have to be true.* That is what it means to say an argument's structure is successful in the strongest possible way.

When the premises of an argument provide complete support for the conclusion, the argument is called *deductively valid* or simply *valid.*

> In a deductively valid argument, if the premises are true, then the conclusion must also be true.

You can also express the idea of deductive validity in other ways:

A. It is not possible for the conclusion to be false while the premises are true.
B. One cannot consistently assert the premises and deny the conclusion.

An argument not deductively valid is deductively invalid. Since deductive invalidity (like validity) refers only to an argument's structure and exists without regard to the truth of the premises and conclusion, it is possible for an argument to have all true premises, and a true conclusion, but be deductively invalid. The following is an example of such an argument:

C. Lyndon Johnson was president of the United States.
   Lyndon Johnson was not a Republican.
   _____
   So Lyndon Johnson was a Democrat.

All the claims made here are true, but the argument is invalid. It is possible for someone to be a non-Republican president and still not be a Democrat; though unlikely, he or she could be an independent, for example. Evaluated by deductive standards, this argument does not provide support for its conclusion: it is invalid.

6.4 Techniques for Showing Invalidity

If the premises of an argument are *all* true and the conclusion is false, the argument, by definition, is invalid. This is the only instance in which knowing whether the statements are true helps you to decide whether an argument is valid. In the following chart a question mark indicates that the truth or falsity of the statements is insufficient to determine whether the argument is valid or invalid.

		When premises are:	
	All true	All false	Some true and some false
True	?	?	?
False	Invalid	?	?

And conclusion is:

Since you know that an argument that has true premises and a false conclusion is invalid, you can test arguments intuitively by proposing this crucial question:

Suppose the premises were true; could the conclusion be false?

If you can answer "yes," the argument is invalid. You can force this question by (1) creating a scenario in which the premises are true and the conclusion false and by (2) discovering a logical analogy in which an argument with the same structure contains true premises and a false conclusion.

6.4.1 Refutation by Scenario

Consider this argument:

> D. All billionaires are wealthy.
>   J. Paul Getty was wealthy.
>   _____
>   Therefore, J. Paul Getty was a billionaire.

You may just see that this argument is invalid. But if you needed to convince someone—perhaps yourself—that it is invalid, you could create the following scenario:

> Suppose it is true that all billionaires are wealthy (this is not hard to suppose!). Suppose also that Getty had only $800,000,000; he would no doubt be a very wealthy man. But since $800,000,000 is less than $1 billion, Getty would be a wealthy man who was not a billionaire. This scenario is possible, and in it the premises are both true and the conclusion false. Therefore, the argument is invalid.
> Consider another example:

> E. All negotiators hope to get the best deal they can get.
>   Jared negotiated the deal he hoped to negotiate.
>   _____
>   Thus, Jared got the best deal he could get.

Here is a scenario that shows E to be invalid:

> 1. Suppose all negotiators do hope for the best deal they can get. Jared, who is negotiating the price for a house he wants to purchase, hopes for the best deal he can get. Going into the negotiations, he identifies what he takes to be the best he can hope for, say a selling price of $87,000 (the house had intially been offered at $98,000, and the assessed value was closer to $94,000 in a buyer's market). At a certain point in the negotiations the sellers offer to take $87,000, and Jared concludes that this is the best he can expect. Thinking that asking for more might cost him the good deal he has now been offered, he accepts that price. Unbeknownst to Jared, the people with whom he was negotiating were willing to accept a much lower price because they were desperate to sell but had succeeded in concealing that fact. He got *the deal* he hoped for, but not *the best deal he could have negotiated*. In this scenario all the premises turn out to be true and the conclusion false, so the argument must be deductively invalid.

Suppose you had offered the following scenario:

2. Jared is fed up with thinking of negotiating in competitive and individualistic terms. Instead, he thinks that negotiations should seek mutually satisfactory results for all concerned, even when this means one party does not do as well as he might otherwise. No one should leave the negotiations, or find out anything later, that will make him feel cheated or as if he had been forced to decide without full information. At a certain point Jared decides that the deal being offered ($91,000) is good enough and accepts it. He thinks a better deal could have been negotiated, but would be inconsistent with his values.

This last scenario does not show argument E to be invalid, for it fails to demonstrate that you can answer "yes" to the crucial question. A scenario can do that only if it makes the premises all true and the conclusions false. In scenario 2 the premises are not all true: if Jared does not hope to negotiate the best deal he can for himself, the first premise is false.

Notice that this method does not require you to show that the premises *are* true or that the conclusion *is* false. (Indeed there are people like the Jared of scenario 2—people who do not always hope for the best deal for themselves at all costs to the other party.) For the purpose of creating a scenario, all you need to do is *suppose* the premises are true, and if it is possible to suppose them true and the conclusion false without contradicting yourself, you can show the argument to be invalid.

6.4.2 Refutation by Logical Analogy

At the Mad Tea-Party in *Alice in Wonderland* (64–66) the Mad Hatter poses a riddle: "Why is a raven like a writing-desk?"

"Come, we shall have some fun now!" thought Alice. "I'm glad they've begun asking riddles—I believe I can guess that," she added aloud.

"Do you mean that you think you can find out the answer to it?" said the March Hare.

"Exactly so," said Alice.

"Then you should say what you mean," the March Hare went on.

"I do," Alice hastily replied; "at least—at least I mean what I say—that's the same thing, you know."

"Not the same thing a bit!" said the Hatter. "Why, you might as well say that 'I see what I eat' is the same thing as 'I eat what I see!'"

"You might just as well say," added the March Hare, "that 'I like what I get' is the same thing as 'I get what I like!'"

"You might just as well say," added the Dormouse, who seemed to be talking in its sleep, "that 'I breathe when I sleep' is the same thing as 'I sleep when I breathe!'"

"It is the same with you," said the Mad Hatter, and here the conversation dropped. . . ."

Alice defends herself against the March Hare's criticism that she should say what she means rather than something else by claiming that saying what one means is the same as meaning what one says, and thus (implicitly) her original statement ("I believe I can guess that") should do just as well as the more precise "I can find out the answer to it." The Mad Hatter, the March Hare, and the Dormouse all refute Alice's argument by posing arguments of their own that are about completely different subjects but that have the same form as Alice's argument.

Their refutations of her argument exemplify a technique called "refutation by logical analogy" (or sometimes "counterargument"). You can see that "I mean what I say" is not the same thing as "I say what I mean" when you compare it with the "sameness" of "I like what I eat" and "I eat what I like."

Refutation by logical analogy relies on certain assumptions. First, the technique assumes that two different arguments sharing the same pattern of reasoning, or *form,* are either both valid or both invalid, because arguments are valid or invalid by virtue of their form. Second, you know that any argument that has true premises and a false conclusion must be invalid. If the logical analogy (the counterargument) has all true premises and a false conclusion, it must be invalid. So if the original argument has the same form as the logical analogy, it too must be invalid.

Consider the following argument:

F. All cats are felines.
   All cats are animals.
   ―――――――――――――――
   So all felines are animals.

Is this argument deductively valid? You can't tell by questioning the truth of the premises and conclusion. All the statements in F are true, and you know that arguments with true premises and a true conclusion may turn out to be valid or invalid. But if you consider the following analogous argument, you can see that F is invalid:

G. All ewes are sheep.
   All ewes are female.
   ―――――――――――――――
   So all sheep are female.

Notice first that F and G share the same form; they employ the same pattern of reasoning. They differ only in subject matter. You can see the pattern even more clearly by substituting symbols to abstract the form from the subject matter:

All A are B.
All A are C.
So all B are C.

This scheme clarifies the form of both arguments. Sometimes you can provide such schemes, but many times it is very hard to do so accurately.

Notice second that argument G is clearly invalid; the premises are both true and the conclusion false. When refuting by logical analogy, you must be sure that the analogy is uncontroversially invalid. If the premises are not clearly true and the conclusion clearly false, neither you nor your audience will be convinced.

Consider these two refutations by logical analogy of an argument Nixon used in his famous "Checkers Speech." The first is successful, the second not. Nixon argued:

H. If I took the money for personal profit, then it was wrong.
   I did not take the money for personal profit.

   Therefore, it was not wrong.

Here is a successful refutation by logical analogy:

I. If a fire is burning in this room, then oxygen is present in this
    room.
    A fire is not burning in this room.

    So no oxygen is present in this room.

The analogical argument I successfully refutes H because it satisfies both conditions: it has the same form as H, and it is clearly invalid because the premises are unproblematically true and the conclusion false.

Here is an unsuccessful refutation:

J. If a fire is burning in this room, then oxygen is present in this
    room.
    There is oxygen present in this room.

    So a fire is burning in this room now.

J is in fact invalid (notice that its premises are all true and the conclusion false). But since it does not have the same form as I, it cannot be used to demonstrate the invalidity of I.

Creating a scenario or logical analogy in which the premises are true and the conclusion false shows an argument to be invalid; failing to discover such a scenario or logical analogy, however, does not prove it valid. Finding scenarios and logical analogies requires some imagination. If you can discover one, you can show an argument to be invalid, but if none come to mind, you can conclude only that you have been unable to think of one, not that one doesn't exist. Do not conclude that an argument is valid simply because you are unable to show it invalid.

Exercise 6.4

I. Determine whether the following arguments are deductively valid or invalid by using your intuition. Does the argument *seem* valid? If an argument is invalid, explain as best you can in your own words what is wrong with it.

1. Either the teacher didn't notice the students collaborating on the exam, or he tolerates it. He noticed it all right. He must tolerate it.
2. The weather in January is usually similar to that in February. We had a pretty dry January, so February will also remain relatively dry.
3. If Marilou is at school, then her oboe must be there. But her oboe is not there. So Marilou isn't at school.
4. You have never written a symphony, so you are in no position to criticize one.
5. Since all mammals are warm-blooded, and all anteaters are mammals, all anteaters are warm-blooded.
6. In a million different tosses of a variety of coins, tossed in a variety of ways, in different places, at different times of day, by different people, not a single one landed on its edge. Therefore, a tossed coin does not land on its edge.
7. If I stay home I'll watch MTV, and if I watch MTV I'll neglect my work. So I'll neglect my work if I stay at home.
8. That boxer is still moving well and throwing hard punches. He can't be hurt too badly.
9. Jones says no one should ever be trusted. If he is right, we should not trust his statement. Hence, he is lying.
10. The O. J. Simpson trial has contributed more than any single factor in the last decade to undermining the public's trust in the criminal justice system. It has everything you can imagine to raise doubts: racist cops who perjure themselves and may have even planted evidence, contamination of evidence

by sloppy handling and questionable laboratory conditions, experts whose testimony is later revealed to contain simple statistical mistakes, high-priced lawyers who act as if they don't know they're on the same team and are criticized by the judge for submitting incoherent motions, jury members who have to be removed for keeping illicit diaries for later book deals, other jurors who break down under the pressure of sequestration, and a judge who has to excuse himself from making certain rulings because they involve his spouse, a supervisor in the police department. Is it any wonder people are pretty fed up with the system?

11. A good private university can educate someone for less than the cost of keeping a prisoner in a typical prison. We have to do something to improve the administration of prisons in this country.

12. If Patty Hearst were a terrorist, she wouldn't have published a book about her experiences with the SLA. Since she did publish the book, she wasn't a terrorist.

13. Aquinas's proofs for the existence of God are weak because he was just trying to justify through reason what he already believed on faith.

14. Obviously, we would all be better off if we had more money. So we should raise all prices and incomes by 10 percent, for then we would all (including the self-employed) have more money.

15. Definitions cannot, by their very nature, be either true or false; one simply stipulates how a term is to be defined. For this reason it makes relatively little sense to argue over definitions.

16. I do know that Samantha is innocent, but I could not know that if either her confession or Drake's testimony corroborating it were truthful; therefore, both Samantha's confession and Drake's testimony are untruthful.

17. Asked if he felt the story were accurate enough to constitute responsible journalism, the editor commented, "Well, we couldn't verify what our source said, so in a conservative newspaper it would be edited out. But this isn't a conservative newspaper, so it needn't be edited out."

18. All people who live in London drink tea, and all people who drink tea like it. We may conclude that all people who live in London like it.

19. Inventors are people who see new patterns in familiar things, so all inventors are eccentric, since eccentrics are people who see new patterns in familiar things.

20. All social change requires action, and action sometimes results in violence. So some social change results in violence.

II. Provide scenarios that show these arguments to be invalid.

1. Social change always produces violence, and violence is regrettable. Therefore, social change is always regrettable.
2. All mammals are capable of feeling pain, but reptiles are not mammals. So reptiles aren't capable of feeling pain.
3. He will be admitted to the theater only with a ticket. But he has one. So he will be admitted.
4. Sammy loves Cindy, and Cindy loves Mandy, so Sammy loves Mandy.
5. If Gramm is elected, the economy will be in trouble; and if Dole is elected, the economy will be in trouble. So the economy will be in trouble.

III. Refute each of the following arguments using a logical analogy. If an analogy is inappropriate, explain why.

1. You can't pass a law against dangerous drugs because no one can draw a sharp line between dangerous and non-dangerous drugs.
2. If tea is dangerous, then so is coffee. Coffee is not dangerous, so tea is safe too.
3. All U.S. senators live in Washington, D.C., or thereabouts. Barbara Boxer lives in Washington, D.C. So Barbara Boxer is a U.S. senator.
4. Open advocates of communism in the 1950s had nothing to hide, so they should have had no objection to being investigated.
5. That tree will lose its leaves if it is deciduous. It will lose its leaves, so it is deciduous.
6. Women are the natural people to raise children because they give birth to them.
7. Because life imprisonment is even harsher than the death penalty, we should maintain the death penalty.
8. He won't go unless his friends all go. His friends are all going, so he will go.
9. The bigger the burger, the better the burger. The burgers are bigger at Burger King.
10. Most men drink beer, and most beer drinkers pay taxes, so most men pay taxes.
11. All millionaires have ESP. Rockefeller was a millionaire, so he must have had ESP.

12. Social change always produces violence, and violence is regrettable. Therefore, social change is always regrettable.
13. He will be admitted to the theater only with a ticket. But he has one. So he will be admitted.
14. All mammals are capable of feeling pain, but reptiles are not mammals. So reptiles aren't capable of feeling pain.
15. Sammy loves Cindy, and Cindy loves Mandy, so Sammy loves Mandy.
16. If Clinton is reelected, the economy will be in trouble; and if Dole is elected, the economy will be in trouble. So the economy will be in trouble.

7

Evaluating Arguments II:
Inductive Reasoning

Three kinds of reasoning you encounter, and produce yourself almost daily, require less than the complete proof of a deductively valid argument. These three—analogy, generalization, and explanation—are common kinds of inductive reasoning.

7.1 Analogy

Analogies, simply put, are comparisons between two things. You can use analogies either to illustrate a point or as devices within an argument. It is important to distinguish these two uses of analogies, for some of the criteria for evaluating the one will not apply to the other.

7.1.1 Analogy as Illustration

Analogies can help you understand a point or concept. Often you will find an analogy to be an adjunct to other forms of explanation, a device to make a concept more lively, easier to grasp. Such analogies simply help to clarify a concept; they do not provide an additional reason to think its application is correct.

Such analogies are used to illustrate a point difficult to grasp; otherwise you would not need the analogy. The point to be illustrated is called the *primary subject matter,* and the item it is compared to is called the *analogue.* At the beginning of Plato's *Republic,* Socrates asks an old man (Cephalus) what it is like to be old. He explains why he is asking:

> I enjoy talking with very old people. They have gone before us on a road by which we too may have to travel and I think we do well to learn from them what it is like, easy or difficult, rough or smooth. And now that you have reached an age when your foot, as the poets say, is

on the threshold, I should like to hear what report you can give and whether you find it a painful time of life.

(Plato, Republic 328e)

In order to explain why he is curious about old age, Socrates compares growing old to taking a journey. The primary subject matter is growing old, while the analogue is taking a journey. The analogy functions strictly as explanation; Socrates is not using it as evidence for a claim.

When used as illustration, analogies must satisfy certain criteria in order to succeed.

7.1.1a Familiarity   The analogue must be familiar; it succeeds as explanation only when it relates an unfamiliar concept to one well understood. If the analogue is not more familiar than the primary subject matter, it will not clarify what is obscure in the primary subject matter. In the example, the analogue is more familiar to most of us: young and old alike have taken journeys whereas a smaller number have firsthand experience with growing old. We—especially those of us who are relatively young—know more about journeys than we know about being elderly.

7.1.1b Fittingness   Is the analogue really like the primary subject matter? if so, it is a *fitting* analogy; if not, it is *strained*. In many ways, taking a journey is like growing older. There may be adventures and new experiences, as well as difficult stretches of a journey, just as all these things may be found in life; and just as a journey has a beginning and comes to an end, so does life. The best analogues share a number of important similarities with their primary subject matter, but they need not have everything in common. If they did, they would be more than just analogous—they would be the same kind of thing.

7.1.1c Vividness   With use, analogies become worn and tired. They lack luster. And then they fail to conjure up meaning for a reader. Obviously, since you use an analogy to illuminate a point, you want the analogy to carry meaning. Perhaps in our day the journey analogy has grown tired and trite (though it may not have been when Plato used it). A football game is another analogue now pretty tired from overuse, especially in politics.

7.1.1d On Target   Does the analogy target the essence of the primary subject matter, or does it encourage you to believe something false of it? For example, if you come to think of aging as a reversible process on the basis of Socrates's analogy (since you can turn back to your origin midjourney), the analogy has misled you. Analogies that encourage false beliefs are "misleading." But take care in calling an analogue misleading;

"I TOLD THEM THAT REFUSING TO READ DICKENS IS LIKE REFUSING TO DO ALGEBRA. NOW THEY REFUSE TO DO ALGEBRA."

the potential to mislead resides in all analogues if you pay attention to the wrong features. Sometimes writers avoid the risk of misleading by explicitly identifying the respects in which analogue and primary subject matter are similar.

7.1.2 Analogy in Argument

> If you don't believe in God, then you can't go to heaven. So if you don't believe in the devil, how can you possibly go to hell?
>
> (T. S. Isen)

Analogies can also serve as evidence in an argument. Such arguments, called *arguments from analogy* or *analogical arguments,* function by offering the *analogue* to support a claim about the *primary subject matter.* Analogies offer indirect support for the conclusion.

Consider Bertrand Russell's argument that we have good reason to believe other people have thoughts and feelings similar to our own even when we are not directly aware of those thoughts or feelings:

> The behavior of other people is in many ways analogous to our own, and we suppose it must have analogous causes. What most people say is what we should say if we had certain thoughts, and so we infer that they probably have these thoughts. . . . They behave in ways in which we behave when we are pleased (or displeased) in circumstances in which we should be pleased (or displeased). . . . There are, in short, many ways in which my responses to stimuli differ from those of "dead" matter, and in all these ways other people resemble me. As it is clear to me that the causal laws governing my behavior have to do with "thoughts," it is natural to infer that the same is true of the analogous behavior of my friends.
>
> (Russell 483)

Russell points out that the analogue (Russell himself, or anyone else considering the issue) shares certain characteristics with the primary subject matter (other human beings). He knows that in his own case, thoughts and feelings cause certain responses or behaviors and that others also exhibit these. He concludes that the primary subject matter therefore shares the additional feature as well: thoughts and feelings like his. He reaches the conclusion *through* the analogy.

The logical form implicit in analogical arguments is this:

Primary Subject Matter has characteristics D, E, F.
Analogue has characteristics D, E, F.
Analogue has a further characteristic, G.
Therefore, Primary Subject Matter has G.

Although you cannot rely on a strict set of rules to evaluate all analogical arguments, you should consider these criteria:

7.1.2a Degree of Analogy If the primary subject matter and the analogue share many properties and fewer differences, they have a high degree of analogy. It is then reasonable to expect the further similarity to exist as well. Unfortunately, this guide is extremely rough. A creative person can identify indefinitely many similarities and differences between just about any two things. You could find endless similarities between cats and scissors, for example: both are physical objects; they exist for finite periods of time; they take up space; they can be found in Georgia; they have color; they don't speak French, Latin, or Russian; and so forth.

As always, you want to avoid frivolous responses. Certain features of primary subject matter and analogue stand out prominently in our experience of them. In assessing the degree of analogy in analogical arguments, be sure to consider the *important* similarities and dissimilarities.

7.1.2b Relevance   Are the characteristics the analogue shares with the primary subject matter (D, E, and F in the schema above) relevant to the further characteristic argued for? You may be reluctant to infer that further characteristic if you are skeptical about any relevant connection between the known characteristics and the new one. And if you know that the characteristics are irrelevant to each other, you will see that the conclusion is not supported at all by the similarities presented in the premises.

If instead of bodily expressions of his own feelings, Russell had listed such similarities as vocal cords in his premises, his case for the presence of feelings in others would be significantly weaker. And had he listed irrelevant similarities, such as skin color, his conclusion would be completely unsupported. Russell's actual reference to bodily behavior in both himself and others *is* relevant to his conclusion because the bodily behavior is supposedly the expression of those feelings. Given the causal relation between the shared characteristics (behavior) and the characteristic in question (feelings), Russell's analogical argument gains some strength.

7.1.2c Moderation   Be careful not to claim more of a conclusion than the analogy warrants. Russell would have wildly overstated his case had he concluded that, because he shares the outward signs of feelings with other people, they must feel exactly what he feels in all circumstances.

As you can see by now, analogical arguments do not provide knockdown proofs for their conclusions; they establish them with only some degree of probability. In other words, a successful analogical argument will be only inductively strong, not deductively valid. But, of course, they are not automatically flawed for that reason. Aristotle's advice (from *Nichomachean Ethics*) is worth mentioning in this regard. Aristotle said that every subject matter permits its own degree of precision; we should expect only that which is appropriate to the subject matter at hand. In some cases the best you can do is provide analogical evidence.

Exercise 7.1

I. Consider each of the following analogies. Identify the primary subject matter and the analogue, decide whether the analogies illustrate a point or offer evidence for a conclusion, and evaluate the analogies according to the appropriate criteria.

A. Perhaps I can make the process of repression and its necessary relation to the resistance of the patient, more concrete, by a rough illustration which I will derive from our present situation. Suppose that here in this hall and in this audience, whose exemplary stillness and attention I cannot sufficiently commend, there is an individual who is creating a disturbance, and by his ill-bred laughing, talking, by scraping his feet, distracts my attention from my task. I explain that I cannot go on with my lecture under these conditions, and thereupon several strong men among you get up, and, after a short struggle, eject the disturber of the peace from the hall. He is now "repressed," and I can continue my lecture. But in order that the disturbance may not be repeated, in case the man who has just been thrown out attempts to force his way back into the room, the gentlemen who have executed my suggestion take their chairs to the door and establish themselves there as a "resistance," to keep up the repression. Now if you transfer both locations to the psyche, calling this "consciousness" and the outside the "unconscious," you have a tolerably good picture of the process of repression.

(Freud 194)

B. It is not at first evident how we can get from the repression to the creation of the symptoms. Instead of giving a complicated theoretical derivation, I will return at this point to the illustration which I used to typify repression. Remember that with the ejection of the rowdy and the establishment of the watchers before the door, the affair is not necessarily ended. It may very well happen that the ejected man now embittered and quite careless of consequences, gives us more to do. He is no longer among us, we are free from his presence, his scornful laugh and his half-audible remarks, but in a certain sense the repression has miscarried, for he makes a terrible uproar outside, and by outcries and hammering on the door with his fists interferes with my lecture more than before. Under these circumstances it would be hailed with delight if possibly our honored president, Dr. Stanley Hall, should take upon himself the role of peacemaker and mediator. He would speak with the rowdy on the outside, and then turn to us with the recommendation that we let him in again, provided he would guarantee to behave himself better. On Dr. Hall's authority we decide to stop the repression, and now quiet and peace reign again. This is in fact a fairly good presentation of the task devolving upon the physician in the psychoanalytic therapy of neuroses.

To say the same thing more directly: we come to the conclusion, from working with hysterical patients and other neurotics, that they have not fully succeeded in repressing the idea to which the incompatible wish is attached. They have, indeed, driven it out of consciousness and out of memory, and apparently saved themselves a great amount of psychic pain, but in the unconscious the suppressed still exists, only waiting for its chance to become active, and finally succeeds in sending into consciousness, instead of the repressed idea, a disguised and unrecognizable surrogate-creation (Ersatzbildung), which the same painful sensations associate themselves that the patient thought he was rid of through his repression. This surrogate of the repressed idea—the *symptom*—is secure against further attacks from the defences of the ego, and instead of a short conflict there originates now a permanent suffering.

(Freud 195–96)

C. It is commonly said that the German drive on Paris in 1914 and the unlimited U-boat warfare both "nearly succeeded." But this expression requires analysis, and also differentiation between the issues on land and sea. A partisan watching an evenly contested football match, an engineer watching a vehicle whose weight he does not know exactly crossing a bridge whose strength he has never been able to measure, experience no doubt similar sensations of anxiety and excitement. The processes however are different. A football match like a great battle on land is in a continual state of flux and change. But whether the vehicle will break down the bridge does not depend on chance. It depends on the weight of the vehicle and the strength of the bridge. When both these are unknown beforehand, anxiety is natural. But once it is known that the bridge will bear at least ten tons and the vehicle at the most weighs no more than eight, all misgivings are proved to be unfounded. To say that the vehicle "nearly" broke down the bridge is untrue. There was never any chance of it. Whereas any one of a score of alternative accidents would have given the German Army Paris in 1914, the seafaring resources of Great Britain were in fact and in the circumstances always superior to the U-boat attack. Moreover, the attack was inherently of a character so gradual that

these superior resources could certainly obtain their full
development.

(Churchill 721–22)

D. Shylock: He hath disgrac'd me, and hind'red me half a
million, laugh'd at my losses, mock'd at my gains, scorn'd
my nation, thwarted my bargains, cool'd my friends, heated
my enemies; and what's his reason? I am a Jew. Hath not a
Jew eyes? Hath not a Jew hands, organs, dimensions, senses,
affections, passions? Fed with the same food, hurt with the
same weapons, subject to the same diseases, heal'd by the
same means, warm'd and cool'd by the same winter and
summer, as a Christian is? If you prick us, do we not bleed? If
you tickle us, do we not laugh? If you poison us, do we not
die? And if you wrong us, do we not revenge? If we are like
you in the rest, we will resemble you in that. If a Jew wrong a
Christian, what is his humility? Revenge. If a Christian
wrong a Jew, what should his sufference be by Christian
example? Why, revenge. The villainy you teach me, I will
execute, and it shall go hard but I will better the instruction.

(Shakespeare, *The Merchant of Venice*, 3.1.50–69)

E. Look around the world: Contemplate the whole and every
part of it: You will find it to be nothing but one great machine, subdivided into an infinite number of lesser machines,
which again admit of subdivisions, to a degree beyond what
human senses and faculties can trace and explain. All these
various machines, and even their most minute parts, are
adjusted to each other with an accuracy which ravishes into
admiration all men who have ever contemplated them. The
curious adapting of means to ends, throughout all nature,
resembles exactly, though it much exceeds, the productions of
human contrivance; of human design, thought, wisdom, and
intelligence. Since therefore the effects resemble each other,
we are led to infer, by all the rules of analogy, that the causes
also resemble; and that the Author of Nature is somewhat
similar to the mind of man; though possessed of much larger
faculties. By this argument *a posteriori*, and by this argument
alone, do we prove at once the existence of a Deity, and his
similarity to human intelligence.

(Hume 176–77)

II. Consider the following dilemma involving surrogate mother
hood. A few analogies that might help you develop a solution
are suggested here. Your tasks are (a) to develop the proposed
analogies more fully, explaining what relevant similarities and

dissimilarities need to be considered, (b) to develop your own analogies and explore them in detail, and (c) to critique all of the analogies and explain how some of them help you think about this situation.

Sue Donaldson agreed to be artificially inseminated with Dave Schlepp's sperm, to carry the child to term, and then to hand the child over to Schlepp. In return, Schlepp agreed to pay Donaldson $10,000. Once born, the child was discovered to be microcephalic: his head was abnormally small, and he had almost no chance of normal intelligence or of leading an independent life as an adult. Schlepp refused to take the child and refused to pay Donaldson the $10,000. She sued to collect the $10,000 (plus legal and medical costs) and to force Schlepp to adopt the baby.

Here are some leads for possible analogues to develop and critique: (a) buying and selling perishable goods; (b) buying and selling slaves; (c) an agreement to rent a room of your house for nine months; (d) a prostitute selling the use of her body (adapted from Moore 39).

7.2 Generalizing from a Sample

Another common pattern of reasoning, called *enumerative induction*, involves inferring something about a large group from what you know about a small subgroup. Here's an example:

> Our study of second-year females brings up yet another unusual feature: opossums are among the shortest-lived mammals in the world for their size. Among common opossums in Venezuela we found that of 78 radio-collared mature females, 18 percent lived to breed in a second season, 1.2 percent lived to breed in a third season and none survived to a fourth. In his study of the Virginia opossum in Florida, Aunquist found that 8.3 percent lived to a second season, 3 percent lived to a third, and none lived to a fourth.
>
> (Austad 103)

Austad draws a conclusion about all opossums (that they are among the shortest-lived mammals in the world for their size) from two studies of opossums. One of these involves a sample of 78 females; although Austad does not mention the size of the other sample, we might assume that it is no larger, and possibly smaller, than the Venezuela study's sample. He derives his generalization about opossums, then, from facts about a small number of observed opossums. In general, this is the way enumerative inductions work: they invoke generalizations about a group from facts known about a smaller number of observed cases, a "sample" of the group.

Generalizing from a sample shares much in common with arguing from analogy. Analogical arguments begin with some features of an analogue and come to some conclusion about the features of the primary subject matter by claiming that the two are similar in essential ways. In the exercise about surrogate motherhood, each new analogy presents surrogacy from the perspective of a group to which it might belong, and you might argue that surrogacy shares certain features with the other members of that group (e.g., contracts to sell perishable goods and surrogate contracts are both *contracts*. As this example reminds you, whether the primary subject matter is most usefully thought of as a member of that class may be quite controversial.

Now consider the opossum argument. It sounds very much like the analogical arguments we have been considering. After all, the unobserved opossums are said to be like the observed ones with respect to longevity. But there are some differences worth noting. First, in this argument, if you were to say that the primary subject matter is opossums in general, then you must include the analogue (the observed opossums) as part of the primary subject matter as well (the entire group of opossums). Analogical arguments, however, present something controversial about the primary subject matter by exhibiting it in *something else* more familiar and less controversial. So primary subject matter and analogue have to be different.

Second, it is not at all controversial whether the observed opossums are members of the larger class of opossums in general. If you had any doubt about the species membership of the animals that the studies observed, then you would automatically have serious doubts about the legitimacy of generalizing about opossums on that basis. For instance, if the studies indicated only that some animals are not very long-lived, you may well not be convinced that opossums have short lives. In general, analogical arguments answer the question "What are the features of the primary subject matter?" whereas enumerative inductions answer the question "Can you generalize the features of a large group from those of a smaller subset of it?" You may depict the difference this way:

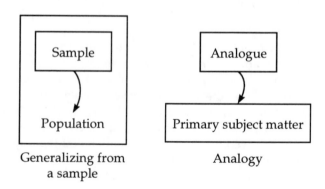

Generalizing from   Analogy
a sample

Clearly, both kinds of argument are useful. Often you will find it impractical (or impossible) to check the truth of a hypothesis directly. You can proceed by considering a more familiar analogue or a smaller, more manageable sample of a larger group. Both kinds of argument are inductive: the support may strongly suggest the conclusion but will not guarantee it. The differences between these two kinds of reasoning, however, suggest different ways of evaluating their success.

The very good reason you can manage a sample more readily than an entire group may lead you to generalize inappropriately from that sample. Enumerative inductions are risky. Nevertheless, even if you cannot study statistics (necessary to understand fully how to generalize from a sample), you can avoid many errors by arming yourself with an understanding of how such arguments work and the general features necessary to their success.

7.2.1 Representativeness of the Sample

Most important, the sample must be representative of the larger group (or "population," as it is standardly called). Can you confidently claim that the instances you have observed are typical of other things of their kind? Consider the sample's size, breadth, and randomness.

7.2.1a Size of the Sample   The more instances you observe, the better your chances of eliminating an unrepresentative *(biased)* selection in your sample. If the opossum study involved only 5 opossums rather than the 78 mentioned, your confidence in your ability to generalize about their longevity would be diminished severely because it is more likely for factors irrelevant to opossum longevity to interfere with the lives of 5 opossums than with 78.

Is bigger always better, then? Unfortunately, no. As your sample increases, each new example provides diminishing returns. The difference between 5 and 78 observed opossums is important, but the difference between 1,005 and 1,078 observed opossums may not come to much.

When, then, is a sample large enough? There is no single answer. It depends on what else you know about the subject itself. On the one hand, a fairly small sample may be adequate if you are studying the skeletal structure of a species of dinosaurs, for you know that skeletal structure is somewhat uniform within a species and that it is subject to a variety of constraints (such as that the weight it bears restricts its structure). On the other hand, if you want to know whether children learn to read better with one kind of instruction than another, you need a much larger sample since many more individual factors can corrupt your results. Only by understanding the subject well can you decide how large a sample you need. There just isn't any shortcut around the need to know a lot about the world if you want to support interesting generalizations.

7.2.1b Breadth of the Sample

The more various the conditions under which the sample cases are observed, the better. The opossum argument involves not just Venezuelan opossums but also some studied in Florida. This variety helps to strengthen the argument since the short lives of the opossums cannot be explained solely in terms of some condition present only in Venezuela and quite irrelevant to the animal itself (such as opossums' being severely hunted there). Additionally, variety in the sample helps rule out idiosyncratic features of the subgroup interfering with your ability to generalize (for example, the Venezuelan variety of opossums having a shorter life span than other varieties). So it is important to gather the data from as broad a sample as possible.

7.2.1c Randomness of the Sample

Randomness, although related to breadth, is yet a bit different from it. A sample is random if each member of the larger group has an equal chance of being selected for the sample. If someone were to poll people attending a fraternity party to form a general estimate of college students' attitudes toward exclusive social organizations, the sample could hardly be considered random. Students opposed or indifferent to such organizations are much less likely to be at such a party and therefore less likely to be included in the sample of students who favor fraternities.

In recent years, fund raisers for a variety of causes have been using mail polls. Recipients are offered an opportunity to have their view on some important issue included as part of a sample of public opinion. The results are (allegedly) used to describe the public's concern about the issue for appropriate legislators, the press, or the board of directors. The obvious flaw in such polls is that even if the samples are quite large and quite broad (covering, for example, a spectrum of economic and geographic areas), they are far from random. People who receive the questionnaire have usually been identified as prospective donors (something the pollsters acknowledge by including a request for donations in the same mailing), suggesting that the recipients may already share the pollsters' view.

7.2.2 Errors in Presenting Generalizations from Samples

When you offer a generalization based on a sample, you need to provide sufficient information for your readers to evaluate the sample's size, breadth, and randomness. Sometimes, you may not be able to judge whether an argument is flawed by its sample's being too small, too narrow, or biased because of the way it is presented.

7.2.2a Insufficient Information   You may simply have too little information. For example, the *National Examiner* reported a survey of kissing habits, breaking down those in various age groups who kissed their partners more or less than once a week, once a day, in broad daylight, in public, on the lips; how many women are put off by beards, men by lipstick; and so forth. If you cared about this information, you would want to know something about the reliability of the study. But nowhere in the article do you find out who conducted the survey, where the sample came from (how broad it was), how large it was, or anything that might help you determine how random it was. You would want to know whether the questionnaires were distributed to college students, urban people, subscribers to *Hustler,* or people in the phone book. Such omissions undermine your ability to use the survey (at least as reported in the article) as evidence for its conclusions. To a much less serious degree, Austad's failure to mention the number of opossums in the Florida study makes it difficult for someone without access to that study to know whether it adds the variety it seems to add to the Venezuelan study.

7.2.2b Does the Data Really Exist?   A quick perusal of such tabloid magazines as the *National Enquirer,* the *Sun,* and the *Globe* should give you a lifetime supply of "reports" of people receiving messages from the grave, animals with psychic powers, miracle cures, sightings of Bigfoot, such unusual occurrences as a man who became homosexual because he received a heart transplant from a female donor, and a variety of amazing feats, such as the report of a man who captured a ghost in hot wax. If you seek something other than entertainment, you must approach such claims with skepticism. You can discount surveys and studies that draw generalizations from data you suspect is phony or innacurate or questionably interpreted (as in the story of the man who knew his dead son was communicating with him because a plant the son had given him, which had died, had suddenly revived; curiously the reporter failed to ask why the son had not himself revived, only sending a third-rate substitute!). Beware when the source of the data is unspecified or unreliable; the very existence of the data may be suspect.

7.2.2c Ignoring Disconfirming Evidence   You may be tempted to support a generalization with only those examples that confirm it, that suggest it may be true. Consider how unreliable such generalizations can be. A *National Examiner* advertisement for a system to beat lotteries offers "POSITIVE PROOF" that the product, one's own "Personal Numbers Report," is efficacious: "Our customers beat the lottery, the horses, bingo, any games of chance using their 'PERSONAL NUMBERS REPORT.' THE RESULTS YOU CAN GET ARE SIMPLY AMAZING!!! We get so many letters from richer, happier people they would fill a book!!!" The ad quotes from nine (alleged) letters written by satisfied customers spanning North America, such as the following: "I was unlucky for years. I received my LUCKY NUMBERS, and immediately hit $500.00, then $1,200.00, then $5,000.00 at Lotto, then $12,000.00. S. R., Porterville, Calif."

How strong is the so-called positive proof? Give it its best chance by suspending whatever doubts you may have about the truth of these letters; that is, assume the data to be real, the letters written by satisfied customers. There may in fact be nine (or even ninety) people who bought the Personal Numbers Report and also won lotteries, bingo, or other prizes. People who pay $12 for their own Personal Number Reports probably also purchase quite a few lottery tickets, attend bingo games, and bet on other things. It would not be surprising for some of them to win something. What you do not discover is how many people purchased the product and won nothing or no more than they were winning without it.

When you generalize from a sample, you must consider the evidence *against* your generalization, the *disconfirming* evidence, if you want to know how reliable the conclusion is. Considering only the evidence for the conclusion, the *confirming* instances, can mislead you since you may find some confirming examples for generalizations known to be wrong. If you wanted to know whether all redheads really are short-tempered, you could find some confirming instances, but it would be more useful for you to discover how many redheads are *not* short-tempered than to continue seeking more who are.

This tendency to seek confirming evidence while ignoring the disconfirming evidence that more accurately suggests the reliability of a conclusion drawn from a sample can be illustrated by the public's interest in biorhythms, an idea that gained some currency a few years back. According to the theory of biorhythms, allegedly discovered independently by Wilhelm Fliess, Hermann Swoboda, and Alfred Teltscher in the last century, everyone goes through physical, emotional, and intellectual cycles of the same length on a regular basis. Central to this theory is a generalization about these rhythmic cycles: the physical cycle lasts 23 days, the emotional cycle 28 days, and the intellectual cycle 33 days for everyone without variation. One experiences high and low points at different times during these cycles, certain days of which are critical, such as those when the low points of all three cycles coincide. Given that the cycles are completely invariable for all people, an individual can chart his own cycle from the day and time of his birth (Radner and Radner 5). One person explained to us that when he is low he often checks his biorhythms. "You'd be surprised to see how often my biorhythm chart predicts that I should be down when I am." What is crucial, of course, in order to know whether the generalization is reliable, is how often the biorhythm chart predicts he will be down when he is *not*. Unfortunately, he hadn't considered this data.

Others have used the generalization about biorhythms to predict such events as airplane and industrial accidents. Here, as in the personal case, you cannot accept the generalization as reliable without considering the disconfirming evidence. In their book *Science and Unreason,* Radner and Radner illustrate how strongly tempted many are to maintain a generalization they want to accept in spite of evidence to the contrary: "In response to a study showing no biorhythm effect in a sample of over 4,000 airline accidents, one author had this to say: 'If Wolcott's results are correct, it proves that no correlation exists for aircraft accidents. It does not prove, however, that no correlation exists for other occupations'" (69). Recall that biorhythms are supposedly invariable for all people, including airplane pilots!

7.2.2d Relevance of the Sample   Finally, you should ask whether the conclusion goes beyond the information supplied by the sample. Is the evidence truly relevant to determining whether the generalization is correct? Some current surveys try to determine what a group of people think about political issues, health and fitness, or qualities they prefer in a mate. Although the sampling in such surveys may be random, broad, and large enough for some generalization to be drawn, you must be careful to ensure that the correct one is drawn. Consider, for example, the generalization drawn from a recent survey conducted and published by *Ladies' Home Journal:*

> Women who want to stay their healthiest would do well to keep stress to a minimum, this survey seems to prove. Of all the factors that link people who suffer from both minor conditions and major illnesses, stress is the most significant. Only 6% of the people who described themselves as very stressed and anxious say their health is excellent, but 50% of the people who say they are very calm also enjoy excellent health.
>
> ("Your Body, Your Health" 92–93)

The results of this survey may be interesting for what they reveal about how respondents *perceive* the relation between stress and health, but they cannot be used to justify the conclusion proposed in the first quoted sentence: that stress and health are linked. First, the report leaves unclear how the questionnaire defined terms such as *stress* and *health,* if it did at all—an example of insufficient information to judge the strength of the argument. But even if that were not problematic, the survey relies upon self-reports of health and stress. It is entirely possible that some respondents perceive themselves as stressed and anxious when they are not (perhaps partly resulting from the vagueness of the terms). Some may even have unreasonable anxieties about their health, reporting stress and lack of good health when in fact they are quite healthy. Self-reports of health are not the most reliable ways of determining actual health. So no matter how representative the sample, you cannot conclude actual health from self-reported health. Although the information supplied by this sample may allow you to generalize about respondents' perceptions, it simply is not relevant to the generalization cited in the article.

Exercise 7.2

Decide whether the following passages contain an analogical argument, generalize from a sample, or do neither. If a passage generalizes from a sample, analyze and evaluate it: (1) State the generalization and describe the sample; (2) explain whether the sample is representative; and (3) explain whether there are any problems besides the sample's lack of size, breadth, or randomness that should make you wary of accepting the generalization on the basis of the evidence provided. If a passage contains an analogical argument, use the criteria from section 7.1.2 (degree of analogy, relevance, and moderation) to evaluate it.

A. William Walsh, employed by the Argonne National Laboratory near Chicago, spends his spare time working with prisoners. Over the years he became obsessed with the possible influence of body chemistry on criminality. . . . The major finding of Walsh's study is that there is a fairly clear *chemical* profile of violent personalities. Measuring the trace elements in the hair of 24 matched pairs of violent and nonviolent siblings and, in a second study, of 96 extremely violent men and 96 controls matched by age, race, socio-economic level, and size of resident city, Walsh found that there were clear differences in the hair samples of the violent siblings and the violent men.

(Adapted from Bunch 457)

B. Rudimentary organs may be compared with the letters in a word, still retained in spelling, but become useless in the pronunciation, but which still serve as a clue in seeking for its derivation.

(Charles Darwin, qtd. in Gould 27)

C. It is worth noting that in the post-war period, many researchers have felt able to employ this ethically "tainted" data. Ms. Kristine Moe, a science and medicine reporter for the *Journal-American* newspaper in Bellevue, Washington, has enumerated at least forty-five research articles published since 1945 which draw upon scientific data from Nazi experiments [conducted on unconsenting subjects in concentration camps], mostly concerned with hypothermia research.

(Schafer 413)

D. Today there are 37 juvenile delinquents awaiting execution on death row. After examining 14 of the current inmates, Dorothy Otnow Lewis, professor of psychiatry at the New York University School of Medicine, found that they had numerous psychiatric, neurological, and cognitive problems that had not previously been identified. What is more, the majority had been abused, both sexually and physically. . . . Based on her research, Lewis and her colleagues have come up with a new psychiatric classification: the limbic-psychotic-aggressive syndrome. According to Lewis, these death row inmates, like other violent juveniles, share a common life history. As kids they suffered severe beatings; as teenagers, many of the violent delinquents repeatedly attempted suicide or experienced paranoid thoughts and visual or auditory hallucinations. In addition, many suffered from symptoms commonly associated with psychomotor seizures, although few ere epileptic. . . . Teenagers she had studied had suffered severe accidents as children: Some had fallen from trees; others had been hit by cars or trucks; one had been shot in the right temple. These accidents, injuring the central nervous system, sometimes caused serious neurological problems, including frequent blackouts, dizzy spells, lapses of memory, dreamlike states, and seizures.

(Raeburn 28)

E. "Study Finds SAT Coaching Waste of Time"

Newton, Mass. (AP)—Special classes to improve scores on the Scholastic Aptitude Test are a waste of time and money for high school students, a new Harvard study has found.

William Fitzsimmons, Harvard's director of admissions, said Monday a study of Harvard freshmen, comparing students who were coached and those who were not, showed no appreciable difference in SAT scores.

In fact, Fitzsimmons said the students who were not coached scored higher on both verbal and mathematics sections than those coached.

. . .

The study was based on a questionnaire given to the more than 1,500 Harvard freshmen last fall.

The study found students who were not coached scored an average of 649 on verbal and 685 on math. Students who were coached, scored an average of 611 on verbal and 660 on math. The tests are graded on a scale of 200 to 800.

("Study Finds SAT Coaching Waste of Time" A3)

F. The Zen teacher Suzuki Shunryuu wrote, "In the beginner's mind there are many possibilities, in the expert's few." The clarity of expertise sometimes depends, that is, upon quite a narrow focus—seeing sharply by virtue of restricting attention to a tightly limited number of elements. There is great value in such controlled scrutiny, and in the authoritative, well-documented reports which it produces. But the meaning of a life and the tone of a relationship also derive from chance encounters, unforgettable conversations, hobbies, and the sometimes funny collisions between public and domestic spheres.

(Elder 11)

7.3 Explanation

When you explain something, you seek not so much to justify the truth of a conclusion as to account for why something you take to be true is so. As you explain why something is true, you need to keep clearly in mind the central problem or question that calls for explanation and to maintain a critical attitude toward alternative explanations. Recall how in "Silver Blaze" Holmes carefully formulates the problem he is addressing and maintains a critical attitude toward it as his inquiry proceeds. In his book *Knowledge as Design,* David Perkins uses the term *truth-mongering* to refer to the all-too-common practice of educators who present truths "as givens to be learned, without context, without critical perspective, without creative application" (xv). Too often you can discover only the results of science (and pseudo-science) and not the real insights: understanding why accepted theories are preferred over their competitors. These are the insights you must seek.

You are, of course, familiar with explanations; you hear and offer them all the time. But what makes an explanation good? What is involved in giving an explanation, and how you can assess its adequacy? To answer these questions, we will consider a model of explanatory reasoning.

7.3.1 A Case Study: "The Bubonic Plague"

The following article raises some questions about the bubonic plague and considers some answers offered for those questions. Read the article and respond to the following study questions. Read the study questions first, so you can keep them in mind as you read the article.

Study Questions:

1. What is the major problem about bubonic plague author Colin McEvedy addresses?
2. What data or facts give rise to this problem?
3. What are the different explanations offered to account for the puzzling phenomenon McEvedy discusses in the article?
4. Select two of the explanations McEvedy rejects and explain why he eliminates them.
5. McEvedy has his own favorite account. Has he proven that it is the right explanation of this phenomenon? Why or why not?

"The Bubonic Plague"[1]

By Colin McEvedy

In the year 1346 Europe, northern Africa and nearer parts of the Middle East had a total population of approximately 100 million people. In the course of the next few years a fourth of them died, victims of a new and terrifying illness that spread throughout the area, killing most of those unfortunate enough to catch it. The disease put an end to the population rise that had marked the evolution of medieval society: within four years Europe alone suffered a loss of roughly 20 million people. The disease responsible for such grim statistics was the bubonic plague, and this particular outbreak, lasting from 1346 to 1352, was known as the Great Dying or the Great Pestilence. Later it was appropriately referred to as the Black Death, a name that has come down through history.

Although the effects of the Black Death may have been particularly catastrophic, striking as it did after a long period in which the disease had been unknown in the West, this was not the first time the plague had ravaged Europe. Some 800 years earlier, during the reign of the emperor Justinian in the sixth century, there was an epidemic of similar proportions. There were also repeated, if less widespread, epidemics in the two centuries following the plague of Justinian's time, and for four centuries after the Black Death. The disease has undergone a precipitous decline since that time, but it still occurs sporadically in various parts of the world today, including the U.S.

From 70 to 80 percent of those who contracted the plague in the 14th century died from it. Indeed, the symptoms usually presented themselves with a ferocity that presaged death within five days. The name bubonic plague, derives from one of the early signs of the disease: the appearance of large, painful swellings called buboes in the lymph nodes of the armpit, neck or groin of the victim. Three days after the appearance of the buboes people were characteristically overwhelmed by high fever, became delirious and broke out in black splotches that were the result of hemorrhaging under the skin. As the disease progressed, the buboes continued to grow larger and more painful; often they burst.

The bursting is said to have been particularly agonizing, capable of arousing even the most moribund patients to a state of frenzy. Yet physicians always regarding the bursting as a good sign, if only because it indicated that the patient was still capable of putting up a fight a week or so after the onset of the illness. Of those who were going to die, probably half were already dead by this stage.

In some cases a person's bloodstream was directly infected, which led to septic shock, massive hemorrhaging and rapid death, a form of the disease known as septicemic plague. In other cases plague was transmitted as a type of pneumonia; in pneumonic plague the victims collapsed, spit blood and were almost always dead within a few days.

Strange as it may seem, in view of the frequency of the disease and the toll it exerted on the population, no one at the time had an inkling of its fundamental nature, its ultimate cause or how it was spread. During the period of the Black Death people were inclined to attribute the disease to unfavorable astrological combinations or malignant atmospheres ("miasmas"), neither of which could be translated into a public-health program of any kind. More paranoid elaborations blamed the disease on deliberate contamination by witches, Moslems (an idea proposed by Christians), Christians (proposed by Moslems) or Jews (proposed by both groups).

It was not until 1894 that the French bacteriologist Alexandre Yersin discovered that bubonic plague is caused by a gram-negative bacteria, *Yersinia pestis*, belonging to a group of bacteria known as rod-shaped bacilli, many of which are pathogenic. Plague bacilli are found at low frequency in many wild rodent populations throughout the world and are transmitted from one rodent to another by fleas. In the case of the bubonic plague the flea often responsible for transmitting the disease is the oriental rat flea, *Xenopsylla cheopis*. When a flea bites an infected rat, it ingests the bacilli, which proceed to replicate within its digestive tract, forming a solid mass that obstructs the flea's gut; the flea is unable to ingest blood and becomes ravenously hungry. In a feeding frenzy it repeatedly bites its animal host, regurgitating plague bacilli into the host's bloodstream every time it does so. These injection sites then act as foci for the spread of bacilli. If the host animal dies, as it is likely to do, the flea moves to the next available live rodent. The disease spreads rapidly in this manner; as the number of live rats decreases, the fleas move to warm-blooded hosts on which they would not normally feed, such as human beings and their domesticated animals, and so an epidemic is launched.

Once the disease enters the human population it can sometimes spread directly from human to human through the inhalation of infected respiratory droplets. The normal mode of spread is by the bite of rat fleas, however; the disease does not persist in the absence of rodents, which are the primary host for both the plague bacillus and the rat flea.

The essential requirement for an epidemic (an outbreak in a human population) is a rodent epizootic (an outbreak in an animal population). This is necessary both to initiate and to sustain the disease in human beings. Of course, the two populations must be in close contact for the transmission to be successful, but it is unlikely that this was ever a significant variable in medieval times. In rural as well as urban areas humans lived surrounded by rats.

The Black Death is thought to have migrated along the Silk Road, the trans-Asian route by which Chinese silk was brought to Europe. There are two reasons for believing this was the case. The first is that outbreaks of the plague were recorded on 1346 in Astrakhan and Saray, both caravan stations on the lower Volga River in what is now U.S.S.R. The second is that during the years 1347 and 1348 the Arab traveler and scholar Ibn Battuta, returning along the Spice Route from a stay in India, first reported hearing news of the plague when he reached Aleppo in northern Syria, not before. That clue excludes transmission by way of the Indian Ocean and Persian Gulf ports.

Most likely the disease erupted first among marmots, large rodents native to central Asia (they are related to woodchucks but belong to a different species) whose fur was an important article of trade throughout that part of the world. According to this historical reconstruction, trappers coming across dead or dying animals collected their furs, delighted to find such an abundant supply, and sold them to dealers who in turn (without worrying about reports of illness among the fur trappers) sold them to buyers from the West. When the bales of marmot furs sent west along the Silk Road were first opened in Astrakhan and Saray, hungry fleas jumped from the fur, seeking the first available blood meal they could find. From Saray the disease is thought to have traveled down the Don River to Kaffa, a major port on the Black Sea, where a large rat population provided the perfect breeding ground for the plague bacillus. Because many of the rats in Kaffa were living on sailing vessels bound for the ports of Europe, the disease had a ready means of transport to that part of the world.

Indeed, it would be difficult to design a more efficient means of disseminating the plague than a medieval ship. The holds of these ships were generally crawling with rats; when the crew slept, the rats took over, running through the rigging and dropping fleas onto the decks below. The cycle of infection, from flea to rat and rat to flea, would be maintained until the rat population was so reduced by the disease that it could no longer sustain the fleas and the plague bacteria they were carrying. Hungry fleas, seeking any host they could find, would then carry the disease into the human population. It is small wonder that by the end of 1347 plague had broken out in most ports on the route linking Kaffa to Genoa in northern Italy.

The two most important ports along this route were Pera, a suburb of Constantinople, and Messina, in Sicily. Both places were stopover points for ships crossing the Mediterranean and became major foci for further dissemination of the plague. The initial impact on the population of Constantinople was graphically described by the emperor Cantacuzenus, who lost a son to the disease in 1347. He recounts how it spread throughout the Greek islands and along the coasts of Anatolia and the Balkans, killing "most of the people." In Messina the first outbreak was recorded in October of 1347, launching an epidemic that quickly spread to include the entire island.

From there in early 1348 the Black Death crossed over to Tunis on the north coast of Africa and then spread by way of Sardinia to Spain. By the time it reached Spain the Black Death had also spread to the heart of Europe, a fact that can be blamed at least in part on the Genoese, who are said to have heartlessly turned away ships from the East carrying their sick countrymen. Not only did such hardheartedness have little effect (the city was as badly hit as any in Europe) but also the diversion of ships to other ports, such as Marseilles and Pisa, hastened the spread of the plague throughout Europe.

By this time the epidemic was raging throughout the Mediterranean. Ships carrying silk, slaves, and fur brought it to Alexandria before the end of 1347; from there it spread south to Cairo, east to Gaza, Beirut, and Damascus and finally along the north coast of Africa to Morocco.

By 1348 the Black Death had jumped from the mediterranean region to the Atlantic coast of Europe. It crossed southwestern France by way of the regional capital, Toulouse, and rapidly passed down the Garonne River to Bordeaux on the west coast. From there it is likely that one of the ships loading claret for the British market brought the Black Death to Great Britain. In 1348 it was first recorded at Weymouth on the south coast of England, and it is believed to have spread to Ireland from Bristol.

From England the plague crossed the North Sea to envelop Scandinavia in its deadly grasp. According to one story, the invasion of Scandinavia can be blamed on a ship that left London in May, 1349, bound for Bergen with a full crew and a cargo of wool. The ship is reported to have been seen some days later, drifting off the coast of Norway. Local people who rowed out to investigate found the crew dead and returned to shore, carrying the wool and—unwittingly—the plague with them. That started a chain reaction as village after village along the Norwegian coast succumbed to the disease. The following year the Black Death ravaged the populations of Denmark and Germany before entering Poland in 1351 and Russia in 1352. This in effect completed the circle; not only had the disease returned to within a few hundred miles of its entry into Europe on the Volga steppe but also after four long and devastating years mortality rates in western Europe had finally returned to normal.

The society that emerged from the period of the Black Death became quite prosperous; the survivors had inherited the fortunes of their deceased relatives and many were able to move into positions of prominence once closed to them. Their good fortune did not necessarily last for long, however. In 1356 a second outbreak of the plague appeared in Germany and spread rapidly throughout Europe. It exacted a particularly heavy toll among the children born since the end of the Black Death.

Thereafter the plague returned to Europe with mournful regularity; indeed, the continent never seemed free of it for more than a few years at a time. Although the later epidemics never matched the Black Death in terms of overall mortality, they nonetheless continued to have a negative impact on population growth in Europe through the end of the 14th century.

At this point an equilibrium was reached between plague and people, and in the 15th century the population began to recover. In particularly hard-hit regions it took more than a century for numbers to return to their original levels, but by the end of the 16th century populations all over were higher than they had been prior to the onset of the Black Death.

Strangely, when the plague did reappear (which it continued to do, albeit less frequently), it often did so with a ferocity equal to any recorded in previous outbreaks. In the last epidemic in France, from 1720 to 1722, half of the population of the city of Marseilles died, together with 60 percent of the population in neighboring Toulon, 44 percent at Arles and 30 percent at Aix and Avignon. Yet the epidemic did not spread beyond Provence, and the total number of deaths was less than 100,000.

By the 16th century it was widely believed the plague spread as a result of contagion: a toxic factor that could be transferred from the sick to the healthy. Human-to-human transmission was thought to take place either directly through physical contact with a sick person or indirectly by the clothes or bed sheets. In response, many towns and villages instituted quarantine regulations. The authorities in England, for example, recommended that plague victims be locked up in their homes or transferred to special "pest houses." An extreme example of adherence to public policy is the famous case of William Mompesson, rector in the small village of Eyam in Derbyshire, who persuaded the entire community to enter into quarantine when the plague erupted there in 1666. One by one the parishioners who remained faithful to their contaminated hearths fell victim to the disease. A mortality rate of 72 percent indicates that the community probably had a morbidity (infection) rate of 100 percent, an extraordinary price to pay for a misconceived theory.

Locking people in their homes is, of course, one of the worst possible ways to fight the plague. The plague is a disease of "locality," most likely to manifest itself when rats, fleas and people are kept in close contact with one another. To confine people is to maximize their chance of being bitten by a plague-carrying flea or infected through close contact with another human being.

Officials recognized that quarantines were dangerous to healthy individuals confined with sick relatives, but they imposed them nonetheless in the belief that some lives must be sacrificed in order to stop further spread of the disease. Because it is rats that carry the plague (and the rats were free to travel), the entire quarantine effort was a waste of time—and lives.

Attempts were also made to quarantine passengers and goods arriving in boats from overseas. When sickness suggestive of the plague was observed among crew members or passengers, the ships were diverted to lazarettos (quarantine stations) until the authorities deemed it safe to release them. At Marseilles in May of 1720, for example, the sailing ship *Grand Saint Antoine* was placed in quarantine for three weeks because eight of its crew had died in the course of the voyage from the Near East. In spite of these efforts to limit the spread of the plague, the disease broke out in Marseilles—first among the dock workers who unloaded the ship's cargo when it was released from quarantine and then in the population at large.

There is little evidence that quarantines of this type were ever very effective. Venice was one of the first seaports to introduce quarantine regulations, early in the 15th century, enforcing them by imposing the death penalty to anyone who broke the rules. Yet Venice suffered from the plague as much as any city in Italy, presumably because it was impossible to prevent rats aboard quarantined ships from jumping ashore, carrying the plague with them.

Finally, after innumerable cycles of onslaught and retreat, the plague disappeared from Europe. London's last experience with the disease, the Great Plague, began in 1665 and ended in spectacular fashion with the Great Fire of 1666. At that time it was natural for Londoners to believe they owed their deliverance to the purifying conflagration. Later it was suggested Londoners owed their resistance to the plague to the reconstruction that followed the fire and the fact that the rebuilt city boasted brick houses and wide, rubbish-free streets in place of the higgledy-piggledy structures and malodorous alleys of medieval times.

This explanation is attractive but does not hold up under scrutiny. One reason is that the fire destroyed only the central part of London, the area least affected by any of the outbreaks of plague earlier in the century, leaving untouched the overcrowded suburbs that had provided the disease with its main lodging in previous times. A second reason is that other cities in Europe, such as Paris and Amsterdam, became plague-free during the same period—a phenomenon that could not be linked to the Great Fire of London.

A somewhat more convincing (but still flawed) theory suggests that the disappearance of the plague coincided with a slow rise in prevailing standards of health and hygiene. Although hygiene cannot be eliminated as a factor, it does not explain why subsequent outbreaks followed the standard course, complete with high rates of mortality, but were farther and farther away from the center of Europe each time they appeared. It was almost as if Europe were developing some form of resistance to the plague that kept the infection from propagating in the usual way. In the north the path of retreat was to the east; in the Mediterranean it was to the south. The later the epidemic, the less it seemed to be capable of spreading. This, moreover, was at a time when, according to every available index, traffic by land and by sea was increasing.

When the role of rats was finally established late in the 19th century, it was suggested that the subsidence of the plague could be explained by changes in the population dynamics of the black rat, *Rattus rattus*. During the 18th century it had been observed that the black rat, the historic carrier, had been largely displaced by a new species, the brown rat *(Rattus norvegicus)*, which would have been a much poorer vector of the plague: the brown rat is as susceptible to the plague bacillus as the black rat but does not normally live in close proximity to humans. Brown rats typically live in dark cellars or sewers, whereas black rats overrun the upper rooms and rafters of a house. Because the oriental rat flea has a maximum jump of 90 millimeters (a little more than 3.5 inches), the difference in preferred habitats may have been enough to isolate humans from plague-infested fleas.

The brown-rat theory seems plausible but does not fit the geography: the brown rat spread across Europe in the 18th century from east to west, whereas the plague retreated from west to east. The brown rat was in Moscow long before the city experienced a particularly severe epidemic of the plague in the

1770s; it did not reach England until 1727, more than 60 years after that country's last bout of the plague.

The late Andrew B. Appleby of San Diego State University suggested an alternative theory, namely that a certain percentage of black rats became resistant to the plague over the course of the 17th century and that the resistant animals would have increased in number, spreading across Europe during the next 100 years. Although these rats might still be infected by the plague bacillus, they would not die from it and therefore could not support a large population of fleas, rendering it unnecessary for the fleas to seek other hosts. This theory, however, does not conform to what is known about resistance to plague in animal populations. As Paul Slack of the University of Oxford has pointed out, rat populations often develop resistance when exposed to a pathogenic bacterium or virus, but such resistance is short-lived and is therefore unlikely to have been responsible for broad-based immunity to the plague.

A more plausible theory suggests that a new species of plague bacillus, *Yersinia pestis*, may have evolved that was less virulent than the previous strain. Being less virulent, it might have acted as a vaccine, conferring on infected animals and humans a relative immunity to more virulent strains of the bacterium.

The bacteriological theory is acceptable on several grounds. First, it conforms to the dictum, proposed by the American pathologist Theobold Smith, that "pathological manifestations are only incidents in a developing parasitism," so that in the long run milder forms of disease tend to displace more virulent ones. Second, it explains why the decline of the plague is associated with a failure to spread beyond local outbreaks: a disease cannot travel far when the number of people susceptible to it is low. Third, it is supported by the existence of a close relative of the plague bacillus, *Yersinia pseudotuberculosis*, which does not induce visible illness in rats but does confer on them a high degree of immunity to the plague.

Did *Y. pseudotuberculosis*, or a relative with similar properties, gradually spread through the rodent population of early modern Europe, making it impossible for *Y. pestis* to gain a foothold there? Although no direct evidence exists to support that hypothesis, it seems more reasonable than any other.

The discovery and widespread use of antibiotics has conferred on human beings a different form of protection from the plague. Although the disease still occurs with regularity throughout parts of Africa, South America and the southwestern U.S. (in 1986, 10 cases were reported in the U.S.), it is never again likely to reach epidemic levels now that we know how it spreads, what public-health measures are appropriate, and how to treat plague cases as they occur. Nevertheless, many questions about the plague are as yet unanswered. For example, the mode of transmission in rural areas, where rat populations are discontinuous, is entirely unclear. And what explains the distribution of the plague throughout the world today? Why are only certain rodent populations reservoirs of the disease whereas others are entirely free of it?

7.3.2 Getting Clear About the Problem

Explaining and justifying, while not always easy to distinguish, are importantly different enterprises. When you set out to justify a claim (that is, to provide evidence that it is true), you do not presuppose it to be true, for its truth is just what is in question. You may discover the claim to be false. But when you explain something, you presuppose it to be true. You do not attempt to explain the fact that the moon is edible because you do not consider it to be edible in the first place. You saw a dramatic example of the inability to explain something not true in "Silver Blaze": Gregory and Holmes are unable to solve the mystery as long as they describe the puzzling phenomenon as an intentional murder. In searching for the culprit they were trying to explain something that had not, in fact, happened.

First, then, you need to describe the phenomena you wish to explain. Begin by answering two questions:

1. What are the data or phenomena to be explained?
2. What do you find puzzling about this situation?

"The Bubonic Plague" provides a useful model of explanatory reasoning. McEvedy presents a complex set of data about the nature, transmission, and historical spread of bubonic plague. He presents quite a bit of data, all of which turns out to be relevant to his aim, but not all of it is necessary to state the central problem he addresses. The data generating the central problem may be summarized this way: Most people are familiar with the epidemic bubonic plague that occurred in the fourteenth century (the "Black Death"). During a period of just a few years, the plague spread rapidly from Asia through the Middle East and North Africa to Europe and back to Asia. Some 70 to 80 percent of those infected died, usually within five days. Plague epidemics were recorded as early as the sixth century (when there was an epidemic of similar proportions) and continued into the eighteenth century, with occasional smaller outbreaks right into this decade. Despite the long experience with plague, no one had an inkling how it was caused or how to avoid it until late in the nineteenth century. Nevertheless, after the fifteenth century, though the plague reappeared as ferociously as it had in the fourteenth century, it did not spread as readily as it had in earlier outbreaks. Eventually, the plague largely disappeared from Europe.

These are the main facts that call for explanation. What's puzzling is this: given the ferocity of this disease and the rapidity with which it spread prior to the fifteenth century, why did plague largely disappear from a place (Europe) it had so thoroughly devastated so many times? What was different?

7.3.3 Generate Hypotheses

An answer to such a question is called a *hypothesis*. McEvedy reviews quite a few answers others have suggested. Because inevitably you will find many possible answers to a puzzling question, you need to be careful not to settle too quickly on any one without considering the other possibilities. Why doesn't Johnny learn to read? Perhaps it may be the teaching methods are not a good fit for his learning style; or perhaps his parents are not helping him at home sufficiently; or maybe he hasn't been able to concentrate because of some physical deficiency, perhaps inadequate nutrition; or maybe Johnny has as-yet-undetected brain damage. The possibilities are almost endless. It could be a disservice to Johnny, his teachers, his parents, or his breakfast to settle too quickly on any one of these without considering other possibilities.

In "The Bubonic Plague" McEvedy considers six hypotheses:

H1: Europe was purified of the bubonic plague by the Great Fire of London in 1666.

H2: The reconstruction of London after the great fire of 1666 created an environment inhospitable to bubonic plague, thereby leading to its eventual disappearance from Europe.

H3: Increased awareness of health and hygiene practices decreased the incidence of bubonic plague.

H4: The displacement of the black rat by the brown rat, which is not as good a vector for plague, resulted in the disappearance of plague.

H5: Beginning in the seventeenth century, an increasing percentage of black rats became resistant to bubonic plague, thereby eliminating the need for infected fleas to leave their preferred hosts (rats) for human hosts, to whom they move only when living rat hosts are unavailable.

H6: A new strain of the plague bacillus evolved that was less virulent than previous strains, enabling it to act as a vaccine, conferring on infected animals and humans a degree of immunity to the more virulent strains of the plague bacterium.

How you generate a list of potential hypotheses depends in part on what the problem is. You can certainly use many of the idea-generating techniques we have discussed in this book. Depending on the problem, it might be useful to freewrite, engage in dialogue, or brainstorm. It is important to realize, however, that there is no substitute for having a lot of background information at your disposal at this stage, especially the more complex the problem. Recall that in "Silver Blaze," Holmes's knowledge

about such things as the habits of men with mistresses, the gregarious-
ness of horses, the problems faced by Gypsies, and the smell of opium
guided his thinking of alternatives to the obvious (but wrong) hypothesis
of Inspector Gregory.

A complex situation such as the plague's failure to spread as far as it
had previously calls for extensive background information before you
can consider hypotheses. Each of the hypotheses McEvedy considers arises
out of some further information about the situation. H4, for example,
requires you to know that the brown rat displaced the black rat at the
relevant time, that plague is transmitted via bacteria-infested fleas hosted
by rats, and that the different habits of the black and brown rats make the
subsidence of plague epidemics more likely. One important element in
generating hypotheses, then, is to know as much as possible about the
phenomena surrounding the puzzling situation.

7.3.4 Test Your Hypothesis

Nobel physicist Richard Feynman told a story about a group of people
in the South Seas, who, having seen airplanes loaded with goods land
during the war, wanted to see this good fortune continue. So they built
a runway, lit fires along its sides, and built a hut for a man to sit in
with wooden pieces on his head that looked like headphones (equipped
with bamboo antennae). Then they waited for the airplanes to land.
They had a hypothesis based on the behavior they observed of the
people who had been associated with the puzzling appearance of cargo
planes (311).

It isn't enough to have a hypothesis that you think explains the puzzling data. You need to see whether your hypothesis will stand up under
scrutiny. You need to follow Sherlock Holmes and subject your pet theories about the way the world works to critical scrutiny. Without that, you
engage in what Feynman called "cargo cult science": achieving the outward appearance of scientific inquiry without attaining what is crucial to
its substance. But how do you get past the appearances to the substance?
Consider a few examples from "The Bubonic Plague."

Take H2, the explanation that plague disappeared from Europe when
the rebuilding of London after the great fire of 1666 destroyed the hospitable environment for plague-carrying rats. McEvedy cites the following
objections to H2:

> This explanation is attractive but does not hold up under scrutiny. One
> reason is that the fire destroyed only the central part of London, the
> area least affected by any of the outbreaks of plague earlier in the cen-
> tury, leaving untouched the overcrowded suburbs that had provided
> the disease with its main lodging in previous times. A second reason is

that other cities in Europe, such as Paris and Amsterdam, became plague-free during the same period—a phenomenon that could not be linked to the great fire of London.

How do the objections work? Look at the second objection. McEvedy checks H2 by a prediction based on it:

P1: London was more plague-free than cities that had not rebuilt.

He knows that P1 is false. Because it should be true if H2 is true, he knows H2 must be rejected.

The argument against H2, then, can be represented as follows:

If plague disappeared from Europe because the rebuilding of London after the great fire of 1666 destroyed the hospitable environment for plague-carrying rats, then London was more plague-free than cities that had not rebuilt from the fire.

But London was not more plague-free than cities that had not been rebuilt from the fire.

Therefore, plague did not disappear from Europe because the rebuilding of London after the great fire destroyed the hospitable environment for plague-carrying rats.

Or you can represent it schematically:

If H2 is true, then P1 is true.
But P1 is false.

Therefore, H2 is false.

McEvedy infers P1 from H2 in order to predict what he should find if the hypothesis is true. The prediction must encompass something he can actually check out by reliable methods (for example, observation). If a prediction based on a hypothesis turns out to be false, the hypothesis is *disconfirmed*; if a prediction turns out to be true, the hypothesis is *confirmed*.

7.3.5 Auxiliary Assumptions

McEvedy's refutation of H2 depends on his being able to make a prediction from the hypothesis. Strictly speaking, though, he cannot infer from the hypothesis (that rebuilt London was more plague-free than other cities) unless he makes certain assumptions. For example, even though other cities did not rebuild, they may already have had the kind of environment London acquired in 1666. In order to infer P1 from H2, he must assume that these other cities lacked the relevant advances the London rebuilding brought.

Such assumptions, called *auxiliary assumptions,* allow you to check the truth of the prediction you make from the hypothesis; otherwise the prediction will not help you test the hypothesis. Often you will be unable to find a statement that you can derive (by itself) from the hypothesis *and* check by some reliable method. Auxiliary assumptions need not cause problems as long as they are themselves safe to rely on.

7.3.6 Disconfirming a Hypothesis

You test your hypotheses by trying to disconfirm them; that is part of the critical attitude. If you make a prediction based on a hypothesis and find the prediction false, you have *disconfirmed* the hypothesis. Because the prediction (P1) is false, you can say that the hypothesis (H2) is disconfirmed. Recall the schematic argument:

> If H2 is true, then P1 is true.
> But P1 is false.
> ―――――――――――――――
> Therefore, H2 is false.

This is a valid argument form (called *modus tollens*). You can test its validity by trying to produce an argument in this form with true premises and a false conclusion; you can't do it. Since arguments in this form are always deductively valid, then given true premises, the conclusion must also be true. So long as you can rely on the truth of these premises, you can be sure that you should reject H2 as an explanation for the disappearance of plague in Europe.

7.3.7 A Special Case: Nondisconfirmable Hypotheses

You need to be on your guard against turning hypotheses into impenetrable fortresses, immune from even the possibility of attack. If nothing could count as a reason to reject your hypothesis, you can't rely on it simply because it has not been disconfirmed.

Consider this example. In 1973 a group of psychologists led by D.L. Rosenhan wanted to discover how able the professional staffs at mental hospitals were at distinguishing sanity from insanity. Eight of them admitted themselves voluntarily to such institutions without letting the hospitals know what they were doing. Aside from presenting themselves as having heard voices (one sign of schizophrenia) before coming to the hospitals, they behaved "normally" throughout their stays. Surprisingly, the staffs—from psychiatrists to orderlies—never caught on that these people lacked the psychological problems that ordinarily provide grounds for admission to a mental hospital. Despite the fact that the pseudopatients feigned no symptoms of any psychological disorders once in the hospitals, their "sanity" went unnoticed.

Perhaps even more disturbing than the professionals' failure to discover the pseudopatients' "sanity," the psychiatrists interpreted their "normal" behaviors as confirming the initial diagnoses. For example, when the pseudopatients kept notes of their experiences, one professional marked on a pseudopatient's chart that he had engaged in "writing behavior." In another case, a pseudopatient pacing the hall from boredom was interpreted as pacing from nervousness. Rosenhan concluded that little or nothing the pseudopatients could have done would have convinced the staff that these patients were not suffering the disorders they had been diagnosed as having. The reason was simple: though one would suppose some kind of evidence exists that could lead professionals to think that a patient is not schizophrenic, the staffs *were treating* the diagnoses as certain, not open to disconfirming evidence. As a result, the staffs reinterpreted all behaviors that might provide evidence against the diagnoses to fit the diagnoses, insulating the diagnoses from all possible criticism and refutation (Rosenhan 250–58). When you treat hypotheses in this way, you make them "nondisconfirmable."

Nathaniel Hawthorne's comment on George Washington and the cherry tree is instructive: he said that he was a better man than Washington because, whereas Washington *could not* tell a lie, he *could, but would not*. Disconfirmable hypotheses are, for a similar reason, preferable to nondisconfirmable hypotheses. Nondisconfirmable hypotheses may seem to give you an advantage, but it is only a chimera. No evidence arises to show them in error, but you avoid refutation only because you insulate them from the very possibility of critical scrutiny. They are, quite literally, too good to be true.

One further point is noteworthy. Assuming that the Rosenhan study does not throw into question the very concepts of sanity and insanity (some would claim it does), it shows that even a hypothesis that is disconfirmable can be treated as if it is nondisconfirmable. In other words, hypotheses are not necessarily disconfirmable or nondisconfirmable by themselves; often the distinction depends on how you treat them.

7.3.8 Confirming a Hypothesis

Suppose you make a prediction based on a hypothesis, and the prediction turns out to be true. Do you know then that the hypothesis is true? Unfortunately, confirming a hypothesis is much more difficult than disconfirming one. Sometimes when the prediction turns out to be correct, you say it confirms or gives supporting evidence of the truth of the hypothesis, but not always.

Consider the explanation McEvedy favors for the disappearance of bubonic plague. That explanation (H6) hypothesizes that the plague disappeared from Europe because a new, less-virulent strain acted as a vaccine, conferring on infected animals and humans a degree of immunity to the more virulent strains of the plague bacterium. McEvedy offers three reasons to believe this is the most plausible explanation for the disappearance of plague:

> The bacteriological theory is acceptable on several grounds. First, it conforms to the dictum, proposed by the American pathologist Theobold Smith, that "pathological manifestations are only incidents in a developing parasitism," so that in the long run milder forms of disease tend to displace more virulent ones. Second, it explains why the decline of the plague is associated with a failure to spread beyond local outbreaks: a disease cannot travel far when the number of people susceptible to it is low. Third, it is supported by the existence of a close relative of the plague bacillus, *Yersinia pseudotuberculosis*, which does not induce visible illness in rats but does confer on them a high degree of immunity to the plague.

All three of these grounds give some support or confirmation to the hypothesis. The second and third grounds exemplify the pattern you have been studying. Consider the third ground. McEvedy again relies on a prediction (call it P2): On the basis of H6 he expects such a less-virulent bacterium to be found. To derive this prediction, he requires the auxiliary assumption that the same forces that led to its diminution in the eighteenth century operate today to keep the incidence of plague low. In fact, scientists have found a close relative of the virulent bacterium that fits the description given in the hypothesis: it is capable of conferring immunity on rats while not giving them the illness itself. This finding gives some measure of support to H6.

But it is important to realize that the finding is only a *measure* of support: confirmation is not on a par with disconfirmation. If you can disconfirm a hypothesis, you can be confident it is false. But if you confirm a hypothesis, you have simply provided some evidence in support of it; it may still turn out to be false. Look at the logic of the argument confirming H6:

> If plague disappeared because a less-virulent strain that inoculated many hosts appeared, then this less-virulent plague bacterium can be found.
>
> A less-virulent plague bacterium, *Yersinia pseudotuberculosis*, has been found.
>
> ---
>
> Therefore, the disappearance of plague is explained by the appearance of a less-virulent strain that inoculated many hosts.

Or put it schematically:

If H6 is true, then P2 is true.
P2 is true.
_____

Therefore, H6 is true.

This argument is not deductively valid. Even if all the premises are true, the conclusion may still be false. To see that this is so, consider the following logical analogy:

If George Washington drank a lot of jet fuel, he would be dead now.
George Washington is dead now.
_____

George Washington drank a lot of jet fuel.

The premises are both true: jet fuel will kill you if you drink it, and Washington is dead. Of course, he couldn't have drunk jet fuel because it didn't exist while he lived, so the conclusion is false. Any argument in the same form is invalid.

This particular argument form is called *affirming the consequent.* What's interesting about affirming the consequent is that although arguments in this form are usually not worth much, sometimes they are still valuable because they help to confirm a conclusion. We have to decide when such arguments are worthless and when the presence of confirming evidence constitutes a genuine reason to believe the hypothesis has some support. But how do we decide?

Just as a prediction to disconfirm a hypothesis must be both derivable from the hypothesis and testable, so too must these conditions hold for confirmation. But in addition the prediction for confirming a hypothesis must be improbable! That seems an odd requirement, but it is nevertheless an important one.

Recall Sherlock Holmes's use of the lame sheep to confirm his hypothesis about the disappearance of Silver Blaze and the death of John Straker. Holmes argues that if Straker had intended to perform an operation to make Silver Blaze lame, he probably would want to practice the operation on some other animal first. Holmes predicted, in other words, on the basis of his hypothesis that Straker had practiced on some other animal. Noticing the sheep, he surmised that they may well be the animals Straker practiced upon. He was right; they had become inexplicably lame a few days earlier.

From this hypothesis, Holmes made a prediction that turned out to be correct. Suppose, instead, that Holmes predicted that Straker had behaved normally toward Silver Blaze in the presence of other people in previous days, employing the auxiliary assumption that Straker would want others to think he had nothing to do with Silver Blaze's becoming lame. Unlike the prediction of lame sheep, this one would be of no use in confirming the hypothesis, even if correct, becase it would likely be true even if the hypothesis were false. One would expect Straker to behave normally *whether or not* Holmes's theory is correct. So its being a true prediction cannot lend any support to Holmes's theory. It is less likely, however, that some other animals would be lame just prior to Silver Blaze's disappearance *unless* Holmes's theory were true. So the prediction of the lame sheep is useful in supporting Holmes's hypothesis in a way that other predictions might not have been.

Thus, a true prediction confirms a hypothesis only if the prediction is unlikely to be true unless the hypothesis is also true.

Vague predictions, an all-too-common way of disguising a lack of support for a claim, fail this criterion. For example, consider this horoscope: "Aries: Don't ignore your social obligations today, even if they are a bit demanding and you have to attend more than one event. Each gathering could be fortuitous" ("Astrograph" B5). Notice that this horoscope does not predict that anyone's social obligations *will* be demanding, but only that *if* they are, they shouldn't be ignored. That, of course, is not bad advice whether or not you are an Aries! The reason offered not to ignore them—the prediction—is cast in such guarded terms ("could be fortuitous") that it would be very hard to know that the prediction had turned out false. What counts as fortuitous here? Suppose you settle somewhat unrealistically on monetary gain. How much gain? A little? No gain, but at least no loss? Some loss, but (thankfully) not too much? And once you settle what counts as fortuitousness, will the prediction be false if an Aries loses more or gains less than is fortuitous? Might an unfortuitous gathering still be one that *could* have been fortuitous and therefore be consistent with the prediction? As a prediction that, if true, supposedly lends some support to astrology, this one is too vague to be of any use as a test.

7.3.9 Other Kinds of Confirmation

McEvedy's first reason for accepting H6 differs from the second and third. Simply put, he argues that since parasites need their hosts to survive, evolution tends to favor those strains of the parasite that do not kill off the host species altogether. And because plague bacteria are parasites on the fleas, rats, and humans they infect, he would expect that the more-virulent strain of the plague might be displaced over time by a less-virulent form. Instead of deriving a prediction from the hypothesis, McEvedy here argues that the hypothesis explains the disappearance of plague in a way that is consistent with what he knows in general about the behavior of parasites (which plague bacteria are) and evolutionary theory. That is, the hypothesis gets its support by being consistent with theories accepted on independent grounds. So we cannot expect *all* cases in which confirming evidence is supplied for a theory to fit the model we have supplied. But it will work for a great many.

SKELETON OF NEWLY DISCOVERED DINOSAUR SPECIES
RECONSTRUCTED FROM TWO FOSSILS
(DISPUTED BY SOME EXPERTS)

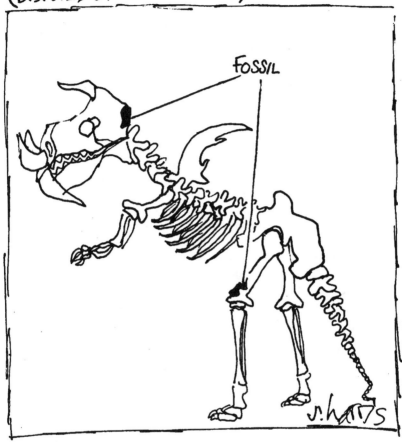

FOSSIL

Exercise 7.3

I. For each of the following, express in your own words: (1) the data
that gives rise to the puzzle and (2) the puzzle that the data gives
rise to. (3) If the passage proposes a test of the hypothesis, explain
why you think it a good or poor test, and (4) if the hypothesis is
supported or refuted, explain whether it is well done.
   A. This is the problem that Darwin faced, for his creationist
      opponents did view each species as unaltered from its initial

formation. How did Darwin prove that modern species are the products of history? We might suppose that he looked toward the most impressive results of evolution, the complex and perfected adaptations of organisms to their environments: the butterfly passing for a dead leaf, the bittern for a branch; the superb engineering of a gull aloft or a tuna in the sea.

Paradoxically, he did just the opposite. He searched for oddities and imperfections. The gull may be a marvel of design; if one believes in evolution beforehand, then the engineering of its wing reflects the shaping power of natural selection. But you cannot demonstrate evolution with perfection because perfection need not have a history. After all, perfection of organic design had long been the favorite argument of creationists, who saw in consummate engineering the direct hand of a divine architect. A bird's wing, as an aerodynamic marvel, might have been created exactly as we find it today.

But, Darwin reasoned, if organisms have a history, then ancestral stages should leave *remnants* behind. Remnants of the past that don't make sense in present terms—the useless, the odd, the peculiar, the incongruous—are the signs of history. They supply proof that the world was not made in its present form. When history perfects, it covers its own tracks.

(Gould 28–29)

B. R. Robin Baker at the University of Manchester in England studied recently deceased corpses. By using stains for iron, he found a layer of iron compounds in the sinuses of four of his five subjects. Iron, of course, is one of the elements that exhibit strong magnetism. Various researchers have proposed that the magnetic material in other species (fish, pigeons, dolphins, bees) are aids in navigation, orienting the creatures to the earth's magnetic field. Baker, who has published work on humans' ability to find direction in response to a magnetic field, proposed that the finding of iron in the sinuses is related to his earlier findings.

(Adapted from Bunch 164)

C. Honeybee venom, wasp venom, and phymatid venom injected into the leg of an orb-weaving spider all cause the spider to detach the affected leg. Because the response is so swift—only a few seconds—the venom has little chance to reach the spider's body. Spiders that do not discard their legs when stung in the leg usually die. Thus, discarding the legs has definite survival value.

Katydids and three other families of spiders also display similar leg-shredding behavior when stung. While this behavior in itself does not prove that some spiders feel pain, the components of the venom associated with leg detachment suggest that these spiders do feel pain. Melittin, histamine, phospholipase A2, and serotonin, found in venoms, are known to cause human pain.

(Bunch 169)

II. The English physician Edward Jenner is well-known for his development of a smallpox vaccine in the late eighteenth century. One could be infected with more or less serious forms of smallpox, and people who survived the less severe form did not become reinfected. Before Jenner's discovery, people would sometimes scratch themselves with material from sores formed by the milder form of smallpox as a method of preventing more serious forms of the disease. Unfortunately, this method was unreliable. It involved the risk of inflicting oneself with a deadly case of smallpox.

Dr. Jenner noticed what dairymaids knew well: that an attack of cowpox (a less serious disease that infects both cows and humans) seemed to confer some immunity to smallpox. Jenner wanted to test this hypothesis. Ultimately, his famous experiment led to a vaccine for smallpox. Here is how the *Encyclopedia Britannica* reports this test:

> The story of the great breakthrough is well known. In May 1796 Jenner found a young dairymaid, Sarah Nelmes, who had fresh cowpox lesions on her finger. On May 14, using matter from Sarah's lesions, he inoculated an eight-year-old boy, James Phipps, who promptly developed a slight fever, and a low-grade lesion. On July 1 Jenner inoculated the boy again, this time with smallpox matter. No disease developed; protection was complete.
>
> ("Jenner")

A. What auxiliary assumptions was Jenner employing in his reasoning?

B. Is the *Britannica* correct—did Jenner know that "protection was complete"? How could Jenner's reasoning have gone wrong?

III. For the following, identify the hypothesis, state a prediction that follows from the hypothesis, identify the auxiliary hypotheses needed for your prediction, and formulate an alternative hypothesis.

A. A plastic surgeon who specializes in face-lifts recently commented that his youngest patients are frequently actresses. He believes that actresses' faces "fall" as a result of extensive massaging when they put on and take off their makeup.

B. According to Stephen Jay Gould, Cyril Burt wondered about the intellectual achievements of Jews, and attributed them, in part, to the inherited myopia that keeps them off the playing fields and adapts them for poring over account books.

IV. Ignaz Semmelweis, a physician in the Vienna General Hospital in the 1840s, discovered that a higher proportion of women delivering babies in the First Division than in the Second Division contracted childbed fever, a sometimes fatal illness. Between 1844 and 1846 the average annual mortality rate in the First Division was over 8 percent, while it was just over 2 percent in the Second Division.

A commission concluded that rough examinations by inexperienced medical students, who received obstetrical training only in the First Division, were to blame. Semmelweis rejected this explanation, first because the injuries resulting from giving birth are much greater than those caused by rough examination, and second because midwives receiving training in the Second Division were as rough as the interns. Furthermore, even when the number of examining interns was reduced, the mortality rate continued to climb.

The rooms were arranged so that the priest bearing the last sacrament to a woman dying in the sick room had to pass through the First Division, but not the Second. Some hypothesized that the priest's presence (preceded by an attendant ringing a bell) was making patients along his route susceptible to childbed fever through fear. Semmelweis convinced the priest to eliminate the bell and avoid the First Division in approaching the sick room, with no effect on the mortality rate.

In 1847 a physician was wounded by a scalpel during an autopsy, developed symptoms similar to childbed fever, and died. Semmelweis thought that "cadaveric matter" ("putrid matter deriving from cadavers") introduced into his colleague's bloodstream was responsible. Additionally, the medical staff came directly from dissections in the autopsy room to examine women in labor. Their superficially washed hands retained a characteristic, foul odor. Semmelweis concluded that the patients in the First Division were also dying of blood poisoning from the cadaveric material carried on the hands of the medical staff.

This hypothesis accounted for the different rates of childbed fever. The training of midwives in the Second Division, unlike that of the medical students, did not include anatomical instruction involving dissection of cadavers. The women who had delivered babies on the street and then entered the First Division were rarely examined after admission, and they had a lower rate of childbed fever. To test his idea, Semmelweis ordered the staff to wash their hands in a solution of chlorinated lime before examinations. In 1848 the mortality rate from childbed fever dropped to slightly higher than 1 percent in the first division.

(Adapted from Hempel 3–7)

A. Display Semmelweis's reasoning to disconfirm the view that childbed fever is caused by alarm at the presence of the priest. Are there any auxiliary hypotheses necessary to this argument?

B. Display Semmelweis's reasoning to confirm his hypothesis that "cadaverous matter" was being spread during examination by the medical staff.

C. Semmelweis's discovery certainly seems important and useful. After all, when the medical staff washed their hands more fully, the incidence of childbed fever went way down and stayed down. Could Semmelweis nevertheless be wrong? Explain how he could be wrong and how he could design a test to find out.

8

Fallacies

A fallacy is an error in reasoning, usually a particularly persuasive one. As the term *fallacy* is used in the field of logic and critical thinking, it does not mean "false" or "falsehood" (as it is sometimes used in every-day English); the term is usually reserved for arguments and inferences, which are neither true nor false. Nor does *fallacy* necessarily suggest deception or trickery. Generally we reserve the terms *sophistry* and *propaganda* for the intentional use of fallacious reasoning to deceive. An argument can be fallacious whether or not the author is trying to deceive, or even knows it is fallacious. A person can be taken in by his own fallacious inference. In the most general sense, fallacious reasoning prevents an argument from providing adequate support for its conclusion.

Many reasoning errors, especially those most likely to catch you off guard, have names. Gaining a vocabulary to describe the major types of fallacious appeals may help you to avoid them in your own reasoning and to avoid being victimized by such errors in others'. In addition, you can discuss argumentation more easily if you know the vocabulary commonly used by others.

However, be wary of seeking too many different types of fallacies or focusing on the technical terminology itself. Some texts identify hundreds of fallacies, all with names to be remembered. At some point, trying to learn the finer distinctions between fallacies of the same general type does not repay the effort to master them, and labeling an error may come to substitute for genuinely understanding why it is an error. Rather than give a long catalog of fallacies, therefore, we focus on some major types of fallacious appeals, with examples of the most commonly identified fallacies. Strive to understand the reasoning and, above all else, why it fails or succeeds.

Not only are there many different labels for fallacies, but fallacies are also classified differently by various authors.[1] Nothing of great theoreti-

---

[1]Any classification of fallacies runs into the problem that a particular fallacy seems plausibly classifiable under a number of headings. For example, *ad hominem* arguments will be classified here as mistreatment of opposition, but they could equally well be seen

(Cont.)

cal import rests on which way we classify fallacies; what is important is to provide groupings that aid you in identifying, understanding, and avoiding potential errors. In section 3.8 we suggested seven questions to explore as you construct arguments. If you fail to consider one of these questions, you may produce a fallacious argument. Because in this book we have focused on these strategies for developing arguments, we will also organize our presentation of fallacies according to the checklist of questions.

8.1 Have You Defined the Context Clearly?: Fallacies Relating to Context

When constructing an argument, you consider what is and is not relevant. Two ways in which mistakes concerning relevance can produce fallacious reasoning are (1) introducing something irrelevant that diverts us from the real issue, and (2) ignoring something relevant that, if brought to light, might prevent us from arriving at the conclusion offered. The first variety—diversion—occurs in a number of ways, including emotional appeals and certain kinds of appeal to authority. The second—omission—can also take a number of different forms, including suppression of evidence and false dichotomy.

8.1.1 Fallacies That Distract by Introducing Something Irrelevant

8.1.1a Illegitimate Emotional Appeals   In the original *Star Trek* television series, the character of Mr. Spock represented a logical thinker free of all emotion, thus presumably able to reason more perfectly than any human. Certainly, emotions can interfere with clear thinking in a number of ways. Reasons that appeal to our prejudices, stereotypes, and desires are often quite effective in persuading people, even when the reasons are not very good. But the Spock image of correct reasoning as free of emotion is a misleading caricature. Not all arguments that appeal to emotions are fallacious; an argument can both appeal to the emotions and be logically correct. An appeal to the audience's emotions is not fallacious if the emotions are relevant to the issue and if the reasons given provide support for the appropriateness of those emotions. For example, if in dis-

---

as bringing in something irrelevant. In fact, they do both, and both ways of seeing them are correct. This is not surprising; as the nineteenth-century logician Augustas De Morgan put it, "There is *no* such thing as a classification of the ways in which men may arrive at an error; it is much to be doubted whether there ever *can be*" (qtd. in Copi 89).

cussing what punishment is appropriate for rape you point out how seriously this crime violates the victims, you may well appeal to your audience's sense of indignation. Such an appeal will not automatically be fallacious. Certainly, indignation about rape is not out of place, and pointing to the seriousness of the violation of the victim supports claims about appropriate punishment for rape.

If, however, you appeal to emotions that are not relevant to your claim or, worse, distract from your claim, you make an illegitimate emotional appeal, as did the student during the Vietnam War who was caught cheating on a final exam but asked the instructor to pass him anyway, claiming he would be drafted if he flunked out of school. Such an *appeal to pity* is traditionally called *argumentum ad misericordiam*.

Appealing to strong popular sentiments can also be fallacious, typically taking a form called an *appeal to the gallery* (in Latin, *ad populum*). Some advertisers take advantage of the public's strong sentiments against foreign imports by clearly labeling their products as manufactured in the United States by Americans. If the implicit reason is that the place of manufacture is relevant to choosing which products to purchase, then the appeal is not fallacious. One might argue, for example, that certain foreign imports are of lesser quality or that they have unfairly flooded certain markets. But lacking such background arguments, the appeal is illegitimate, asking people to buy because of the positive sentiments they have toward Americans without examining how strong their case is against foreign imports.

Another example of an *ad populum* appeal is found in Nixon's famous Checkers Speech. He seeks his audience's sympathy by relating in detail the story of how the Nixons' little dog, Checkers, was given as a gift to his daughters. Of course, no one who had accused him of impropriety in relation to campaign donations meant to impeach his acceptance of the gift of a dog for his children. Though irrelevant to the real issue, Nixon was able to exploit the strong positive sentiments associated with the very thought of taking away a child's dog.

8.1.1b Arguing from Ignorance   Another fallacy that results from resting a conclusion on irrelevant support is to conclude that just because no evidence against a claim exists, the claim is true, or just because no evidence for a claim exists, the claim is false. If upon entering a city you do not see a sign prohibiting the discharging of firearms within city limits, and you conclude that shooting your gun is therefore permitted there, you would be committing the fallacy known as *arguing from ignorance*. Similarly, a voter who concludes that a politician must be in favor of abortion because she has not come out against it has committed the same fallacy.

But arguments are not always fallacious when they appeal to lack of evidence: if you look around your bedroom in a reasonably normal state of consciousness, the fact that you don't see an elephant is an appropriate ground for concluding that there is none in your room. And similarly, when your fiancée suggests setting the wedding date for next week so you can live together as a married couple as soon as possible, her omission of any mention of ever having been and still being legally married to someone else would give you a reasonable presumption that she is not in fact married already.

What makes these cases different from fallacious arguments from ignorance is that in them you have good grounds for thinking that if things were different than you are concluding them to be, the evidence for that difference would be obvious to you. Since it isn't, you may conclude that things are as they seem. If an elephant were in your room right now, it would be pretty hard to miss. Since you aren't noticing any elephants right now, you may reasonably conclude there is none. The marriage case is a little different since someone's being married to another person would not necessarily intrude on your awareness as an elephant's presence would. But in this case you assume that a person you trust sufficiently to marry would not keep such a relevant fact from you. Of course, you could be wrong, but it is nonetheless a reasonable presumption given appropriate evidence of your fiancée's trustworthiness.

Similarly, when a judge instructs a jury to find a defendant not guilty if the prosecution fails to provide evidence of guilt beyond a reasonable doubt, the judge has not invited the jury to argue from ignorance. A guiding principle of our law is that the defendant is presumed not guilty unless sufficient evidence has been provided to show otherwise. A "not guilty" verdict, therefore, really means that the defendant has not been proven guilty, and not, as many people mistakenly assume, that he is innocent of the crime he is alleged to have committed.

8.1.2 Fallacies That Ignore Relevant Information

8.1.2a Suppressed Evidence   In "Silver Blaze," Inspector Gregory's argument for his theory was found unsatisfactory as much for what it omitted as for any flaw in what it included. For example, he ignored the facts that the dog didn't bark when Silver Blaze was removed from the stable, that the opium was placed in a dish with a strong enough flavor to mask its taste, and that John Straker was carrying a bill with someone else's name on it. Until those facts were accounted for, the evidence pointing toward Fitzroy Simpson could not be considered complete, and ultimately his theory had to be rejected for its inability to account for such facts.

Sometimes it's what we don't consider that makes our reasoning go wrong. In Chapter 7 we discussed the problem that arises for generalizations when one fails to consider disconfirming evidence: for example, we can't tell whether all corporations are interested in caring for the environment only when it profits them to do so solely by considering examples of corporations that fit that description. We also have to consider whether we can find corporations that protect the environment even when it hurts them to do so. That is, we have to look for evidence that, if true, would defeat the claim we are contemplating.

Suppressed evidence is a fairly common fallacy. Much advertising offers no evidence for the worthiness of the advertised product, but when they do provide reasons, ads typically omit any evidence against the quality of their product. Many movie ads, for example, include positive comments from critics, such as "One of the year's best movies" or "Hilariously funny—Gene Siskel gave it a thumbs-up." But when was the last time you saw an ad for a new movie that mentioned that Roger Ebert gave it a thumbs down?

8.1.2b False Dilemma   Another way ignoring relevant information can produce fallacious reasoning is called a *false dilemma* (or *false dichotomy*). If you know that a certain number of alternatives exist, and that all but one can be ruled out, you can justifiably infer that the remaining one is true. That is the process of elimination, and it is based on sound logical principles. But if you pose an issue incorrectly as a choice between only two alternatives when there is, in fact, some reasonable third option, you commit the fallacy of false dilemma. False dilemmas are fallacious because they presume that there are only two alternatives when in fact there are more; they therefore ignore something importantly relevant. (Of course, we can also commit the same error by assuming that there are only three options when there are really four, and so on.)

In April 1995, *Time* magazine did a cover story on miracles, highlighting the story of young Elizabeth Jernigan, who was diagnosed as having a brain tumor when less than a year old. The tumor turned out to be a rare malignant meningioma—a form of cancer "which has killed everyone who has ever had it." Doctors performed surgery to remove the tumor but couldn't get it all. Elizabeth grew worse. Fluid built up around her brain, and more surgery would be needed to insert shunts to relieve the pressure. The family prayed; her grandparents asked a priest to anoint her with oil, according to biblical instructions for healing. Prior to the surgery, Elizabeth was suddenly found to be free of the fluid; the doctors couldn't find any to drain. When they operated again to remove the rest of the tumor, they could not find any evidence of cancer. "The family call it a miracle. Even a resurrection."

The implicit argument leading to the conclusion that Elizabeth was cured by a miracle involves a false dilemma, since it relies on the assumption that either science can explain the healing or Elizabeth was cured by the miraculous intervention of a supernatural being. But there are other options that need to be considered, including the mundane possibility that something caused her healing that scientists do not yet understand. Human physiology is enormously complicated, and there is much that is not understood. Further, many diseases are self-limiting, disappearing after a period of time (or going into "remission") with no treatment at all. Spontaneous remission or healing, as well as the placebo effect (in which a person who is given a treatment—such as a sugar pill—known to have no physiological effect on an illness but derives some benefit from it anyway) are not uncommon, though they are not completely understood. Yet another possibility is that the illness was misdiagnosed in the first place (or perhaps laboratory results were mislabeled). So we cannot assume that the only options are that either doctors can explain how Elizabeth was cured or a miracle occurred.

Recently in Redlands, California, voters passed a proposition that provided special funding (through extra taxes) for paramedics. Those who voted for the proposition voted for this special source of funding; those who voted against the proposition voted against paramedics' receiving this special source of funding. Most of the arguments in favor of the proposition (for example, those in letters to the *Redlands Daily Facts*), however, posed this choice: either the community passes the proposition, or it will have no paramedics. But there were other alternatives— for example, the city could have provided funding in its general operating budget.

Not all cases in which someone reasons from a limited set of choices involve a false dilemma. The musical group Pearl Jam recently challenged the exclusive rights of the Ticketmaster company to sell tickets for events scheduled in many major arenas. They attempted to stage a concert tour without using Ticketmaster's sales network, and ultimately gave up the effort when they claimed to be unable to find adequate concert halls not under Ticketmaster's exclusive contract. If their claim is true, the dilemma appears to be genuine: for major concert tours, either a rock group schedules through Ticketmaster or not at all.

8.2 Have You Considered Important Views on Your Topic?: Fallacies Relating to Inadequate or Improper Use of Sources

When you review what others are saying about your topic, you determine who the reliable sources are, what you can learn even from nonexperts, and what objections might be put forth against your view.

"HOW ABOUT: 'THE SURGEON GENERAL HAS DETERMINED THAT MARIJUANA MAY OR MAY NOT BE DANGEROUS TO YOUR HEALTH, DEPENDING ON WHICH AUTHORITIES YOU BELIEVE'."

© 1996 by Sidney Harris

8.2.1 Improper Appeal to Authority

The first two inquiries can lead you to a lot of useful information and ideas. None of us exists in a vacuum. We cannot simply go out and acquire all the information we need on our own. We must rely on others for a vast amount of information that we do not have either the time or the ability to provide for ourselves. But just as we can make mistakes gathering information, inferring or judging, so too can those we rely on. Our reliance on others therefore puts a special kind of burden on us to ensure that the information we then employ in our arguments is reliable. While we are frequently justified in our reliance on others—on "authorities"— that reliance can also be fallacious. The most common fallacy deriving from the use of sources is *improper appeal to authority*.

You can get clearer about the appropriateness of relying on a purported authority by asking these questions:

A. *Is the person cited as an authority well qualified in the field in question?* For example, consider the following argument:

> Our university had better reexamine its policy forbidding sexual rela-
> tions between faculty and students. Dozens of schools, including quite
> a few from the Ivy League, have what they consider effective sexual
> harassment rules that stop short of forbidding sexual relations between
> students and faculty, including the top schools in and out of the state.
> Our policy is clearly more restrictive than it needs to be.

Do these other universities know more about the situation than we do?
Other schools are appealed to as authorities in this argument partly because of their prestige (appealing to celebrities as authorities on questions about which they have no special knowledge is a common error)
and partly because of how popular this move is ("Everyone's doing it" is
also a common error of authority). Be sure to check sources' claims to be
authoritative—not only their training but also their track records in making reliable statements on a subject. Do those making such decisions at
other schools know anything special about rules governing faculty-stu-
dent relations that we don't? Be especially wary of appealing to individuals who may be experts on some questions but not those under discussion. Albert Einstein was well aware of this temptation when he
declined an invitation to run for the Presidency of Israel.

B. *Are you certain what the authority is actually endorsing?* For example,
should you accept the claim that "Anacin contains the pain reliever doctors recommend most for headache relief" as a basis for preferring Anacin
to other headache remedies? Were the doctors this Anacin commercial
cited actually recommending Anacin or only the ingredient it—along with
many other pain relievers—contains?

C. *Is the authority biased?* When someone has a stake in what people
believe to be true, he or she is biased. Often that interest is financial, but
it could also be an emotional attachment to another person, traditional
ways of doing things, or even an attachment to products. Anything that
motivates someone to hope an issue turns out one way rather than another is a source of bias.

If researchers employed by the National Dairy Council assure us that
women should drink milk daily to avoid osteoporosis (a disease involving calcium loss in bones), we would be wise to check with independent
sources as well since the National Dairy Council exists to help promote
dairy products. One source may in fact cause you to question that claim:
in *Diet for a New America,* John Robbins cites numerous independent studies
showing that osteoporosis is not effectively prevented with milk, but in
fact is more likely to occur in people who consume dairy protein than in
those who do not (Robbins 189–202). Be wary of paid endorsements; pay-
ment creates a powerful motivation beyond the desire to say what is true

or even believed by the speaker. Just because a claim has been endorsed by a biased source, however, does not mean it is necessarily false. The fallacy is more subtle: it is simply that you cannot tell to what extent bias has clouded a person's judgment or led her or him to falsify details or suppress inconvenient evidence.

D. *Is there wide disagreement among authorities about the issue in question?* A popular magazine published the following in 1874:

> Louis Agassiz, the greatest scientist of his day, examined Darwin's claims for his theory of evolution very carefully and finally decided that it could not be true that man was descended from the ape and its earlier animal ancestry. Within six months the greatest German biologists, and the most learned anthropologists now living, have declared that the Darwin theory of the origin of man could not be true. In spite of the opinions of these, the . . . leading investigators of the century, the theory of Darwinism is being taught in the universities of America. There is such a thing as a little knowledge leading to a great error, and this is an example.
>
> (Quoted in Kahane, 5th ed. 42–43)

In 1874 great controversy surrounded the correctness of Darwin's theory. When experts disagree, the opinion of one could be set against the opinion of others on the opposite side of the issue. In such a case, appealing to any of their opinions as authoritative is fallacious.

Sometimes you should not rely entirely upon an appeal to authority even when it is satisfactory because some questions cannot be settled solely by expert testimony. For example, consider the following advertisement:

> The acoustic guitar has only improved slightly since its distant origin. And whatever improvements were made were the result of trial and error—luck. That's why Gibson chose a new method in its search for a better acoustic guitar—the scientific method. The result is a fascinating breakthrough in acoustic guitars—the Mark series.
>
> Gibson researched the Mark design for two years with the help of such noted scientists as Dr. Adrian Houtsma, Professor of Acoustical Physics at MIT, Dr. Eugene Watson, Professor of Acoustics at Penn State, and the celebrated chemical physicist and Director of the Institute of Molecular Biophysics at Florida State University, Dr. Michael Kasha, whose guitar designs have won the praise of Maestro Andres Segovia.
>
> Of course we also listened to our most valued advisors, the musicians who *play* the instruments. And we weren't satisfied until we started getting consistent comments from the finest studio pickers in Nashville (the acoustic guitar capital) like, "I definitely like this sound. Think you can make me one?" Or, "What you like for it to sound like on tape is what you hear right here. In fact, I'd like to hear how 50 of 'em would sound."

Although you could quibble with some of the details here (for example, the anonymity of the Nashville pickers may make you hesitate in giving that appeal much weight), overall this is a reasonable appeal to authority. The scientists seem well qualified on acoustical design, and praise from Andres Segovia for the design of acoustical guitars is certainly pertinent to evaluating Kasha's expertise. But you'd be very foolish to buy a guitar solely on the basis of authoritative claims. Perhaps you can best consider this an argument why it would be worthwhile to check out the Gibson. In the end, you'd also better like the way the thing sounds.

8.2.2 Countering Your Opposition Unfairly

Knowing what arguments are likely to be raised against your position helps you think about it in useful ways. It can help you develop the details of your own case and can increase your ethical appeal by showing your readers that you take the issue seriously enough to consider opposing arguments. But there are some ways of using opposition that produce fallacies. These occur primarily when you haven't really accorded the opposition the respect it deserves.

8.2.2a Attacking the Person   If, when you respond to someone's arguments or criticisms of your views, you ignore her points and instead attack her as a person, you commit the fallacy called *ad hominem* argument (Latin for "against the man"). If, for example, you refused to listen to former President Nixon's arguments about U.S. involvement in Central America, your implicit argument would have been *ad hominem*:

> Nixon resigned in disgrace.
> _____
> Thus, Nixon's views cannot be true.

Notice that in an *ad hominem* argument the attack on the person's character need not be untrue or unjustified; Nixon did indeed resign in disgrace. But that point is irrelevant to whether some of his views on foreign policy are correct. Even those who resign in disgrace may have useful insights. A famous example of an *ad hominem* attack is Spiro Agnew's response to his critics in 1969. He said, "A spirit of national masochism prevails, encouraged by an effete corps of impudent snobs who characterize themselves as intellectuals." Agnew was engaging in somewhat literary name-calling rather than showing why their criticisms of him were incorrect.

Closely related to this kind of *ad hominem* attack is another: pointing out that a person is being hypocritical (called *tu quoque*). If a person's belief system is not the issue at hand, pointing to hypocrisy won't really refute your opposition. Hypocrisy is a flaw, but knowing that a person's beliefs are inconsistent doesn't tell you *which* of those beliefs is false. Practicing what one preaches is important, but failing to do so doesn't make the sermon incorrect. Knowing a person is a hypocrite does not, by itself, justify your rejecting his or her claim. To do *that* you need to examine the claim and the reasons for and against it.

An attack on a person is *ad hominem* when you use his or her character, other beliefs, or motivation to distract from the real issue. Of course, if the person's character, belief, or motivation is the subject of discussion, the attack may not be *ad hominem*. Such an attack might be appropriate if, for example, the person is running for political office, testifying in court, or trying to sell you a used car. And even if the person is not the issue, knowing that he has a vested interest in a certain point of view should alert you to examine what he says vigilantly. Just be careful not to convert the call to be cautious about what someone claims into a refutation all by itself of what he is saying.

8.2.2b Straw Man   Another fallacy that arises from abusing an opposing stance is called a *straw man* argument. Such an argument appears to refute a position, but really it diverts our attention by challenging a *weaker* position that, despite appearances, is not held by those under attack. The following argument against legalizing drugs is a straw man:

> Here's what you can expect if we legalize drugs: There won't be any drug crimes anymore, because we simply made everyone who abused drugs law-abiding by definition, regardless of what they do; and there won't be any need for drug dealers to stand outside school playgrounds anymore, because kids will be able to buy dope from vending machines, tobacco shops, and candy stores; as with sex, people will say that since kids are going to do drugs whether or not parents like it, we'd better not bury our heads in the sand—better to have classes that teach safe drug use in schools. Perhaps they can give out the samples of marijuana and cocaine at the same time condoms are distributed?

No serious advocate of legalization has suggested that drugs be made available to minors or that any behavior engaged in under the influence of drugs be decriminalized. As you can see, straw man arguments caricaturize a view and, in so doing, fail to direct serious criticism against the real claim under discussion.

8.2.2c Red Herring   *Red herrings* are similar to straw man arguments, except that while a straw man creates a misleading version of another's position to attack, a red herring raises an entirely new, irrelevant argument rather than answer an objection to a view. (The term *red herring* comes from the practice of deliberately misleading dogs from a trail in order to teach them to follow it. The strong smell of an animal

carcass such as a cooked herring was dragged across the trail to confuse the dogs.)

In July 1995 President Clinton agreed to normalize relations between
the United States and Vietnam. Some who objected pointed out that Clinton had promised during the election not to do so until all those still
missing in action from the Vietnam War had been accounted for, something that had not been accomplished. It would be a red herring to defend President Clinton's action against the charge of inconsistency by
pointing out that normalization is in the best economic interests of the
United States, which was, after all, already at a disadvantage because
companies from other countries had established a foothold while U.S.
firms were not permitted to trade with Vietnam. That defense suggests
that normalization may be the best policy, but it does not answer the
charge that Clinton was breaking a campaign promise.

After a number of highly publicized cases of young people running
away from home with adults they had met via the Internet, some people
have become concerned that children face dangers from molesters who
might establish contacts in this way. One response to this concern (we
found it via the Internet) was that the risk of such contacts being established via Internet is no greater than the dangers children already face
elsewhere in life. This response is a red herring, because knowing that
the dangers on the Internet are not greater than elsewhere does not respond to the charge that they exist and ought to be considered. The
Internet-defender's answer is a somewhat subtle diversion and exempli-
fies the kind of red herring you have to watch out for—the ones that tend
to focus attention on an issue similar enough that the shift may go
unnoticed.

8.2.2d Ridicule

> [On peace groups funded by Ben & Jerry's:] Probably a bunch of people
> out in California standing on top of Mt. Shasta going 'Om, om,' trying
> to . . . send good vibes to Mikhail Gorbachev or whoever is running the
> Soviets so they won't nuke us.
>
> (Rush Limbaugh, qtd. in Rendall, Naureckas, and Cohen 87).

At the far end of the spectrum in responding inappropriately to your
opposition is the practice of substituting humor for any real response to
what they are saying. Critical engagement with serious ideas need not be
humorless, and it's healthy to be willing to poke fun at ourselves. But as
much as we enjoy a good laugh at our own or someone else's expense,
humor is not a substitute for reasons to agree or disagree with an idea.
The quotation at the beginning of this section from Rush Limbaugh is an

example of the most abusive form of this use of humor: *ridicule*. By trying to make other people look ridiculous, the ridiculer encourages us not to take their view seriously. Of course, ridicule does not really give us a relevant reason to reject someone's idea, but our desire not to align our-selves with someone who looks ridiculous is a powerful tool in the hands of the ridiculer.

8.3 Have You Clearly Specified Your Position?: Fallacies Relating to Specifying Conclusions

You know now how important it is to state your conclusion as carefully as you can, distinguishing it from related claims for which you are not arguing. Misstating your conclusion can lead to fallacies.

8.3.1 Drawing the Wrong Conclusion

Sometimes people draw the wrong conclusion, however carefully the evidence is marshaled. When O. J. Simpson's lawyers fought to have au-topsy photographs of Ronald Goldman and Nicole Brown Simpson ex-cluded as evidence, they were fearful that the photos might entice the jury to commit the fallacy of drawing the wrong conclusion. Here's how that might happen: although the photographs could show something rel-evant about the way in which these victims were killed (and for this rea-son Judge Ito permitted them as evidence), the primary impact might well be to focus the jury's attention on the horror of being murdered. If that happened, there was a risk that the jurors could confuse their desire to punish someone for such a horrible crime with the conclusion that it was the defendant who committed that crime.

Consider this argument:

> Computer technology changes very quickly. You invest a lot of money in hardware only to see it go out of date in a year or two when it won't run the newest software being produced. Then your kids are endlessly pestering you to buy this or that add-on: CD-ROMS, modems, scan-ners, and who knows what else. If your computer runs at 75Mhz, in two years you'll wonder why you didn't wait to buy one that runs at 500. Much better to stick to your typewriter than get started investing your hard-earned cash in a computer.

The fact that computer technology does change rapidly, however true, is not really a reason to think you couldn't put your "out of date" computer and its software to good use for a long time—just like an "out-of-date" typewriter! The only reason a computer becomes out of date is that other people have begun to use new products you could not use with your computer. But with no computer at all you couldn't use them anyway, so the conclusion is not the right one to draw from this evidence. A better conclusion would be that keeping up to date with new technology is for most of us an illusion that should not blind us to the fact that what is out of date may still be quite valuable.

Often you are encouraged to draw a wrong conclusion by language that merely suggests a conclusion without stating it. Much advertising is of this sort. For example, an advertisement for an expensive, name-brand, over-the-counter remedy that says something like "Studies have shown that only the active ingredient in Zamboogle Pain Reliever reduces inflammation while it also does your dishes and walks your dog" suggests that *only* the advertised brand will do all this for you. But that may well be incorrect. The right conclusion to draw from the "studies" is that you should seek products with the active ingredient, and that active ingredient may be found not only in the advertised product but also in generic brands being sold at half the price.

Clearly, this fallacy could also be considered as introducing irrelevance (section 8.1.1) or as insufficient grounds (section 8.4.2), but we place it here because it is worth noting that you can avoid the error if you are careful to identify *which* conclusion you are trying to support and if you determine that the evidence you are considering will indeed support *this particular* conclusion.

8.3.2 Overly Hedged Claims

When someone hedges a bet, he makes a second bet that protects against any loss from the first. Similarly, one can hedge a claim against its turning out to be false. There are a number of ways to make claims safer. You can limit the extent of your claim, substituting *most, many,* or *some* for *all*. Or you can qualify the degree to which you are committed to its truth, claiming *it is almost certain that, it is arguable that, may,* and *perhaps*.

Qualifying what we say is sometimes a good idea—too bold a statement might not be supportable. A more-qualified statement can also be more accurate. But qualifications can go too far: it is possible to qualify or hedge a claim so much that it really says very little and, thus insulated from criticism, may deceptively suggest a substantive statement. Some people, in fact, call these qualifying expressions *weasel words*, since they suck the content out of a statement as weasels suck the content out of an egg and leave a shell that deceptively appears to have something in it. As we saw in Chapter 7 when discussing nondisconfirmable hypotheses, contrary to appearances immunity to criticism is not a desirable quality. Overly hedged conclusions, vague predictions, and nondisconfirmable hypotheses are the stock in trade of pseudoscience masquerading as real insight. One advertisement for a weight-loss program refers to "dramatic proof" obtained by (an unnamed) "leading medical school in California" that shows that "you may lose as much as 6 to 9 lbs. in a single weekend" if you use the "Doctor's Wonder-Treatment for Obesity." Of course, you may not lose that much; it's all a question of whether you like to look at the bottle with one drop left as 1 percent full or 99 percent empty.

8.4 Have You Selected Acceptable Evidence?: Fallacies Relating to Unacceptable Premises

Are you using reasons that are obviously true or plausible? Are they matters of common knowledge? If not, can you defend their truth?

8.4.1 Questionable Premises

As we saw in Chapter 6, one of the criteria of sound reasoning is to begin with premises that are true or plausible. If they are not intermediate conclusions—that is, if you do not provide evidence for them—then they could be justifiably believed without further evidence. Some arguments are fallacious because they run afoul of this condition: they begin with a *questionable premise.* If we have reason to doubt a claim or, worse, know it to be false, then of course we cannot accept an argument that depends on it.

Talk-show host Rush Limbaugh has become famous for his use of questionable premises. Here are a couple of examples from a June 1994 report exposing many of his inaccuracies by the organization Fairness and Accuracy in Reporting (FAIR):

Limbaugh: On Whitewater: "I don't think the *New York Times* has run a story on this yet. I mean, we haven't done a thorough search, but I—there has not been a big one, front-page story, about this one that we can recall. So this has yet to create or get up to its full speed—if it weren't for us and the *Wall Street Journal* and the *American Spectator,* this would be one of the biggest and most well-kept secrets going on in American politics today."
(TV, 2/17/94)

Reality: We'll let Limbaugh in on the secret: The *New York Times* broke the Whitewater story on March 8, 1992, in a front-page, 1700-word report by Jeff Gerth. The *Times* published more than a half-dozen additional front-page Whitewater stories in the two months immediately prior to Limbaugh's utterance.

Limbaugh: On Iran-Contra special prosecutor Lawrence Walsh: "This Walsh story basically is, we just spent seven years and $40 million looking for any criminal activity on the part of anybody in the Reagan administration, and guess what? We couldn't find any. These guys didn't do anything, but we wish they had so that we could nail them. So instead, we're just going to say, 'Gosh, these are rotten guys.' They have absolutely no evidence. There is not one indictment. There is not one charge."

(TV, 1/19/94)

Reality: Walsh won indictments against 14 people in connection with the Iran-Contra scandal, including leading Reagan administration officials like former Secretary of Defense Caspar Weinberger and former national security advisers Robert McFarlane and John Poindexter. Of the 14, 11 were convicted or pleaded guilty. (Two convictions were later overturned on technicalities—including that of occasional Limbaugh substitute host Oliver North).

(Rendall, Naureckas, and Cohen 91, 81)

These examples might remind you of a point we made in Chapter 1 (in our discussion of Holmes's reasoning skill): critical thinking depends on having a lot of background information about the world at your disposal.

Another common version of the fallacy of questionable premise is appeal to *questionable statistics*. When, for example, an article in a tabloid on how to tell whether your mate is cheating tells you that "in 75% of cases, the woman is proven correct in her worries. But men are correct 99% of the time," you should probably be pretty skeptical about the numbers, especially when the source is "a nationally acclaimed infidelity expert who's been snooping on unfaithful husbands and wives for 22 years"—that is, a private detective who has most likely not investigated the issue beyond his own experience. Even if the article's author didn't just invent these figures, such a statistic hides assumptions. Presumably the "infidelity expert" deals only with people suspicious enough to pay someone to investigate. Do those men who simply confront their spouses, just live with their suspicions, or seek divorce without the aid of a private detective also get it right 99 percent of the time? Be wary of the false appearance of precision that numbers can create: merely attaching a number to a phenomenon doesn't make the number meaningful.

8.5 Have You Supplied Premises That Together Provide Sufficient Support for Your Conclusion?: Fallacies Relating to Insufficient Grounds

In addition to being true, your reasons should provide solid support for your conclusion. If they do, someone who accepts them as true should also accept your conclusion as true or likely to be true. Many fallacies are variations on the theme of premises that do not provide sufficient grounds for their conclusions (also called *non sequiturs*, Latin for "it does not follow"). Among these are fallacies traditionally known as *formal fallacies*. The formal fallacies produce deductively invalid argument forms that may nonetheless tempt us to make the wrong inference. *Informal fallacies* relating to insufficient grounds, on the other hand, have less to do with invalid argument form than other kinds of "leaps."

8.5.1 Formal Fallacies

Formal fallacies result solely from the form of an argument. As you recall from section 6.3, a *deductively valid* argument is one in which it would be impossible for the premises to be true while the conclusion is false. So an argument is deductively <u>in</u>valid when it is possible for the premises to be true while the conclusion is false. Again, as you recall from section 6.4.2, arguments are valid or invalid because of their logical forms. Certain of the invalid forms are sufficiently common and enticing that they have been named. There are many of these, but we will mention only a few examples to whet your appetite to study more formal logic!

Formal fallacies include such errors as *affirming the consequent* and *denying the antecedent*. Arguments using conditional statements ("if . . . then . . ." statements) can be constructed in four ways, each combining a conditional statement with a further premise that either affirms or denies some part of the conditional. Two of these combinations produce valid forms, and the other two produce formal fallacies. You have already encountered one of these fallacies in connection with confirming hypotheses, *affirming the consequent:*

> If Ann is drawing a square, then Ann is drawing a polygon.
> Ann is drawing a polygon.
> _____
> So Ann is drawing a square.

Of course, even if the premises are true, Ann may be drawing some polygon other than a square, say, a triangle or a rhombus, so this conclusion does not follow from these premises.

Another way to produce a formal fallacy using conditional statements is by *denying the antecedent:*

> If Josephine has terminal cancer, then she will die.
> Josephine does not have terminal cancer.
> _____
> So Josephine will not die.

Again, the premises may be true while the conclusion is false: Josephine may well not have terminal cancer, but she will die from some other cause (after all, Josephine cannot escape mortality just by escaping cancer!).

These arguments are invalid because of their logical form—their pattern of reasoning. Any argument that proceeds according to these patterns will be invalid. You can see these fallacious patterns more clearly by setting out schema that represent them. For example, the fallacy of denying the antecedent follows this pattern:

If P, then Q.
It is not the case that P.

So it is not the case that Q.

But not all arguments using conditional statements are fallacious. Recall the pattern so important in disconfirming hypotheses:

If P, then Q.
It is not the case that Q.

So it is not the case that P.

Arguments in this form (called *modus tollens*) are valid. Consider this example:

If the polar ice caps have been melting since the dawn of human history, then there would be some record of the oceans rising substantially. But there is no record of the oceans rising substantially.

So the polar ice caps have not been melting since the dawn of history.

To go very far in understanding formal fallacies, though, one needs to study formal logic beyond the scope of this book. In the remainder of this chapter, we will focus exclusively on what are known as informal fallacies.

8.5.2 Informal Fallacies Relating to Insufficient Grounds

8.5.2a Causal Fallacies   Determining what causes what can be a lot harder than it looks at first blush. Many fallacious arguments arise because of mistakes in thinking about causes. One especially common causal fallacy is known as the *post hoc fallacy*, short for *post hoc, ergo propter hoc*, a Latin phrase meaning "after this, therefore because of this." Here's one:

For his 72nd birthday Wally received a cellular phone, and after three years of using it almost daily, he was diagnosed with brain cancer. Clearly, holding the phone so close to his head was responsible.

Perhaps Wally's cancer was caused by the cellular phone, but the mere fact that he acquired cancer after using the phone doesn't show the phone to be the cause. Similar arguments could lead us to conclude that his turning 75, being Irish, or living in a brick house with green shag carpeting were the causes of his cancer. Even when it seems plausible to claim that an incident is a cause, the fact that it preceded the effect does not by itself show us that it was the cause.

Another causal fallacy is *confusing cause and effect*. If Sloppy Sam's roommate makes this argument, we hope it is only a joke: "How clever Sam's mother is to visit only on those days when Sam puts a lot of effort into cleaning!" If it's not a joke, he would be confusing cause with effect. Undoubtedly Sam's mother is kind enough not to drop in unannounced, and Sam cleans a bit more thoroughly in anticipation of her visits.

It can be fairly easy to confuse cause and effect in some cases. A recent newspaper report (Doheny E2) mentions that if you are an adult you are more likely to be bitten by a rattlesnake if you are a male with tattoos. Why is that? How does a tattoo cause you to be bitten by a rattlesnake? Is it because snakes are somehow attracted to tattoos? If you draw that conclusion, you are confusing cause and effect. The tattoos do not cause the men to be bitten; rather, having tattoos and being more likely to be bitten are both effects of the same cause. That is, men with tattoos are more likely than other adults to have certain personality characteristics, and it is those characteristics that lead them to want tattoos, to get drunk, and to play a losing game of chicken with snakes.

Yet another fallacy involving causes is the *domino argument*. As children know, if you line up a series of dominoes just right, you can knock over the whole series if you hit just the first one. If steps in a series are indeed causally related, once things get going it may be difficult to stop the process. It can be important, then, to recognize domino-like relations. It's better to eat nutritious meals in the first place, for example, than to be fighting off diseases related to poor nutrition later.

Of course, every child who has played with dominoes also knows that even when they are set in a series, hitting the first one does not always take down the rest. The dominoes may not be set in quite the right relationship. The domino fallacy occurs when we illegitimately treat events that are not causally related as if they were steps in a causal process—that is, we *wrongly assume* that the events are related like dominoes that have been set together just so. The "domino theory" from the Cold War period is the classic example from which the fallacy takes its name. It held that the spread of communism occurs like a line of connected dominoes—when one country falls, the next will do so also. The theory was one of the main justifications for U.S. involvement in Vietnam.

You may find a typical form of the domino fallacy in objections to proposed actions. One worries that if we allow A, then that will lead to B, which in turn leads to C, until we are ultimately forced to live with the horrible K. The conclusion is that we must not allow A in the first place. The fear that smoking marijuana leads people to try other drugs, which in turn leads them to trying more addictive drugs, and ultimately leads to their being strung out on heroin is another classic domino argument.

A related kind of argument based on a series of steps doesn't involve causality, but can also be called a domino argument. It goes like this: We had best not take a first step, however well justified it may be, if it leads to a series of other steps that in turn lead to some undesirable outcome. The causal form of the domino argument is exemplified by the fear that allowing openly gay men and women to remain in the military will lead to diminished respect for military authority, which in turn will lead to discipline problems, which ultimately will lead to a less-well-prepared military. Therefore, we had better not let them remain. The noncausal form is exemplified by the fear that if we acknowledge adolescents' strong sexual curiosity and teach them anything other than sexual abstinence (say, how to use condoms should they decide to go ahead and have sex anyway), we will not be justified in drawing any limits to teenage sexual behaviors. Therefore we had better not begin by acknowledging their strong curiosity.[2]

8.5.2b Hasty Generalization   We saw in Chapter 7 that one can go wrong in arguing from a sample to a generalization in a number of ways (see section 7.2). Unrepresentative samples, samples that are too small or those biased in some way, all lead to the fallacy of *hasty generalization*. One particularly common form of the fallacy is generalizing from anecdotal evidence. Suppose Harry (a white male) claims he was passed over for a promotion to a management job in favor of someone less qualified because the company felt pressure to place more minorities in management positions. If we conclude from Harry's anecdote that affirmative action encourages the promotion of less-qualified people, we will be making two mistakes. First, we will be mistaken to take Harry's story at face value: while it's possible he was passed over in favor of someone less qualified, it is also possible that, not being in a position to evaluate the competition's qualifications in an unbiased manner, Harry underestimated

---

[2] Domino arguments are sometimes called *slippery-slope arguments*. Unfortunately, line-drawing arguments are also occasionally called slippery slopes. The name makes sense for both fallacies—if you raise one end of a slippery surface to create a slope, an object at the higher end will slide down unless there is something to impede it. The metaphor works for differences of degree along a continuum (line-drawing arguments) as well as for a causal process that seems difficult to stop (domino arguments). To avoid confusion, we call neither slippery slope here.

what his fellow worker brought to the job. That is, the premise is certainly not one we should accept without further evidence, and if we were to do so we would be committing the fallacy of questionable premise. Second, even if we accept Harry's claim as true, we cannot make any generalization about the functioning of affirmative action programs in general until we know how representative this instance is. Is it a typical case or an aberration? Does affirmative action function differently for government contracts and for university admissions? While anecdotes may relate personal experience that should not be ignored, reliance on them as a basis for generalizations frequently invites us to ignore the larger question of how good a sample we are considering.

8.5.2c Questionable Analogy   As we saw in section 7.1.2, arguments can turn on analogies. Such arguments can fail for a variety of reasons. Egregious cases of bad analogies are considered by many authors to commit the fallacy of *faulty comparison* or *questionable analogy*. For example, after voters amended the California State Constitution to limit the number of terms state legislators could serve, State Assemblyman Tom Bates challenged this law in court on the grounds that the Supreme Court had recently thrown out laws that states had passed imposing limits on U.S. congressional representatives. Defenders of the new term limits argued, however, that the analogy between the Supreme Court's overturning of states' imposing term limits for U.S. Congress and states imposing them for their own legislatures is flawed. To limit the members of Congress, you have to amend the federal Constitution, which the overturned laws did not do. To put eligibility limits on the state legislature, you have to amend the state constitution, which is exactly what Californians did when they passed Proposition 140 (Cooper A1).

8.6 Have You Considered Your Audience?: Fallacies Relating to Audience

How much detail do you need to provide your audience about the assumptions necessary to your argument? Are you omitting some things in order to hide them from criticism? The concern here is a little different than that in section 8.4. Here we are asking not whether the premises are acceptable, but rather whether your readers accept them. Your premises may be true, and you may think you know that they are true, but if your audience does not accept them, you have not provided persuasive grounds for your conclusion. If you don't provide appropriate support for a claim, your argument may fail to persuade your audience.

8.6.1 Begging the Question

You beg the question when you assume to be true that which is at issue, that is, what you are setting out to prove. Usually the assumption is implicit, so you need to identify it in order to reveal the fallacy.

The French philosopher René Descartes pointed out an obvious kind of question-begging argument (in the letter of dedication to his famous *Meditations on First Philosophy*) that explained his interest in providing additional proof of the existence of God. He wanted to overcome the problem posed by those who maintain that we should believe in God because the Bible tells us to, and, when pressed, say we should believe what the Bible tells us because it is the work of God. When the authority of the Bible as evidence for God's existence is supported in this way, Descartes observed, the "question has obviously been begged."

More subtly, some American women recently challenged the Catholic church's refusal to ordain women by maintaining that there isn't any reason women cannot perform the functions of priesthood as well as men. Had the Pope replied that women cannot be priests because the authority of the Church has always rested with men, as is evidenced by the fact that Jesus and his disciples were all men, he would have begged the question. It is the very tradition of male dominance that the women's challenge calls into question. Such a challenge to a tradition cannot be answered simply by saying that the tradition exists.

One can beg the question in a number of interesting ways. By refusing to accept proposed counterexamples to a claim, you may be using a *question-begging definition*. Suppose someone claims to have discovered from his experience that "good parents don't spank their children." If, when confronted with evidence of people who are both good parents and who spank their children, he insists that such people are not really good parents despite any evidence one brings to bear on the case, his claim is not a discovery at all. He has simply secured it by defining "good parent" as "parent who would never spank a child." His claim has been made "true" by definition, but he hasn't given us any reason to accept his (unusual) definition.

Another way to beg a question is to ask certain kinds of questions, called *leading* or *complex* or *loaded questions*. These are questions that assume what is at issue. If a parent who knows his child has not yet decided whether to attend his alma mater, Ziggledy Zaggledy U, asks "When will you be sending in your acceptance letter to Ziggledy Zaggledy U?" he has asked a leading question. The mother who asks, "When are you going to settle down and get married?" without first determining that her son wants to be married commits the same fallacy. More subtly, when Ted Koppel asked Senator Robert Dole whether he was "intelligent enough to know that" his proposal to drop the arms embargo so that Bosnians would be better able to defend themselves also had dangers (as Dole was charging President Clinton's policy had), Dole indeed showed that he was intelligent enough—by evading the question, since answering it as asked implied either that his approach was fraught with dangers or that he wasn't very smart. Questions that begin with phrases like, "You do, of course, know that . . ." are psychologically loaded—no one wants to admit that she doesn't know what she should, of course, know.

8.6.2 Assuming Something Known to Be at Issue

Related to the fallacy of begging the question is that of assuming something you should be arguing for. The difference between this kind of argument and a question-begging one is that here the claim you assume is not also the conclusion. It is merely a premise you suspect your audience would not accept. If you know that your readers doubt a premise crucial to your case, you need to provide an argument for it. For example, if one were to explain why Japan's emperor deserves to be treated with reverence by appealing to the emperor's descent from the Shinto gods (*kami* in Japanese), he had probably better not assume that his American audience accepts the claim of direct descent from gods.

8.7 Are Your Ideas Expressed Clearly and Accurately?: Fallacies Relating to Language

Is the language you use clear? Unambiguous and precise? Do you present data and viewpoints accurately and fairly? Some fallacies result from particular facets of language and the way they may be manipulated in arguments. Sometimes a fallacy results from unclear language, such as the exploitation of ambiguous or vague expressions; other times the emotive power of language manipulates us into accepting a slant on something that we might not otherwise accept.

8.7.1 Exploiting Vagueness: Line-Drawing Arguments

We have already seen (Chapter 5) that reasoning can be unclear because it employs vague language—i.e., because it lacks a level of precision needed in context. In addition to making writing unclear, vagueness can become a source of fallacious reasoning when the lack of precise boundaries is exploited illegitimately in arguments. If you ask your readers to acknowledge that the difference between each instance in which a vague concept applies is only a matter of degree, and then if you ask them to infer *from that alone* that no real distinction can be made between the extremes, you have argued fallaciously. This fallacy is sometimes called the *line-drawing fallacy* since it demands that a genuine difference between two things on a continuum can exist only when there is a line drawn at some precise point to separate the two.

A recent proposal for a constitutional amendment prohibiting flag desecration elicited this response from a reader of the *Los Angeles Times:*

> If Congress passes a constitutional amendment prohibiting flag-burning, then where do we draw the line on freedom of speech? If I were dissatisfied with this country, could I burn a flag bearing only 49 stars in protest? After all, it would not be the official ensign. I suppose it could be argued that I had violated the "spirit" of the law, in which case it should be illegal to desecrate anything that resembles Old Glory, or perhaps even any American symbol. Why don't we simply make dissent illegal? That would eliminate any gray areas. Why would anyone want to speak out against the freest country on earth?
>
> (Boyer B4)

Boyer suggests that the idea of a symbol's being protected by law against desecration is too vague. Because no reasonable distinction could be drawn between those items the amendment would protect and those it would not, Boyer reasons, and since symbols are important to political expression, this vagueness threatens freedom of speech. As stated, the argument commits the line-drawing fallacy—it simply doesn't follow from the fact that the boundary isn't sharp that no reasonable distinctions between cases could be made. Of course, that doesn't mean the distinctions that may be proposed should such an amendment pass will be reasonable or that they won't threaten freedom of speech. It's just that you cannot make that judgment simply by noticing that the concept of a symbol is vague.

In general, the line-drawing fallacy occurs when we confuse two different points. On the one hand is the legitimate point that it can be difficult to make certain distinctions sharply. On the other hand is the quite-different point that any two items that can be distinguished only vaguely are not truly different. The line-drawing fallacy invites us to draw the second point as a conclusion from the first.

8.7.2 Exploiting Ambiguity: Equivocation

Equivocations exploit ambiguity in an argument, shifting the meaning of an expression mid-argument. An argument may use an expression in more than one way without equivocating. But if the premise is plausible only when an expression is interpreted one way, and the inference is strong only when it is interpreted differently, the argument commits the fallacy of equivocation. For example, this argument equivocates in a rather obvious way:

Safety equipment is a good investment for horseback riders.
Safest Helmets, Inc. makes the best safety equipment.
_____
So purchasing shares of Safest Helmets, Inc., is a good investment for horseback riders.

In order to consider the first premise plausible or true, you must interpret the idea of investing one way (riders should purchase safety equipment), but in order to use the premise as support for the conclusion, you must interpret it to mean another kind of investing (riders should own shares in the company that makes the equipment). So the argument equivocates. Unfortunately, the equivocations you are likely to meet in real life are not always as crude and easily detected as this one!

8.7.3 Slanted Language and Other Proof Surrogates

Consider the force of offensive words concerning sexuality, gender, bodily functions, or racial, ethnic, or religious identity, such as *nigger, kike, honky, fag,* or *broad.* In addition to enabling us to describe the world—refer to things, state facts, attribute properties and relations to things, assert the occurrence of events, and so forth—language enables us to color our descriptions in emotional tones. Usually we do so not by adding words to our descriptions of what is happening, but by using words that both describe and evaluate (or express an attitude) at the same time. The power a term has to raise emotions can be called its *emotive charge,* and the charge can be either positive (e.g., *democracy, freedom, efficiency*), negative (e.g., *wasteful, dishonest, deficit* and all those listed above), or neutral (e.g., *picture frame, skating rink*), though a charge may vary from context to context and audience to audience (e.g., *marijuana, power*).

Even though the emotive charge of words makes language dynamic, it also opens up opportunities for a large variety of "proof surrogates"—devices that substitute for argument, that suggest conclusions without really providing any reasons for the beliefs they encourage.

The conscious manipulation of slanted language is part of what we call *propaganda.* Political campaigns offer many examples of such manipulation. For example, in the 1992 presidential election, GOPAC (a Republican political-action committee) published a brochure with advice for Republican campaigners, including the suggestion that words be selected from two lists: one for use when describing the good guys, and one for use when describing the opposition. Here are the two lists (Delwiche):

Positive words and phrases GOP candidates were told to use when speaking about themselves or their policies:

Active(ly)	Debate	Light	Prosperity
Activist	Dream	Listen	Protect
Building	Duty	Mobilize	Proud/pride
Candid(ly)	Eliminate good	Moral	Provide
Care(ing)	time in prison	Movement	Reform
Challenge	Empower(ment)	Opportunity	Rights
Change	Fair	Passionate	Share
Children	Family	Peace	Strength
Choice/choose	Freedom	Pioneer	Success
Citizen	Hard work	Precious	Tough
Commitment	Help	Premise	Truth
Common sense	Humane	Preserve	Unique
Complete	Incentive	Principle(d)	Vision
Confident	Initiative	Pristine	We/us/our
Conflict	Lead	Pro-(issue) flag,	Workfare
Control	Learn	children,	
Courage	Legacy	environment	
Crusade	Liberty		

Negative words and phrases GOP candidates were told to use when speaking about their opponents:

"Compassion" is	Decay	Incompetent	Shallow
not enough	Deeper	Insecure	Sick
Anti-(issue)	Destroy	Liberal	They/them
flag, family,	Destructive	Lie	Threaten
child, jobs	Devour	Limit(s)	Traitors
Betray	Endanger	Pathetic	Unionized
Coercion	Failure	Permissive	bureaucracy
Collapse	Greed	attitude	Urgent
Consequences	Hypocrisy	Radical	Waste
Corruption	Ideological	Self-serving	
Crisis	Impose	Sensationalists	

When we decide in advance to paint our opponents with negatively charged words and ourselves with positively charged words, we are engaging in intentional manipulation.

Proof surrogates do not manipulate only by painting with positively or negatively charged words. *Euphemism* uses the relatively neutral or positive charge accompanying some words to downplay some fact that is unpleasant or downright nasty: the neutral language, seeming more objective, obscures the unpleasantness of something.

The Nazis employed many euphemisms, calling the intentional murder of millions of people the "Final Solution of the Jewish Question." If you have a problem and find a permanent solution, that must be a pretty good thing, right? "Relocation to the east" meant being sent to one of the death camps, such as Auschwitz or Treblinka. Even in the extermination camps Nazi bureaucrats maintained detailed records, including fabricated causes of inmates' death. The cause listed was never execution or gassing; instead a random illness might be named, or the euphemism "Special treatment."

One need not look so far as the Nazi regime to find the use of euphemism to soften the impact of something that would sound considerably less pleasant if called by its right name. Euphemisms used to mislead have also been called *double-speak*. Governments and bureaucracies use them all the time, so much so that people speak of *governmentese, bureaucratese,* and related double-speak languages. During the Vietnam War, soldiers who were killed by bullets or missiles fired by soldiers from their own side were victims of "friendly fire." President Reagan, having pledged not to raise taxes, cleverly achieved "revenue enhancement" through increased "user fees." And while it is just as harsh to be jobless as a result of "corporate downsizing" as it is to be laid off, somehow it doesn't sound quite so bad.

It should be noted that not all euphemisms are intended only to mislead or deceive. Sometimes it is a matter of tact or politeness to speak euphemistically. When we speak to a small child of euthanizing a pet as "putting it to sleep," we are balancing the regard for truth with the sensitivities of the child. And when we express condolences for the "passing" of a loved one, we are similarly respecting the feelings of the person to whom we are speaking. And when we refer to bodily functions such as defecation, most people prefer to hear euphemisms over more accurate descriptions.

Another proof surrogate is *innuendo*. When Ann Richards ran for governor of Texas, one of her opponents in the Democratic primary, Jim Mattox, found out that some prison newsletter had endorsed Richards; he produced an ad that said, "Vote for Jim Mattox: *He* hasn't been endorsed by anyone on death row." The ad, of course, suggested without saying so (and without saying anything false) that Richards was the favored candidate of death row inmates and that she probably deserved the endorsement because she was sympathetic to criminals (Ivins 277).

Asking certain kinds of loaded questions (see section 8.51) also results in innuendo. The classic example is, "Are you are still beating your grandmother?" If you answer "No," you acknowledge that you were, but are no longer, beating your grandmother. Another blunt example is, "Were you born stupid, or did you have to work at it?"

Sometimes it's the lack of emotive charge that causes trouble. Because of the stature of science and its aura of objectivity, labeling something scientifically carries a kind of persuasive power. Objective-sounding scientific terminology, combined with the authority we often attach to scientific sources, inclines us to accept as value-free some statements that, were they put in plain English, we might at least wish to debate. For many years psychiatrist Thomas Szasz has called attention to this danger within psychology.[3] He points out that defining certain behaviors as symptoms of illness (as opposed to moral vices or sins) provides a kind of justification for our intervention in people's lives that might not otherwise be there. For example, some people disapprove of someone who has an unusual amount of sex (especially if the sex is not with a spouse) on moral or religious grounds, but calling someone a nymphomaniac or sex addict classifies the behavior as symptom of an illness, something that doctors are needed to cure, whether or not the patient wants to be cured. The point is not that all psychological classification is suspicious but that we should be wary of value claims that are presented as if they are neutral, value-free facts.

Exercise 8

I. The author of the following letter concerning flag-burning mentions the fact that Betsy Ross was her relative. Why does she mention that relationship? In what ways might it affect your willingness to accept her argument? Should it? Explain how the argument of the letter fares in terms of appeals to authority and emotion.

> Re: "House Panel OKs Proposal to Ban Flag-Burning," May 26: More than 200 years ago an ancestor of mine, a young widow whose husband had died at the start of the Revolutionary War, became part of our country's history when she was commissioned to sew the first American flag. She was Betsy Ross, my great-great-great-great-grandmother. For this reason, my feelings concerning the proposed constitutional amendment to prohibit desecration of our flag are personal as well as patriotic.
>
> Few people know that Betsy later remarried and also suffered the loss of her second husband in the Revolution. Eventually she was married a third time to John Claypole, who had been injured and imprisoned during the war but survived, and from whom I am descended.
>
> At great price our family, along with many others, purchased the freedom that we take for granted today. With their pain, their

---

[3] See for example his *Sex by Prescription,* where he discusses the idea of sexual disease and sex therapy, or *Law, Liberty and Psychiatry,* where he discusses the use of psychiatric classification to deprive people of freedom.

blood and their lives they established a secure home for the liberty that is our heritage. But the revolution was not fought for the sake of the piece of cloth that Betsy sewed. It was for the country, which the flag only symbolizes, and for our freedom that this sacrifice was made.

America cannot be harmed by the destruction of its symbols, but it can be damaged by abridging the freedom for which so many have died—even if this very freedom allows a sensation-seeker to burn a flag.

Those who seek to dishonor their country by trampling on symbols are only dishonoring themselves. Like a child throwing a tantrum, their goal is to draw media attention, and their actions should be fittingly dealt with. Let's not make constitutional martyrs out of these people in the name of patriotism! Instead, give them the treatment they really deserve. Ignore them!

(O'Brien B4)

II. Early in the campaign for the election of 1996, a Republican fund-raising poster stirred up some controversy. The "Liberal Democrat Wanted Poster" named 28 Democrats and said they were "wanted for voting against at least 7 out of the 10 provisions of the Contract with America and for aiding and abetting President Clinton's big government, pro-tax, anti-family, anti-military agenda in the House of Representatives." Some charged that the poster was really intended to inflame prejudices, as it targeted only 28 of the 90 Democrats who opposed the Contract with America—6 white male, 9 female, 10 African-American, 8 Jewish, and 1 Hispanic representative. In addition, some of the Democrats charged that the poster could put the lives of those targeted on it in danger. The following letter was published in *USA Today* in response to these charges:

> Liberal complaints about the Republican "wanted poster" are ridiculous. Every Democrat on the "wanted poster" is an extremist. Extremists should be identified. This is the same group that wants to label every conservative an extremist.
>
> Rep. Ron Dellums, D.-Calif., was involved in a scandal involving overdrawing his House bank account. Ordinary citizens don't have this luxury.
>
> Rep. Maxine Waters, D.-Calif., made excuses for the rioters in Los Angeles. In doing so, she gave comfort to extremists, who are bent on using violent means to achieve their goals.
>
> Rep. Barney Frank, D.-Mass., fixed parking tickets for a close male friend.
>
> A "wanted poster" is far too easy on them.
>
> (Bloyer 10A)

Analyze Bloyer's letter: Explain what fallacies, if any, it commits.

III. After appropriately reconstructing those of the following passages that contain arguments, explain in your own words why the arguments succeed or fail. Identify any fallacies you detect, and explain your identification. If there is no fallacy, see if you can identify any fallacies that *seem* to be present and explain why the passage is not really fallacious in that way.

1. Darwin's claim boils down to this: some of your relatives are monkeys. Is this really believable at all?

2. Einstein, among many other great scientific minds, believed that God's existence is shown by the marvelous complexity of the natural laws operating in the universe. Thus, the existence of God, far from being disproved by science, is proved by it.

3. President Clinton was right to fire Dr. Joycelyn Elders. She had a lot of really lame ideas—what sensible person would show kids how to masturbate in school? And how would teachers do that—in groups or by individualized instruction?

4. T.V. commercial: "Mikey likes it!"

5. [To the Editor:] "I've had it up to here with people like Judge John T. Noonan of the 9th U.S. Circuit Court of Appeals. This hypocrite strains at a gnat when he allows a scumbozo like Robert Harris a second chance at life because of a technicality. This judge plays God and promotes a sanctity-of-life doctrine that flies in the face of Scripture. Ecclesiastes 8:11 says 'because sentence against an evil work is not executed speedily, the heart of the sons of men is fully set in them to do evil.' This means that the death penalty is, indeed, a deterrent to murder."

   (Sather A5)

6. Periodically suggestions are made to amend the rules for election to the presidency so as to make a majority of the total national popular vote all that is needed for election. If so, winning by a large plurality in the most populous states in the far east and far west will become sufficient for election, and candidates who appeal primarily to these voters will have the best chance. Consequently, the President will not represent the interests of the whole country if the rules are changed in this way.

7. If every word is a name, then every sentence that contains more than one word is a list of names. Lists are neither true nor false. But many sentences are either true or false. Therefore, some words are not names.

8. I had a Ford Pinto once, and it was awful. Seems it was in the shop just about every other week, until they recalled it because it was a death trap. Since then, I've bought only foreign cars. But it's not just me—my uncle Roy had a Thunderbird that must have paid half the mortgage on his mechanic's house! You can't tell me foreign cars aren't better than the ones produced in Detroit.

9. The basic principle of preventive detention is simple: Someone who is preparing to commit a crime (such as a man going around a parking lot trying car doors) is apprehended and held until he can be searched, fingerprinted, and investigated. That way he can be kept from performing the criminal act. So I simply cannot understand the outcry against the City Council's new preventive detention ordinance, which allows the police to take into custody anyone suspected of harboring criminal intentions.

10. Actions that injure other people should always be of concern to society and are justifiably prohibited by law, but so-called crimes without victims (such as gambling, prostitution, drug addiction) are not of this sort. Consequently, crimes without victims should not be prohibited by law.

11. During a recent trip to Idaho I was impressed with that state's law that requires spaying or neutering of any animal being adopted f the shelters. This new law seemed to be working: there are fewer strays and unwanted animals in Idaho than in just about any other state. As a result of their new law, Idaho is about the most humane state around.

12. Some think it would be just fine for City Hall to be staffed by Communists and homosexuals. Don't trust your future to people who don't think like you. A vote for Smith is a vote for good, old-fashioned family values.

13. Bertrand Russell wrote an essay justifying the value of philosophy, and it is very eloquent. But Russell was himself a philosopher for around 70 years. Surely anyone who put so much of his life into an endeavor will be eager to convince you of its value, especially if he has as much pride as Russell

did. If you really want to know the value of philosophy, you'd better ask someone who isn't quite so devoted to it.

14. You will be arrested if the authorities discover your pet weasel. But you won't be arrested. So the authorities won't discover your weasel.

15. [Fred Leutcher, president of Fred A. Leutcher Associates, Inc., the only commercial supplier of execution equipment in the country, regarding electric chair design:] "Current cooks," Leutcher says, "so it is important to limit the current. If you overload an individual's body with current— more than six amps—you'll cook the meat on his body. It's like meat on an overcooked chicken. If you grab the arm, the flesh will fall right off in your hands." Leutcher is reassuring. "That doesn't mean he felt anything. It simply means that it's cosmetically not the thing to do. Presumably the state will return the remains to the person's family for burial. Returning someone who had been cooked would be in poor taste."

(Lehman 27)

16. You're probably wrong to reject Tang because it's not a completely natural product. It's probably fairly nutritious. After all, NASA selected it for use by the astronauts.

17. "Art Torres . . . invited us to follow him around for a day of his life in the Assembly. This is what his busy day was like.
    Nine o'clock—Art Torres arrives at the capitol. The Assembly begins its work with a prayer and the Pledge of Allegiance. Then Torres introduces a bill that will improve school meals. He tries to persuade the members of the Assembly to vote for his bill. When the vote is taken, the bill is passed. This time, his ideas have won.
    Twelve o'clock—Art Torres has lunch with his staff. They talk about problems in his district, or the part of Los Angeles that he represents.
    One thirty—Art Torres goes to a Health Committee meeting. He is chairman. The thirteen members of his committee study every bill that has something to do with health. On this day, they listen while an assemblywoman explains a health bill she has suggested. Everyone on the committee asks questions. Citizens share their ideas about the bill. Then the Health Committee will decide what changes, if any, should be made to the bill before it is sent to

the Assembly for a vote. Or the committee may decide *not* to send the bill to the Assembly.

Seven o'clock—Art Torres has dinner with a group of doctors. He tells them about several health bills that are before the Legislature. They discuss what should be done now to improve the California health system in the future. ... Art Torres thinks everyone should take a turn in public office. He plans to teach people about politics. In this way, he will be able to help future members of the Assembly and Senate do a better job for the people they represent."

(*California History: The Study of Our State* 212–13)

18. This statement was made by a juror in the first of two trials of the four police officers charged with using excessive force in the beating of Rodney King. King was struck approximately 50 times by a number of officers. The officers were acquitted in this trial: "Everybody agrees that the first time one of the officers struck King with a night stick it did not constitute excessive force. Therefore, if we are to conclude that excessive force was indeed used, then sometime during the course of the beating there must have been a moment—a particular blow—at which the force *became* excessive. Since there is no point at which we can determine that the use of force changed from warranted to excessive, we are forced to conclude that it did not become excessive at any time during the beating; and so the officers did not use excessive force."

19. When a person plagiarizes, he or she represents someone else's work or idea as his or her own when it is not. But if a person buys a paper from someone who understands how it will be used, then that person implicitly relinquishes his or her rights to the work, and the buyer obtains them. Presuming the paper properly cites its sources, it cannot be considered plagiarism to hand in such a paper as if it were one's own.

20. Did you see her go through the red light? Boy, elderly drivers are really pathetic!

21. You can accept what the *Catalog* says about graduation requirements; the *Catalog* is the official publication of the university. (If you don't believe me, check page 34 of the *Catalog*.)

22. "After reading your article on the Porsche 911 Carrera 2, I was reminded that while stationed in Japan in 1962 I ordered

a '62 356 S90—the top-of-the-line Porsche at the time. The as-delivered price was $3777. If my calculations are correct, the money spent for a plain-Jane Carrera 2 in 1990 would have bought 15.5 S90s in 1962. Incredible."

(M.G. Long, letter to *Car and Driver*)

23. Bob thinks the Celtics have a shot at winning the championship this year. Can you believe people can be so stupid? Maybe he thinks Bob Cousy and Bill Russell still play for them? Next time we see him, remind me that I've got some swampland in Florida to sell him.

24. If the creation story is a true, literal description, then the earth existed for three days before the sun was created. But the concept of a "day" is defined by reference to the sun. Surely, then, the creation story in Genesis cannot be taken literally.

25. Even if polar ice caps melted, there would be no rise in ocean levels. . . . After all, if you have a glass of water with ice cubes in it, as the ice melts, it simply turns to liquid and the water level in the glass remains the same.

(Rush Limbaugh, qtd. in Rendall, Naureckas, and Cohen 17)

26. Former Secretary of Agriculture Earl Butz: "The small farm is just too inefficient to be profitable. I say to the small farmer, get big or get out."

27. [Excerpt from advertisement in tabloid]: WHAT WOULD YOU GIVE FOR A BEAUTIFUL **BUST?** Stop wishing and dreaming. A beautiful bosom—one that you've always wanted can be yours in the privacy of your home. Why be unhappy, or settle for less. We are proud to introduce **FORM U** the breast creme formulation that will give you the beautiful bust you have always longed for. **FORM U** is perfectly safe and has been used by thousands of women with great success.

> **FORM U I** A creamy emulsion designed for the woman who wants a little "extra" for a more glamorous figure.
> **FORM U II** Our formula for the woman who desires a more proportioned bust.
> **FORM U III** is the ultra-performance creme designed for the small-breasted woman.
> **FORM U V** *(NEW) Super Potency* Our most potent prescriptive available for the petite-breasted woman.

With your **FORM U** breast creme order, you will receive the brochure "BEAUTIFUL BREASTS—WHAT YOU SHOULD KNOW." What would you give for gorgeous breasts? Breasts that give you confidence and assurance. With **FORM U**, satisfaction is guaranteed or your money back. You have nothing to lose and everything to gain.

(The Sun, July 25, 1995)

28. No president is above the law. Just as President Nixon was endlessly investigated by the press, subjected to congressional hearings and a number of bills of impeachment, and ultimately forced to resign from office because of Watergate, President Clinton cannot be allowed to remain as president unless he is shown not to be involved in any wrongdoing in the Whitewater affair.

29. AMA ad against smoking: "100,000 doctors have quit smoking. (Maybe they know something you don't?)"

30. "If Zionism is such a wonderful idea, why don't you live in Israel?"

31. MacDonald's sign: "Over four billion sold."

32. Sign on a competing restaurant: "Less than four billion sold."

33. Andrew Marvell's "To His Coy Mistress," 1681:

> Had we but world enough, and time,
> This coyness, Lady, were no crime.
> We would sit down, and think which way
> To walk, and pass our long love's day.
> Thou by the Indian Ganges' side
> Should'st rubies find: I by the tide
> Of Humber would complain. I would
> Love you ten years before the flood,
> And you should, if you please, refuse
> Till the conversion of the Jews;
> My vegetable love should grow
> Vaster than empires, and more slow;
> An hundred years should go to praise
> Thine eyes, and on thy forehead gaze;
> Two hundred to adore each breast
> But thirty thousand to the rest;
> An age, at least, to every part,
> And the last age should show your heart.
> For, Lady, you deserve this state;

Nor would I love at lower rate.
But at my back, I always hear
Time's winged chariot hurrying near,
And yonder all before us lie
Deserts of vast eternity.
Thy beauty shall no more be found,
Nor, in thy marble vault, shall sound
My echoing song: then worms shall try
That long preserved virginity,
And your quaint honour turn to dust,
And into ashes all my lust:
The grave's a fine and private place,
But none, I think, do there embrace.
Now, therefore, while the youthful hue
Sits on thy skin like morning dew,
And while thy willing soul transpires
At every pore with instant fires,
Now let us sport us while we may,
And now, like amorous birds of prey
Rather at once our time devour,
Than languish in his slow-chaped power.
Let us roll all our strength and all
Our sweetness up into one ball,
And tear our pleasures with rough strife,
Through the iron gates of life;
Thus, though we cannot make our sun
Stand still, yet we will make him run.

(Marvell 53–54)

34. "What seems clear is that those who regularly cite the Bible
to condemn an activity like homosexuality do so by reading
it selectively. Do ministers who cite what they take to be
condemnations of homosexuality in Leviticus maintain in
their lives all the hygienic and dietary laws of Leviticus? If
they cite the story of Lot at Sodom to condemn homosexuality, do they also cite the story of Lot in the cave to praise
incestuous rape? It seems then not that the Bible is being
used to ground condemnations of homosexuality as much as
society's dislike of homosexuality is being used to interpret
the Bible."

(Mohr 155)

35. From Dave Barry's *Stay Fit and Healthy Until You're Dead*
(illustration by Jerry O'Brien):

VEGETARIANS ARE EASY TO SPOT AT ROADSIDE REST STOPS

Illustration by Jerry O'Brien

IV. Here is a question relating to the fallacy of confusing cause and effect for you to reflect on: In his dialogue *Euthyphro* (10a), Plato raised the question whether what is holy (or right) is holy because the gods approve of it, or whether the gods approve of it because it is holy. Which is cause, and which is effect? Many people believe things are right because a deity approves of them (or commands us to do them), but Plato argued that this must get the cause and effect backward, since it would leave the gods in the position of approving arbitrarily whatever they approve. They can't approve of good things *because* they recognize their goodness—for in this view there is no goodness to recognize prior to approving these things! Was Plato right in thinking this a case of confusing cause and effect? What do you think?

V. Consider the following advertisements. Assess each one for its strength as an argument that you should buy the product in question. Where the ads make emotional appeals, determine whether they are legitimate or fallacious appeals. Do you find any other fallacies in them? Do the visual presentations make any difference to your assessment of the logical force of the ads—e.g., can fallacies be produced without words? Do any of these ads do so?

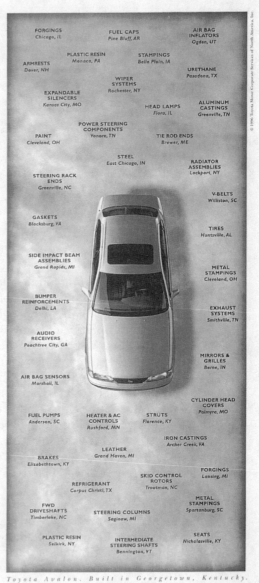

BUYING quality PARTS is not a FOREIGN idea to us.

OVER THE last five years, Toyota in America has purchased more than $20 billion in parts and materials from 510 U.S. suppliers.* Today, more than half the Toyota vehicles sold in America are built at our plants in Kentucky and California. Local investment that contributes to America's place in the global economy - it all makes good sense, in any language.

Toyota Avalon. Built in Georgetown, Kentucky.

INVESTING IN THE THINGS WE ALL CARE ABOUT.   TOYOTA

Some parts that go into our American-built vehicles are purchased overseas. For more information about Toyota in America visit our web site at http://www.toyota.com/antenna/usa.html or write Toyota Motor Corporate Services, 9 West 57th Street, Suite 4900-SI, New York, NY 10019

Courtesy of Toyota Motor Corporation Services

Help stop a different kind of child abuse.

This abuse is back-breaking. And spirit-breaking. The taskmaster is poverty and it takes fragile lives and brutalizes them with 12-hour workdays...inadequate food...little health care...very low — if any — wages...no hope for ever getting anything better.

As hard as parents of children like these struggle, they simply can't provide for them. And they are forced to put their children to work at jobs far above their strength and abilities. These little ones have no childhood.

But you can help. You can ease the suffering of these children. Become a Save the Children sponsor and help stop the horrible abuse that poverty inflicts on children around the world.

Your monthly gift of just $20 to Save the Children will be combined with the gifts of other caring sponsors to benefit an entire community of children. Instead of direct hand-outs, your gifts will help establish community

self-help programs, enabling your girl or boy to receive the food, medical care and education he or she so urgently needs.

Please call or mail the coupon below today and say you'll become a Save the Children sponsor. Only 65¢ a

day from you will help rescue a girl or boy from the most horrible kind of child abuse — and replace it with vitality and hope.

Please call 1-800-257-4949 or mail the coupon below today.

I want to help put an end to a different kind of child abuse.

☐ My first monthly sponsorship contribution of $20 is enclosed.
    I prefer to sponsor a ☐ boy ☐ girl ☐ either in the area I've checked below.
    Please send my child's photo and personal history.

☐ Where the need is greatest
☐ Africa   ☐ Caribbean   ☐ Middle East
☐ American Indian   ☐ Himalayas   ☐ South America
☐ Asia   ☐ Central America   ☐ United States

Name_____
Address_____ Apt._____
City_____ State_____ Zip_____

☐ Instead of becoming a sponsor at this time, I am enclosing a contribution of $_____
☐ Please send me more information.

Established 1932. The original child sponsorship agency. YOUR SPONSORSHIP CONTRIBUTIONS ARE U.S. INCOME TAX DEDUCTIBLE. We are indeed proud of our use of funds. Our annual report and audit statement are available upon request. ©1993 Save the Children Federation, Inc.

Save the Children.
50 Wilton Road, Westport CT 06880

Courtesy of Save the Children

The Ruger 22/45 .22 rimfire pistol features both a grip angle and magazine latch virtually identical to the 1911 Model .45 ACP, and the proven Ruger Mark II action. The Zytel grip frame is strong yet light, and is unaffected by salt water, sweat, oils, and bore cleaning solvents. The grip's matte black finish will not crack, chip or peel, and never needs refinishing. Whether you are looking for the perfect plinking pistol, an inexpensive way to practice, or an accurate sidearm for hunting small game, the Ruger 22/45 is a great choice.

Three configurations available: stainless-steel 4 ¾" standard barrel, stainless-steel 5 ½" bull barrel, and blued 5 ½" bull barrel.

Suggested retail prices from $237.50 to $330.00
Instruction manuals for all Ruger firearms available free upon request. Please specify model.

Sturm, Ruger & Company, Inc.
146 Lacey Place
Southport, CT 06490

RUGER
Arms Makers for Responsible Citizens

Courtesy of Sturm, Ruger & Company

"I HAVE TWO LOVES IN MY LIFE... I MARRIED ONE AND I MOW WITH THE OTHER."

Most people have strong feelings when it comes to their John Deere lawn tractor.

Maybe it's because over 96 percent of John Deere owners are satisfied with their tractors. Which makes John Deere lawn tractors number one in owner satisfaction, when compared to other brands.*

Or maybe it's a combination of features that make these owners so happy. Features like hydrostatic Twin Touch™ two-pedal foot control. Powerful overhead valve engines with cast-iron cylinder liners and full-pressure lubrication. Or the extra-tight 20-inch turning radius, to name a few.

Then again, there's also the fact that John Deere lawn tractors have the highest resale value of any lawn tractors on the market.** (Of course, getting John Deere owners to part with their lawn tractors is another story.)

But of all the things that make John Deere owners the most satisfied, one thing's for sure. While most people have only one love in their life, John Deere owners are lucky. They can count on two.

N O T H I N G   R U N S   L I K E   A   D E E R E®

 *Irwin Broh & Associates, Inc. 1995 Customer Satisfaction survey. **Based on resale value information obtained from the Intertec® Outdoor Power Equipment Blue Book®

Courtesy of John Deere Co.

PART III

Public Writing

9

Style

To this point we have touched on issues relating to language in a number of ways—code words, the effect of your tone on your ethical appeal, slanting, vagueness and ambiguity—but have said nothing of style. You cannot ignore style in writing. You cannot separate the style from the message; they are intimately related. Style is not ornament on the tree of meaning; it is the very texture of the bark, the leaves, the blossoms and seeds. The language you use to make meaning contributes to that meaning and modifies the ways in which others understand you.

9.1 What Is Style?

What is style, anyway? It's hard to pin down. Some claim that it's "my individuality," "the way something comes across," "my personal expression"; you hear vague words describing it, such as *flowery, plain, convoluted, stuffy, smooth.* But none of these descriptions helps you to know what to do to achieve a certain style. For that you need more precise terminology that refers specifically to those elements of writing you can manipulate to determine and alter style: *diction,* the words you use, and *syntax,* the way you put those words end to end.

Jonathan Swift, the eighteenth-century satirist, defined style as "proper words in proper places." He stressed exactly those features of writing that determine style: the words you use and how you arrange them. The tricky part, the part that requires your judgment, comes in his word *proper.* What makes a word or a sentence proper? There is, of course, no simple answer, no single rule to follow, nothing absolute. No word or sentence is, in and of itself, proper. You can determine whether a word or sentence is proper—appropriate—only by looking at the entire rhetorical context: what does the writer wish to say, whom is the writer addressing, and how does the writer wish to come across to the reader?

Hamlet says, "I'll lug the guts into the neighbor room" (3.4.219). Is that proper diction? Of course it is—given his meaning and the situation. Hamlet has just confronted his mother about her complicity in murdering the King, Hamlet's father, discovered someone hiding behind the curtain eavesdropping, and, thinking the intruder is his Uncle, the new King and his father's murderer, stabs him. However, he kills not his Uncle but Polonius, whom he chastises: "thou wretched, rash, intruding fool, farewell! / I took thee for thy better. Take thy fortune." Later, after making peace with his mother, Hamlet lugs Polonius' guts. The words themselves convey important meaning; Hamlet expresses not simply the act of removing the body but, more importantly, his attitude toward his deed and toward Polonius. Consider your reaction to recasting *lug* and *guts:* I'll carry his body, I will remove the carcass, I will bear poor Polonius hence. Readers respond to and derive meaning from the words we use; they do not simply absorb the dictionary meanings of those words.

You are probably far more attuned to style, and its consequences, than you think. At a formal dinner you ask, "Will you please pass the butter," not, "Gimme the butter." When you apply for a job or admission to a university, when you ask for a raise or a change of program, you use different words and arrange them in different patterns than you do when you write to a friend complaining of how unfairly you were denied that job, that admission, that raise, that change in program. You adapt your language, your style, according to how you wish to present your subject and yourself to your readers. Your style says what you often leave unspoken.

Usually you alter your style quite without thinking, without recognizing that you already have many different styles, all of which are your own. Unfortunately, because you seldom think consciously about style, you are less in control of it than you can be and may make gaffes that elicit responses from your readers you don't expect and are chagrined to discover. (The classic example is the student who complains, in stilted and convoluted English, how harshly he was graded, only to discover that the tortured writing weighed more heavily in support of the grade than did his arguments in favor of a higher one.)

This chapter will help you to become more conscious of your options in manipulating diction and syntax and more capable of creating a style that conveys the message you wish to convey. Just as wide knowledge is necessary to discover and evaluate arguments, so a broad vocabulary and understanding of syntax is helpful in mastering style. Nevertheless, studying a series of stylistic options will help you to gain greater control of your expression—and, hence, your meaning.

9.2 Formality and Informality

Perhaps the most familiar distinction of all is that between formal and informal writing. The distinction is at least partly a fiction, for you cannot accurately categorize all writing as either formal or informal; most writing falls somewhere in the middle. Imagine not two separate entities but a continuum from the very formal to the very informal. Nevertheless, it is by understanding what constitutes the extremes—formal and informal—that you will be able to achieve the style you wish. You have been studying formal writing for many years now, and you will be expected to use it effectively in academic and business writing. By describing the kind of diction and sentence structure associated with the extremes, you can become more aware both of what contributes to formality—and what may lead you astray—and how you can vary diction and syntax to achieve the level of formality you desire.

Consider this sample of a very informal style, the antithesis of formal writing:[1]

> If you really want to hear about it, the first thing you'll probably want to know is where I was born, and what my lousy childhood was like, and how my parents were occupied and all before they had me, and all that David Copperfield kind of crap, but I don't feel like going into it, if you want to know the truth. In the first place, that stuff bores me, and in the second place, my parents would have about two hemorrhages apiece if I told anything pretty personal about them. They're quite touchy about anything like that, especially my father. They're *nice* and all—I'm not saying that—but they're also touchy as hell. Besides, I'm not going to tell you my whole goddamn autobiography or anything. I'll just tell you about this madman stuff that happened to me around last Christmas just before I got pretty run-down and had to come out here and take it easy.
>
> (Salinger 3)

How did Salinger choose his words and arrange them to achieve the informal voice of Holden Caulfield? Look first at his diction.

Not all the words are short or ordinary (consider the exaggerated "hemorrhages"), but many are colloquial ("really," "thing," "lousy," "stuff," "pretty," "touchy"), if not altogether slang ("crap," "touchy as hell," "goddamn autobiography," "madman stuff"). They are the kind of words you use with a friend who shares with you a semiprivate vocabulary and who does not need a more exact explanation. They lack the precision associated with more formal diction. This closeness between speaker and listener is supported by Caulfield's addressing the reader as "you" and his using contractions throughout. These are the hallmarks of informal diction: colloquial phrases, "you" to mean "anyone," and contractions.

---

[1] Our comparison of Salinger and Dickens is derived from Gibson 53–59.

But diction alone does not account for the informality of this passage. Far more important—and more subtle—is syntax. Note how long Salinger's sentences are. The length of sentences by itself does not influence formality. What matters is the way the parts of the sentences are joined. Salinger creates Caulfield's voice by stringing short phrases together with "and" and "but." *And* and *but,* together with four other words—*for, so, yet, or/nor*—join information by giving equal weight to the various parts, hence their name *coordinate conjunctions.* There are only these six, so it is possible to memorize them. They give readers the feeling that Caulfield is thinking as he is speaking, saying one thing, which reminds him of something else, which he then adds with an *and,* and so proceeds to string together a sentence. He has not thought out his ideas before saying them, and he does not seem concerned with their relative importance to each other or to the reader. The sentence structure, like the diction, captures the immediacy of the moment but lacks the precision of formal writing.

Notice how all of Salinger's sentences, whether following this pattern of coordinate units or not, give the same impression of ideas just tumbling out as they come to Caulfield's mind. Caulfield says, "They're quite touchy about anything like that, especially my father," beginning with a general statement and then emending it as he reflects on what he has just said. He continues, "They're *nice* and all—I'm not saying that— but they're also touchy as hell," interrupting the coordinate pattern ("They're *nice* and all, but they're touchy as hell") with a full sentence, a comment on the first part of the sentence about his parents' being nice. And it is even an oblique statement meaning the opposite of its surface content: I'm not saying they aren't nice.

Informal writing does not mean license; there are no errors in Salinger's writing. Rather, informal writing consists of loosely constructed sentences and ordinary diction speeded up with contractions and interruptions, all of which give the impression of spontaneity and oftentimes of a congenial writer who is chatting with the reader.

Now compare Salinger's style with some formal writing, first by looking at Dickens' portrayal of David Copperfield, to whom Caulfield refers in the passage quoted above. Copperfield begins his story this way:

> Whether I shall turn out to be the hero of my own life, or whether that station will be held by anybody else, these pages must show. To begin my life with the beginning of my life, I record that I was born (as I have been informed and believe) on a Friday, at twelve o'clock at night. It was remarked that the clock began to strike, and I began to cry, simultaneously.
>
> (Dickens 1)

The rhythm of these sentences causes Dickens' writing to strike readers very differently than Salinger's. Notice the construction of the first sentence: two parallel subordinate clauses preceding the main clause of the sentence. This is not the spontaneous thinking on paper we found in Salinger. It is crafted so that the sentence structure supports—indeed, makes—the meaning of the sentence: that there are two alternatives (expressed in the same grammatical pattern, "whether..., whether..."), and that these alternatives are subordinated, and thereby connected, to the main idea in the sentence, that the book itself will hold the answer. You can see more of this balanced structure in both of Dickens's following sentences.

The words themselves are quite ordinary, but the writing does lack the slang, the use of *you* to mean *anyone,* and the contractions that characterize the most informal writing. And just as informal writing does not excuse errors, so formal ought not to be confused with stuffy writing. Dickens' writing, quite formal, avoids those multisyllabic abstractions and circumlocutions that so often deaden prose. Formality comes from the rhythm of the sentences, the subordinate patterns—not from big words. Formality is also characterized by the precision of both diction and syntax. The subordinate structure aids both writer and reader in seeing the relationships between ideas within a sentence.

Let's take a look at another piece of formal writing, the opening paragraph of Martin Luther King's "Letter from Birmingham Jail." King wrote this letter from jail on April 16, 1963, to eight Alabama clergymen who had criticized his methods of protesting segregated eating establishments in Birmingham.

> My Dear Fellow Clergymen,
>   While confined here in the Birmingham City Jail, I came across your recent statement calling our activities "unwise and untimely." Seldom, if ever, do I pause to answer criticism of my work and ideas. If I sought to answer all of the criticisms that cross my desk, my secretaries would be engaged in little else in the course of the day and I would have no time for constructive work. But since I feel that you are men of genuine good will and your criticisms are sincerely set forth, I would like to answer your statement in what I hope will be patient and reasonable terms.
>
> (King 76)

Like Dickens, King subordinates some ideas to others and places the subordinated phrases and clauses primarily at the beginning of sentences to offer a context for the main part of the sentence. Also like Dickens, King uses parallel structure for parallel ideas. His third sentence begins with a subordinate clause introducing two parallel main clauses: "If I sought to answer all of the criticisms that cross my desk, my secretaries would be engaged in little else in the course of the day and I would have no time for constructive work." The last sentence in this paragraph has the same construction we examined in Dickens, two parallel subordinate clauses leading up to the main part of the sentence: "But since I feel that you are men of genuine good will and [since] your criticisms are sincerely set forth, I would like to answer your statement. . . ." It is largely these subordinate structures (with the subordinated unit often preceding the main clause), along with the parallel phrasing, that lend the prose its formal quality.

Again, the diction is quite ordinary. Notice that when *you* refers specifically to an individual, here to the group of eight clergymen, it does not affect the level of formality, just as the word "I," used by both Dickens and King, can be formal. (*I* certainly affects the style of writing, making it more personal, but that is a separate consideration. Both informal and formal writing can be personal, as these examples illustrate.)

Most of us write most of the time somewhere in between a very formal or very informal style, using both coordinate and subordinate sentence structures. Consider Russell Baker's opening to his essay "Collegiettes":

> For the first time ever, there are more women than men enrolled in American colleges. The immediate implications of this are bound to upset people who need stereotypes to preserve the illusion of stability in a chaotic universe. Joe College, for example, now becomes a false metaphor for the college student. . . .
>
> What does it mean for football, which has traditionally been to college what the nightstick is to police? Does it make sense for a college population dominated by women to have the bulk of its athletic budget spent on a sport that can be played only by 200-pound women with shoulders like stevedores' and legs like oak trees?
>
> Of course not, but then it has been a long time since college football made much sense to anybody except the professional-league operators who use it as a state-subsidized farm system for developing young players. Successful college teams now come almost exclusively from state universities whose money comes from legislatures run by old (male) grads to whom touchdowns are sweeter than libraries.
>
> (Baker 13)

The passage is witty, charging along with ordinary diction, neither simplistic nor difficult. The sentences range from the informally elliptical "Of course not, but . . ." to the longer, subordinated final sentence. But you find neither extreme, none of Salinger's strings of ideas joined by *and* and *but* nor Dickens's and King's carefully balanced sentences or introductory, parallel, subordinated clauses. Almost all of Baker's sentences open with the subject of the sentence and proceed to elaborate his point; if they include subordinated phrases and clauses (and many do), these come after rather than before the main idea. Baker's style is neither as chatty as Salinger's nor as distanced as Dickens's and King's. It falls in the middle of the informal–formal continuum.

What does it take to alter a style along this continuum? Simply changing the sentence structure and diction will change the tone; the subject matter, by itself, will not determine the style. Holden Caulfield could have said, "Because my childhood bores me and because my parents, rather private people, would be embarrassed if I reveal my family's secrets, I will concentrate on the events surrounding my collapse." Obviously you react differently to this Caulfield because he is a different person. The style of a passage conveys its own meaning, and readers respond to that meaning as well as to what the words ostensibly denote.

"Mr. Kellwood is looking for someone to assist him in recasting his journals into a form suitable for a wider audience. The tone should be urbane, warm, and scholarly—somewhat in the manner of Lewis Thomas, but, of course, about plywood."

Drawing by Lorenz; © 1988. The New Yorker Magazine, Inc.

What happens to Baker's passage if you rewrite it informally?

> Who can make any sense out of college football these days, you know,
> now that so many women're going to college—more even than men—
> and football costs so much money, and the women can't play, but isn't
> football part of college, just like a nightstick is part of a policeman?
> Well of course the pros would cry foul if they had to cough up the
> money to train the young jocks, and the government boys—the ones
> who OK the tax dollars—would be put out if they couldn't get their fix
> of touchdowns.

Reading this version, you are probably less inclined to take Baker seriously, and for a good reason. The loosely building sentences suggest that Baker has not thought through his position carefully and that he is just fielding ideas as they come to him. Possibly the ideas will strike you as important enough to develop yourself, but that is not the same as a writer fashioning his prose so that the reader will follow his point of view.

You choose a style that is appropriate to your subject, to your reader, and, above all, to the situation. Your content—what you say—will not determine your style; your diction and syntax do that. But your subject may suggest an appropriate style. The *New Yorker* cartoon on the previous page derives its humor from just this. You must ensure that what you say and how you say it complement each other.

Exercise 9.2

I. Rewrite a passage of your own (perhaps the opening of your own autobiography), making it very formal, imitating Dickens's opening parallel subordinate clauses and King's balanced sentences, and then very informal, imitating Salinger's loose, coordinated style. By practicing the extremes, you will be better able to judge where your general writing falls along the continuum from very informal to very formal.

II. Write two letters, each one asking for something you want from someone who is in a position to give it to you. Write the first one formally, addressing it to someone to whom you would ordinarily write formally. Write the second letter, another rendition *of the same information*, informally. Write it to someone to whom you would ordinarily write informally. Your letters can be evaluated both on the strength of your arguments and on your ability to achieve—and maintain—a formal and informal style.

9.3 A Modern "High Style"

The label *high style* (along with *middle* and *low style*), however inexact, dates from at least the fourth century B.C.E. It has been used to describe an ornate style of writing, often metaphoric, with sentences intricately patterned. Although this sort of ornate writing has long been out of fashion, the desire to create a style that transmits the importance of ideas remains strong. How can you elevate your ideas so that your reader will think them important? A formal style, as defined above, will help make them clear; some attempts to making them seem important, however, run counter to clarity.

You may discover that your own writing includes words chosen less for their meaning than for their impressive sound, and the sentences constructed less to clarify relationships than to showcase the diction.

When you examine your own writing with a view toward recasting it more or less formally, for instance, you may discover that it doesn't fit on the continuum described above at all, not even in the middle of it. You may discover something else altogether: few connectives of any kind, many *to be* verbs *(is, are, has been)*, many nouns, often long nouns. When nouns predominate, writing become sluggish (you may have heard the term *stuffy*). Nouns name things; they don't move a sentence along.

Consider some writing in which nouns predominate. This passage analyzes audiences' willingness to applaud at political speeches:

> The semantics of applause are exceptionally straightforward by any standards. The action of applauding is invariably a display of *affiliation* which, in the context of political speeches, expresses support or approval for the assertion that it follows. Such an action may be treated as having a positive value, deriving from its expressive properties, for each individual who undertakes it; for the purpose of this discussion that value may be treated as fixed. In seeking to realize this value, however, each individual runs the risk of incurring costs. As Asch has demonstrated, most people have a basic fear of social isolation and prefer to express opinions or judgments that are in concert with their peers. Each individual audience member, faced with a political assertion with which he or she agrees, is therefore placed in a situation of choice in which the positive expressive value of applauding may be outweighed by the negative cost of being found to be alone in the expressive act.
>
> Thus the payoff from each act of applauding depends, for each individual, on whether other audience members applaud. The responses of others, however, are to varying degrees uncertain. The position of each audience member is analogous to that of the participants in games of pure coordination in which the decision of each individual must be matched with the independent decisions of others if a positive payoff for each is to be realized.

> (Heritage and Greatbatch 111–12)

Notice how differently this passage reads from Salinger's, Dickens's, King's, or Baker's. You read it more slowly, more ponderously, and that's because the cadence of the sentences forces such a reading. You may also have difficulty understanding the passage at first, even though you know the meanings of individual words. The sluggishness of the sentences and your initial difficulty discerning their meaning stem from a preponderance of (1) linking and passive verbs over active verbs, (2) nouns over verbs of any kind, and (3) abstract nouns over concrete nouns.

9.3.1 Linking and Passive Verbs

The *to be* verbs that predominate in this writing function in one of two ways. Either they *link* nouns as in the first two sentences ("The semantics of applause *are* exceptionally straightforward by any standards" and "The action of applauding *is* invariably a display of affiliation . . ."), or they form part of a *passive* construction as in the third sentence ("Such an action *may be treated* as having a positive value . . ."). Both structures sap life out of a sentence, but they do so in different ways.

Linking verbs (*to be* is the most common, but others, such as *feel, seem,* and *appear,* also link nouns) simply equate (albeit imperfectly) one noun with another or with an adjective. Because linking verbs provide no action, no motion, nouns simply pile on top of each other and the reader must remember them or sort them out herself. Moreover, once you establish the basic linking pattern of noun + linking verb + noun, you have few options for making connections between nouns—or ideas. Notice that Heritage and Greatbatch's dominant sentence pattern forces them to rely on prepositional phrases to add more information.

| The semantics | *of* applause |
| are exceptionally straightforward | *by* any standards. |

| The action | *of* applauding |
| is invariably a display | *of* affiliation. |

The prepositional phrases add more nouns, sometimes stringing together several lines of them:

Each individual audience	
member faced	*with* a political assertion
	with which he or she agrees
is therefore placed	*in* a situation
	of choice
	in which

the positive expressive value   *of* applauding
may be outweighed   *by* the negative cost
                                           of being found to be alone
                                           in this expressive act.

The last sentence of the passage quoted above suffers equally from strings of prepositional phrases.

Linking verbs trap you in this unfortunate pattern. You have neither the freedom of the loose, rambling, informal sentences that permit Holden Caulfield to meander from point to point as he assesses and modifies his ideas nor the opportunity that balanced, subordinated, formal sentences provide for relating ideas to each other. When you rely on linking verbs, you force the reader to struggle through your sentences to locate your meaning. Instead, your style should help your readers understand what you have to say.

Passive verbs weaken your sentences not so much by limiting the way you can adapt them to convey your ideas as by hiding their real subject. Compare the passive "Your window was broken" with the active "I broke your window." The first version eliminates the actor altogether (which, of course, makes it so appealing to those who want to avoid responsibility for an action or policy). But more often writers are less dishonest than misdirected. When you read the third sentence in the Heritage passage, you may at first be confused about who is doing the treating since the writers don't tell you, but, if you puzzle it out, you discover quite readily that the writers themselves are treating applause as pleasurable. Not only must readers take the time to reconstruct the sentence (and not all are so indulgent), but they are also not fooled into thinking the writing any more objective than they would had the writers simply been direct about who was doing what. Passive verbs confuse your meaning and weaken the sentence.

Finally, both linking and passive verbs can destroy the rhythm of your sentences. Linking verbs, with their attendant strings of prepositional phrases, thump along in a repetitive pattern, and passive verbs, which require two words—*to be* plus the past participle of the action verb—weigh a sentence down with extra words. Try reading your sentences out loud to hear them. If they sound lifeless, try speaking them. You may find you can eliminate many confusing, ponderous sentences simply by rediscovering the idea in your mind and speaking it freshly.

9.3.2 A Preponderance of Nouns

Linking verbs encourage you to write sentences in which nouns far outnumber verbs, sentences that emphasize the static names of things over their action. But those very names offer you an opportunity to infuse your sentences with action. Examine the nouns in one of Heritage and Greatbatch's sentences you have been analyzing to find the action they hide:

> The action of applauding is invariably a display of *affiliation*. . . .

All four nouns suppress action: *action* can become *act;* the gerund *applauding, applaud; display, display* (the verb); and *affiliation, affiliate.* Try out some options:

> Applauding acts to display affiliation.
>
> Applauding displays affiliation.
>
> Applauding affiliates the audience with the political speaker.
>
> When the audience applauds, they affiliate themselves with the political speaker.

How can you choose among these versions? Look closely at the original and all four revisions. Count the number of nouns surrounding the verb *is.* (This sentence is by no means as excessive as many.) Notice that Heritage and Greatbatch italicize *affiliation;* because they bury the idea in a prepositional phrase, they must stress it artificially, in this case visually. You can stress words naturally by placing them in the main parts of a sentence, the subject or verb. Also notice how the first three rewrites shorten the original sentence. Stripping the original of its burden of extra words clarifies its point. In fact, by the third rewrite, it becomes so clear that you discover in addition that something is missing: who is affiliating with whom? The context of the sentence implies the answer, though only indirectly. The third rewrite fills in the missing information. The fourth makes the sentence more personal, substituting people for abstractions in the subjects and verbs. As soon as you free the action imprisoned in significant nouns and as soon as you eliminate the confusion caused by extraneous words, your meaning becomes clear. You can decide how personal you wish your writing to be by considering your audience and your context.

9.3.3 Abstract and Concrete Nouns

The more abstract nouns outnumber concrete nouns, the more difficult a passage is to understand and the stuffier the style. Consider this well-known revision of a verse from *Ecclesiastes.*

Objective consideration of contemporary phenomena compels the conclusion that success or failure in competitive activities exhibits no tendency to be commensurate with innate capacity, but that a considerable element of the unpredictable must inevitably be taken into account.

(Orwell 169)

Here is the original:

Again I saw that under the sun the race is not to the swift, nor the battle to the strong, nor bread to the wise, nor riches to the intelligent, nor favor to the men of skill; but time and chance happen to them all.

(Ecclesiastes 9:11)

Orwell obviously exaggerates, as you can see by looking over the less-intrusive abstractions of the Heritage passage, but, unfortunately, his parody comes close to much modern writing. His version is stuffy because of the sheer number of syllables (just try saying his sentence quickly!), but it masks information for other reasons as well. Most important, Orwell's translation lacks the examples of the original. These examples don't function as evidence, nor are they individual cases. But each reader can absorb the point, made and remade with successive illustrations, far more readily than by wrestling with the abstractions of Orwell's translation. When you resort to abstractions, ask yourself, "What am I really trying to say?" Does the abstraction really convey the point? (You may wish to review section 3.3 on unpacking code words.) Usually you will need to replace—not append, replace—the abstraction with the concrete words it hides.

9.3.4 The Message Inactive Verbs and Abstract Nouns Convey

Why is this style so pervasive today? What is its attraction? Orwell lamented it in "Politics and the English Language," published in 1946; others have sought to explain its allure in terms of the weight it adds to ideas, making even common sense seem noble, or its ability to obscure—and therefore make palatable—harsh realities. Consider an example of this style, its a proposed policy statement on "Consensual Relationships." What happens to its meaning if you rewrite it?

Consensual Relationships

Because of the respect and trust accorded a professor by a student and the power exercised by the professor in giving praise and blame, grades, and recommendations for further study or future employment, the student's actual freedom of choice is greatly diminished when sexual demands are made. Therefore, consenting romantic and sexual relationships between faculty and student or between supervisor and employee, while not expressively forbidden, are generally deemed unwise. Codes of ethics for most professional associations forbid professional-client sexual relationships.

Therefore, faculty are warned about the possible costs of even an apparently consenting relationship, in regard to the academic efforts of both faculty member and student. A faculty member who enters into a sexual relationship with a student (or supervisor with an employee) where a professional power differential exists, must realize that if a charge of sexual harassment is subsequently lodged, it will be exceedingly difficult to prove immunity on grounds of mutual consent.

Here you find all the elements of this modern high style: linking and passive verbs, sentences elaborated with strings of prepositional phrases, a high proportion of nouns to verbs, and a preponderance of multisyllabic, abstract nouns. What happens to the message, however, if you rewrite it without the slow pace and ponderous diction? Consider a conversational tone:

We know that some of you may become romantically involved with a student or employee, but we think it a bad idea. That student may later charge you with sexual harassment, and you will not be able to defend yourself simply by claiming the student was also eager for a relationship. We're not forbidding you to get involved with a student, but we want to warn you that the grievance committee will be more swayed by a student's complaint than your impression that you were fond of each other.

It seems inappropriate, the message somehow wrong, even if it is clearer. Faculty may feel the writer doesn't properly respect the seriousness of the issue or their feelings. They may think the writer hard-hearted rather than sympathetic to their dilemma. At least the ponderous version implies that the writer believes faculty members struggle to balance their professional responsibilities with their personal feelings and that the institution has their best interests in mind as well as the students'.

Nevertheless, you can write seriously and clearly at the same time. Here are some broad guidelines:

1. **Release the action hidden in the nouns.** That's where you find your active verbs.
2. **Then decide who is acting.** That's how you avoid the obscurity of the passive voice.
3. **Eliminate extraneous nouns and other filler.**
4. **Subordinate less important information to more important information.** That's how you clarify your ideas, focus the

reader's attention on the important ones, and vary your sentences. (Once you've replaced the linking verbs with active verbs, No. 1, you will no longer be trapped by prepositional phrases.)

5. **Replace abstract nouns with the concrete information they hide.**

The policy statement already has some features that can be released. For example, the first sentence opens with the rudiments of parallel introductory clauses reminiscent of Dickens and King (No. 4) and already specifies a professor's power (No. 5). It suffers from its many nouns (No. 3), its passive verbs (No. 2), its many prepositional phrases (No. 1), and the ambiguity (No. 5) of the students' "freedom of choice" being "diminished" (freedom to choose to enter the relationship, or fewer courses from which to select, or fewer professors to write letters of recommendation, or all of these). Here's one possible revision of the first sentence:

> Because students respect and trust professors and because professors exercise power in praising and blaming students, grading their work, and writing recommendations for their future study and employment, students cannot freely choose to enter a relationship when a professor demands (suggests?) it.

The second sentence also piles many nouns onto a single, passive verb that obscures the actor. Who deems such relationships "unwise," the committee that wrote the initial policy, the senate that passed it, the administration that ultimately acts on it? And in the second paragraph, who warns the faculty? Who, in other words, takes responsibility for this policy? Once you know, you can easily recast the rest of the policy into clearer, more vigorous prose without losing the weightiness of the subject.

Exercise 9.3

I. Combine each of these groups of sentences into a single sentence that emphasizes more important information by subordinating less important information. Then read your sentence out loud to ensure that it makes sense—the same sense you intended when you crafted it.

A. 1. Lorenzo de' Medici was called "Lorenzo the Magnificent."
   2. He was a patron to Florentine artists.

B. 1. A punt is an open, flat-bottomed boat with squared ends.
   2. It is propelled by a long pole.

    3. It is used in shallow water.

    4. Oxford students are adept at piloting the punt.

C. 1. Fred sat alone on the bench.

    2. He read yesterday's newspaper.

    3. He suddenly looked alarmed.

D. 1. Sissela Bok was born in Stockholm.

    2. She earned graduate degrees from George Washington and Harvard universities.

    3. She now teaches at Brandeis University.

E. 1. Comets are essentially dirty snowballs.

    2. They formed at the birth of the solar system.

    3. Scientists study comets to understand conditions when the sun and planets came into being.

F. 1. Comets may have altered the last 4.5 billion years.

    2. They have been heated by very bright stars and by supernova explosions.

    3. The heating obliterates the original structure and chemical composition of the comets' surfaces.

G. 1. It is a little past 5 A.M.

    2. They spot the horizontal sewer grate outside the American Museum of Natural History.

    3. They quickly tether a voracious-looking papier-mâché alligator to the grate.

H. 1. For the vast majority of Americans a healthful diet does not depend on consuming any particular nutrient.

    2. A healthful diet depends on the overall structure of the diet.

    3. The overall structure of the diet refers to the total balance of foods we eat.

I. 1. Shakespeare was an actor.

    2. Shakespeare was a theatre shareholder.

    3. Shakespeare was a poet.

    4. Shakespeare was a playwright.

    5. Shakespeare was naturally learned.

    6. Shakespeare astutely observed people and places.

    7. Shakespeare had the "largest and the most comprehensive soul" of modern or ancient men.

    8. John Dryden thinks Shakespeare had the "largest and most comprehensive soul."

II. Consider a business letter written by a student:

Dear Mr. Smith,

The purpose of this correspondence is to address base salary compensation and eligibility for an increase to that base salary set forth in the employment agreement established with you in August 1995. The secondary purpose of this correspondence is to address excessive expenditures being incurred in order to adequately cover the accounts that compromise territory 4 and to explore the possibility of drawing a nominal sum to help offset these costs being incurred, in the form of expense reimbursements.

As stated in the employment agreement, eligibility for an increase of 12 percent to the base salary will be extended at the end of six months' employment. Furthermore, prior stipulation was that in order not to receive an increase in pay, one would have to be doing poorly in relation to his/her growth performance. Therefore, to support this request it is important to note that there has been favorable growth performance, if not significant.

Present performance levels show company profits produced by the territory in excess of $17,000 per month for the past two months. This level of production more than adequately supports present base salary compensation. Furthermore, gross sales projections for the next three months of the new quarter indicate strongly that gross sales will be in excess of $165,000. This projection is based on the addition of three new nationally contracted accounts as well as on the additional military accounts, that are substantial in size, which have recently been established with Afghans Unlimited. Further, the present accounts that comprise the territory base are expanding supply purchases. These are substantial reasons for the projected increases for the next quarter and remainder of the year. Therefore, a 12 percent increase added to the present salary base, which equates to an annual salary of $39,772.72, would be very reasonable and sufficiently supported.

Secondly, the present expenses being exhausted to cover territorial duties are a good deal more than expected. When compared to other territories that have been established at Afghans Unlimited, the outlay of expenditures is more than ordinary. Fuel and maintenance costs to operate the salesman's vehicle are excessive. Therefore, a request for an expense allowance to the sum of $200 per month payable in the form of expense reimbursement is requested to help cover these unavoidable business expenses.

In summary, because of the success being experienced in the territory, near-term business projections, and a prior employment agreement, an increase of 12 percent added to present base salary compensation is being requested. Also, because of the vastness of the territory and the extra expense that is necessary to incur to cover the territory adequately, a sum of $200 per month expense reimbursement is being requested. Your willingness to review these requests is greatly appreciated. Hopefully these substantiated requests will be granted. If there are any questions you might have or if you need further explanation in regard to this correspondence, please communicate through written correspondence or verbally.

Thank you again, and notification of approval is eagerly sought.

Yours Truly,
Frederick Fleece

This writer struggled through many drafts in an effort to develop good ethical appeal and to seem thoughtful, conscientious, and worthy of the raise and expense account he wants. But his prose obscures rather than directs his reader to the support he presents for his requests. Try describing the style of this letter, and then use the five general guidelines to rewrite the letter (or parts of it), maintaining the seriousness this writer obviously wants to project while clarifying his points.

III. Describe the style of the following passages as specifically as you can, noting sentence structure and diction. Then comment on how the style affects the meaning of the passage.

Additionally, you can copy or imitate the styles you admire. Copying passages, a major part of a classical education, allows you to absorb the rhythm of sentences and sounds. Initiating them, writing the same pattern of sentences but on a different subject, helps you to express your own ideas in new sentence patterns, thereby expanding your options for writing.

A. My friends have no friends. They are men. They think they have friends and if you ask them if they have friends they will say yes, but they don't really. They think, for instance, that I'm their friend, but I'm not. It's okay. They're not my friends, either.

The reason for that is that we are all men—and men, I have come to believe, cannot or will not have real friends. They have something else—companions, buddies, pals, chums, someone to drink with and someone to wench with and someone to lunch with, but no one when it comes to saying how they feel—especially how they hurt.

(Cohen B1)

B. The trouble with the kind of wide-open pornography that is rampant today is not that it corrupts, but that it desensitizes; not that it unleashes the passions but that it cripples the emotions; not that it encourages a mature attitude but that it is a reversion to infantile obsessions; not that it removes the blinders but that it distorts the view. Prowess is proclaimed but love is denied. What we have is not liberation but dehumanization.

(Cousins 4)

C. Sooner or later, fight metaphors, like fight managers, go sentimental. They go military. But there is no choice here. Frazer was the human equivalent of a war machine. He had tremendous firepower. He had a great left hook, a left hook frightening to watch even when it missed, for it seemed to whistle; he had a powerful right. He could knock a man out with either hand—not all fighters can, not even very good fighters. Usually, however, he clubbed opponents to death, took a punch, gave a punch, high speed all the way, always working, pushing his body and arms, short for a heavyweight, up through the middle, bumping through on force, reminiscent of Jimmy Brown knocking down tacklers. Frazer kept on coming, hard and fast, a hang-in, hang-on, go-and-get-him, got-him, got-him, slip and punch, what a punch, never was Frazer happier than with his heart up on the line against some other man's heart, let the bullets fly—his heart was there to stand up at last. Sooner or later, the others almost all fell down.

(Mailer 32)

D. To speak then when one was not spoken to was a courageous act—an act of risk and daring. And yet it was hard not to speak in warm rooms where heated discussions began at the crack of dawn, women's voices filling the air, giving orders, making threats, fussing. Black men may have excelled in the art of poetic preaching in the male-dominated church, but in the church of the home, where the everyday rules of how to live and how to act were established, it was black women who preached. There, black women spoke in a language so rich, so poetic, that it felt to me like being shut off from life, smothered to death if one were not allowed to participate.

(hooks 5)

E. For decisions made under conditions of uncertainty, the information individuals have about prospective outcomes and how they use it are central to economic performance. The importance of these factors has led to the establishment of markets and activities for the transfer of information, ranging from advertising to high-tech "information technologies." Inadequacies in individual information have also prompted a

wide range of risk regulation efforts for potentially hazardous jobs and products. Although these policies usually take
the form of a ban or other technological means of altering the
risk, if the chief inadequacy is lack of information, then in
principle, it should be possible to alleviate the source of the
market failure directly with an informational policy.

(Viscusi and Magat 1)

F. Physicians know only too well how uncertain a diagnosis or
prognosis can be. They know how hard it is to give meaningful and correct answers regarding health and illness. They
also know that disclosing their own uncertainty or fear can
reduce those benefits that depend upon faith in recovery.
They fear, too, that revealing grave risks, no matter how
unlikely it is that these will come about, may exercise the pull
of the "self-fulfilling prophecy." They dislike being the
bearers of the uncertain or bad news as much as anyone else.
And last, but not least, sitting down to discuss an illness
truthfully and sensitively may take much-needed time away
from other patients.

These reasons help explain why nurses and physicians
and relatives of the sick and dying prefer not to be bound by
rules that might limit their ability to suppress, delay, or
distort information. This is not to say that they necessarily
plan to lie much of the time. They merely want to have the
freedom to do so when they believe it wise. And the reluctance to see lying prohibited explains, in turn, the failure of
the codes and oaths to come to grips with the problems of
truth-telling and lying.

But sharp conflicts are now arising. . . .

(Bok 225)

G. Some of us who live in arid parts of the world think about
water with a reverence others might find excessive. The
water I will draw tomorrow from my tap in Malibu is today
crossing the Mojave Desert from the Colorado River, and I
like to think about exactly where that water is. The water I
will drink tonight in a restaurant in Hollywood is by now
well down the Los Angeles Aqueduct from the Owens River,
and I also think about exactly where that water is: I particularly like to imagine it as it cascades down the 45-degree
stone steps that aerate Owens after its airless passage
throughout the mountain pipes and siphons. As it happens
my own reverence for water has always taken the form of

this constant meditation upon where the water is, of an obsessive interest not in the politics of water but in the waterworks themselves, in the movement of water through aqueducts and siphons and pumps and forebays and afterbays and weirs and drains, in plumbing on the grand scale.

(Didion 59)

H. When in the Course of human events it becomes necessary for one people to dissolve the political bands which have connected them with another, and to assume among the powers of the earth, the separate and equal station to which the Laws of Nature and of Nature's God entitle them, a decent respect to the opinions of mankind requires that they should declare the causes which impel them to the separation.

   We hold these truths to be self-evident, that all men are created equal, that they are endowed by their Creator with certain unalienable Rights, that among these are Life, Liberty, and the pursuit of Happiness. . . .

(From *The Declaration of Independence*)

I. Of the wall [of China] it is very easy to assign motives. It secured a wealthy and timorous nation from the incursions of barbarians, whose unskillfulness in arts made it easier for them to supply their wants by rapine than by industry, and who from time to time poured in upon the habitations of peaceful commerce, as vultures descend upon domestic foul. Their celerity and fierceness made the wall necessary, and their ignorance made it efficacious.

   But for the pyramids no reason has ever been given adequate to the cost and labor of the work. The narrowness of the chambers proves that it could afford no retreat from enemies, and treasures might have been reposited at far less expence with equal security. It seems to have been erected only in compliance with that hunger of imagination which preys incessantly upon life, and must be always appeased by some employment. Those who have already all that they can enjoy, must enlarge their desires. He that has built for use, till use is supplied, must begin to build for vanity, and extend his plan to the utmost power of human performance, that he may not be soon reduced to form another wish.

(Johnson 118)

10

Making It Public

The process of identifying an important topic, thinking it through, generating and evaluating arguments, and writing up your understanding for someone else can seem quite complicated, consisting of innumerable, overlapping steps. If at this point, however, you conceive of a four-stage process, you can focus your attention on one of the most easily overlooked steps—and yet one that is crucial in conveying your ideas to others.

1. Investigation: gathering information from research and experience, generating ideas and arguments.

2. Writing to understand, to get it right.

3. Writing to make your insights clear to your readers.

4. Editing your work to make it technically correct.

Steps 1 and 2 overlap considerably, as do 3 and 4. But the move from step 2 to step 3 is different. First, you may overlook it altogether. After all, once you have produced quite a number of pages and said much, if not all, of what seems important to say, you may consider the paper finished, except, of course, to edit for punctuation and spelling. Second, you may not know how to progress from step 2 to 3. How do you go about rewriting something that makes sense to you?

Yet rewrite you must, the vast majority of the time. Even the most cogent of arguments will fail if your readers miss your point or are unable for some reason to hear what you have to say. Therefore, however many pages you have written—5 or 50 or more—you must reconsider your paper from the readers' point of view. And it is of necessity a *reconsideration*: with most topics you will find it next to impossible to write a version of your insights accessible to your readers without first writing some version for yourself. You need to recognize the difference between the steps and write them both. Without the first, you will have difficulty writing the second; without the second, your readers may miss your point.

10.1 Writing for Understanding

How can you recognize when you are writing for yourself? The most obvious instances—freewriting, loose associations, and the like—present no problem. But other drafts may give you more pause. Nevertheless, there are clues you can look for. Consider the following letter of application from a student seeking a job:

Dear Sir or Madam:

I would like to be an assistant instructor of flute at the Community School of Music. I hope to gain experience in teaching flute to children, and I would like to practice my newly acquired skills in music and education.

Two summers ago I worked in the City Parks Program where I taught children ages 4 to 14 swimming and roller skating. They needed a lot of patience to learn these skills. I can relate to their troubles because I went through many trials of my own learning to overcome deficiencies in my method and techniques of playing the flute. Once I wanted to quit because I thought the flute could do nothing for me. Now I am working on a degree in music with an emphasis in education. I am also studying flute with Dorothea LaTrobe.

There are three curricular approaches to teaching music to children now popular. First is the Orff-Schulwerk method of learning by doing. Children learn the elements of music by beginning with simplified instruments and playing folk songs and other familiar tunes right away. The second method is Kodaly. Children learn to sing "Do, Re, Me" without learning any words. This method improves sight reading. The third method is the Dalcroze rhythmic movement. Children learn rhythm by feeling it through their bodies.

I think that flute playing must be taught at first as though it is a hobby. Not all people who study flute will become professional flautists, and some flute players may become discouraged if they think that is the only reason to play the flute. It must first be fun and then, later, it may become a profession. But in any case it takes practice and hard work to learn to play the flute.

I have a strong interest in teaching children ages 7 to 14. I think that teaching music at the Community School can greatly add to my ability to teach and to understand the flute.

Sincerely,
Karen Shidosha

How does Karen present herself in this letter? One reader responded that she seems earnest about her own flute playing and, on a theoretical level, about teaching, but questioned whether she could really help the children at the Community School. This reader worried that she might be less interested in her young charges than in trying out the theories of teaching she was studying. Another reader wanted to know why she almost quit playing the flute. This reader surmised that Karen may have been forced to return to her studies and may therefore have trouble motivating young children to play. Yet another reader believed that someone who worked with children in the past would know whether she could teach children. However, this reader also wondered why, after Karen had worked with children ages 4 to 14, she concluded her letter by claiming a strong interest in teaching those between ages 7 and 14.

How can these three readers respond in such different ways to the same letter? If a writer does not direct her readers to the points she wants them to see, they may read their own ideas into the case. They may take the data and combine them in ways that she did not intend. It is not enough to write down all your information and assume your readers will draw the conclusions you want them to draw. More often they will simply be confused or respond in ways that startle and distress you. And that is a significant problem for any writer who wants to communicate ideas to readers.

Karen's letter typifies writing at the second step of our schema. Karen wrote it as she was thinking through her reasons for wanting the job, and this draft greatly aided her in discovering just why she did want to teach flute at the Community School. Three features in particular reveal it to be written more for Karen's understanding than for her readers' needs:

1. The letter is **written from the writer's point of view, not the reader's.** Karen explains clearly why she wants the position but not why the Community School may want her.
2. **The support follows a narrative pattern, a story held together by the sequence of time rather than evidence.** This pattern, especially true in the second paragraph of Karen's letter, is especially useful as a thinking device, to help her remember the details, but it does not aid a reader in understanding the connections between those details.
3. **The support that is not arranged chronologically seems a description rather than an argument.** The third paragraph reads like a "memory dump" of information on Karen's mind, organized as a lesson to memorize rather than an argument to consider (note the introductory sentence stressing the number of points to be made—an aid to the memory—and the transitions

"first," "second," and "third," followed by the name—also an aid to the memory).

Before readers can be persuaded to consider your thoughts, they must be clear not only about what those thoughts are but also why those thoughts deserve attention. Once you have written sufficiently about your subject to discover your most important ideas and arguments, you can place them in the background of your mind and ask what your readers need to know in order to understand them. By keeping your readers and their needs in the foreground of your mind as you rewrite your paper, you will be able to provide them with cues they need to follow your argument.

Begin at the beginning of your paper.

10.2 Introduce Your Readers to Your Work

In Chapter 2 you considered your readers' reasons for reading your writing, their knowledge of your subject, and their attitude toward your approach, all as a means of generating leads. Now you can return to that analysis to aid you in structuring your writing. How can you get them to listen to you in the first place?

10.2.1 Find Your Common Ground

Just because you want to express your ideas to someone does not ensure that he or she is eager to hear them. Consider your reasons for writing and your reader's reasons for reading. Do you share any common ground with your reader? Once you identify common ground, you can use it to broach your subject to your reader.

For instance, suppose you are helping to establish a Humane Society in your town, and you want a good working relationship between the society and local veterinarians. The society will maintain a low-cost shot clinic, but it will be unable to provide surgery or emergency care of animals. Therefore, you plan to ask the local vets to provide these services for Humane Society animals on a voucher system. The vets can redeem the vouchers given them by families for cash from the Humane Society.

First work through an audience analysis. The veterinarians are most likely familiar with the Humane Society, but they may be less than enthusiastic about its arrival. Its low-cost shot clinic may take away some of their business, and the vouchers will involve paperwork and reduced fees. Nevertheless, you think a mutually satisfactory relationship can be forged. How do you make your case?

Suppose you were to argue like this:

> The Humane Society offers many benefits to a community. It shelters
> abandoned and abused animals, places animals in new homes, pro-
> vides low-cost immunization for healthier animals, and discourages
> breeding of unwanted animals. But the Humane Society cannot pro-
> vide some necessary services: surgery and emergency care. The society
> must rely on local veterinarians to provide these important services.
> Local vets can help the Humane Society provide the fullest service
> possible so that it may better influence the city's overpopulation of
> animals.

Will the local veterinarians jump at the chance? Probably not. Why
should they embrace an organization that discourages the breeding that
brings them their livelihood, undercuts their prices for immunization,
and expects them to provide such services as spaying and neutering at
reduced prices? Perhaps such a presentation would work if you were
writing to the community at large, donors, or other Humane Society personnel. Those audiences may see the project, as you do, from the society's
point of view: the Humane Society needs help, and the local veterinarians have the skill and equipment to provide it. But arguing that the vets
should help simply because they are needed for the Humane Society to
accomplish its goal—however civic minded they may be—is unrealistic,
and the implied bid for power in the last sentence may actually scare
them off altogether.

If you want to persuade the vets themselves, try to look at the situation from their point of view. Do you share any common ground with
them? In fact you do. You are all concerned with the well-being of animals. You all want to see as many animals as possible immunized and
well cared for. Use this insight to motivate the vets to read your letter
and consider your request.

> The Humane Society would like to help you provide our community
> with needed attention to animals. Many animals never see one of your
> offices. They have no homes and are often starving and sick. Together,
> we can provide a high standard of care for these animals. The Humane
> Society will be responsible for sheltering unwanted animals, finding
> homes for some, and immunizing all it places. The Humane Society
> can also provide vouchers to reimburse you for spaying and neutering
> those animals. Although we cannot offer as much as you currently ask
> for surgery, we can offset much of your cost and bring you many cus-
> tomers who would not otherwise spay or neuter their pets. And the
> families you help now may return later for other services. We hope that
> together we can provide needed services for local animals.

Such an approach may not persuade all local veterinarians to accept vouchers: some may already have all the business they can handle. But it may encourage enough to consider the idea that the Humane Society will be able to set up its operation.

By establishing common ground at the beginning of your writing, you can lead your readers into your argument and help them put aside (at least initially) some of their reluctance to consider your case.

10.2.2 Establish Your Credibility

Even if your readers are initially drawn in by the common ground you establish, why should they continue to listen to you? That is, how can you establish ethical appeal early on in a paper?

As you recall from sections 1.4.4 and 2.5, readers are inclined to listen to writers who are knowledgeable about their subject, respectful of its complexities and the positions others take on it, and reason well. They make the best case they can, neither claiming more than their evidence warrants nor misleading their readers through unfounded appeals or omissions. They present information accurately; they make their case with integrity. On the one hand, then, your entire paper—its conception and development—establishes your ethical appeal; on the other, you can reveal your knowledge and approach early on, quickly establishing ethical appeal.

To decide just what it is you need first to reveal, consider what is on your readers' minds as they approach your argument. They may not have thought much about your particular case but have sufficient background (or a vested interest) to respond quickly to it. This situation is common to letters requesting something—employment, that veterinarians accept Humane Society vouchers, a whole host of things. In these instances, you will need to be aware of the issues impinging on the readers' decision. What will the Personnel Director be looking for in a letter of application? What are the highest priorities for the veterinarians? The same is true of arguments you make to alert readers that an issue deserves attention, or even in some cases to persuade readers to consider your view of a controversial issue.

Often you will be writing to readers who have thought a great deal about your subject. As you become familiar (through your research and discussions) with the ongoing conversation about your topic—what is being said among those who are thinking and writing about it—you discover where your ideas fit in, whose assumptions you share, whose conclusions seem believable, which contexts seem suggestive. Importantly, you also discover whose thinking you most want to influence. Are you interested in addressing those who share your assumptions but arrive at different conclusions, those whose views you share but who you feel may not be acting sufficiently or (to your mind) rightly on them, or those with whom you disagree fundamentally? Someone who wants to argue against the claim that a woman should have the right to abortion, for instance, may wish to persuade those who share her assumption about the primacy of the fetus's right to life that exceptions should be made nevertheless in cases of rape and incest, or to protest other antiabortionists' tactic of harassing women entering clinics, or to persuade someone who accepts the claim that women should have the right to abortion to reconsider his position. In the same way, someone who wants to argue for women having the right to abortion may wish to persuade those who share her assumption about the primacy of the woman's right to control her body that the state does have the right to intervene at some point in gestation, perhaps the last trimester, or persuade those arguing publicly for abortion rights to craft better emotional appeals, or to persuade antiabortionists to reconsider how their assumption of the primacy of the fetus's right to life leads to the conclusion that abortion is morally impermissible.

Your planning and early writing will help you decide what you have to say and to whom. (It does you little good simply to restate a view to readers who already hold it. You write to clarify it, expand it, reconcile it, overturn it, or energize readers to act on it.) Whichever readers you choose to address, then, will have their own ideas, either about the subject at large or about particular arguments. In order to win their good will, you can show them—early on—that you have considered their position thoughtfully and that you understand the context that gives rise to it; or, if your readers are not too set in their views, you can show that you know the significant problems, issues, and alternative positions on the subject. (The narrower the audience, of course, the more specifically you can respond to their particular view of a topic.) To display your knowledge effectively, to be sure, you must have done your homework. You must indeed be familiar with the best of your readers' possible views and arguments and have evaluated them, using all the skills you worked on in the past several chapters. You must ask, now, how you can show your understanding and assessment to your readers.

Whether you are writing a letter asking for a job or an essay inquiring about an abstract issue, begin by asking where your ideas differ from your readers' and why. The young flutist did not have the experience teaching music to children required by the job she wanted, the Humane Society held different priorities than the local veterinarians, and writers considering abortion differ on any number of points. Discover the differences between your concerns and your readers'. Do they lie with your definition of what is at issue? Do you question their assumptions, take issue with their arguments, or believe that their position is appropriate in only limited circumstances? Whatever your differences may be, you can gain readers' good will by successfully showing them that you understand their point of view.

Although you can acknowledge your readers' point of view implicitly in a short letter by the issues you raise, longer arguments present a different challenge. If you can describe your readers' position in such a way that they agree with your version of it, they may be convinced that you do indeed understand their point of view, and, if you present it sympathetically, they may be convinced, as well, of your respect. You can show them, that is, that your disagreement does not come from carelessness or lack of understanding. You can thereby shift their focus off any initial distrust they may have of someone who disagrees with their view and onto your arguments.

Consider the opening to Ronald Dworkin's essay "On Not Prosecuting Disobedience":

> How should the government deal with those who disobey the draft laws out of conscience? Many people think the answer is obvious: The government must prosecute the dissenters, and if they are convicted it must punish them. Some people reach this conclusion easily, because they hold the mindless view that conscientious disobedience is the same as lawlessness. They think that the dissenters are anarchists who must be punished before their corruption spreads. Many lawyers and intellectuals come to the same conclusion, however, on what looks like a more sophisticated argument. They recognize that disobedience to law may be *morally* justified, but they insist that it cannot be *legally* justified, and they think that it follows from this truism that the law must be enforced. Erwin Griswold, the Solicitor General of the United States, and the former Dean of Harvard Law School, appears to have adopted this view in a recent statement. "[It] is of the essence of law," he said, "that it is equally applied to all, that it binds all alike, irrespective of personal motive. For this reason, one who contemplates disobedience out of moral conviction should not be surprised and must not be bitter if a criminal conviction ensues. And he must accept the fact that organized society cannot endure on any other basis."
>
> The New York Times applauded that statement. A thousand faculty members of several universities had signed a *Times* advertisement calling on the Justice Department to quash the indictments of the Rev. William Sloan Coffin, Dr. Benjamin Spock, Marcus Raskin, Mitchell Goodman, and Michael Ferber, for conspiring to counsel various draft offenses. The *Times* said that the request to quash the indictments "confused moral rights with legal responsibilities."
>
> But the argument that, because the government believes a man has committed a crime, it must prosecute him is much weaker than it seems. Society "cannot endure" if it tolerates all disobedience; it does not follow, however, nor is there evidence, that it will collapse if it tolerates some. . . .

Dworkin begins with his central question, one that neither he nor his readers can ignore and one that has no obvious answer with which everyone agrees. He begins a lengthy and meticulous argument against prosecuting draft offenders by citing the best of his readers' possible views about his subject—and he does so by quoting one of the most respected proponents of that view and a major newspaper's agreement. He dismisses one line of argument as "mindless," but he continues to write respectfully about Griswold's, both explicitly, calling it "sophisticated" and not easily answered and conceding some issues, and implicitly, meticulously considering all aspects of it. By stating it at the outset, accurately and respectfully, Dworkin quickly establishes sufficient ethical appeal to propel his readers into his argument. He may ultimately fail to convince them, and if his ethical appeal were to slip along the way, they may even stop reading, but his opening paragraphs invite them to continue reading and at least to consider his case.

Although Dworkin directs his essay to a wide audience, clarifying issues, augmenting support for those who already agree with his position, and raising issues that may challenge those who disagree or are neutral, his primary objective is clearly to rally support for not prosecuting draft offenders and to offer arguments to those empowered to make such a decision that are sufficient to make one favorable to his way of thinking. His primary audience, then (see Chapter 2), takes on the role of a relatively neutral party, weighing all the evidence and making an appropriate decision. (This is not to say the audience is disinterested or not personally engaged in this highly charged issue, but only that its role is to act as neutrally as possible.) Similar situations abound: the court with its neutral judge or jury, the debate with its judges, the classroom and the academic paper with their respondents. Raising his opposition's best case thereby functions to draw in his most reluctant readers, open the door for him to respond to that case, and indicate his understanding and careful consideration of views that run counter to his own. Considering the opposition's best case takes on even greater importance when you write not to a neutral—or open-minded—reader but directly to one who holds a view so tightly that he is unable even to consider a different one.

In such instances, when writers and thinkers are so emotionally involved or so committed to a particular set of values that they cannot readily respond to your argument, a "Rogerian" approach may be useful. This method of argument, named after the psychologist Carl Rogers, seeks first of all to increase communication. Rogers believed that what most often blocks successful communication is a sense of threat. Therefore, he reasoned, if people feel they are understood, they may be less defensive. He developed a method of therapy in which he repeated what clients told him, acknowledging their concerns, their voice. In his words, he would "listen with understanding." He would attempt "to see the expressed idea and attitude from the other person's point of view, to sense how it feels to him, to achieve his frame of reference in regard to the thing he is talking about." By engaging not only the views but also the values of the other person, Rogers found "the emotion going out of the discussion, the differences being reduced, and those differences which remain being of a rational and understandable sort" (331–33).

Rogerian argument, developed out of Rogers' framework of therapy into a system for public discourse, applies this concept to persuasion. If writers can indicate they have understood their readers, their readers may be less defensive, more willing to listen. Whereas attacking the views of readers with whom you disagree polarizes you and your readers—the more you argue, the more firmly they may resist your claims—a Rogerian approach may allow even hostile readers to give your argument a hearing. Typically you begin a Rogerian argument by introducing what is at issue, stating the readers' position, and explaining the contexts in which that position may have merit. It is necessary to state the readers' position overtly; you will be less successful if you imply understanding indirectly. It is the statement itself, in terms the readers agree are appropriate, that demonstrates you have understood your readers' assumptions, perceptions, and values.

Rogerian argument has another beneficial effect: as you clarify your readers' best arguments, you understand them more fully. Once you understand another person's frame of reference, your own response may change drastically. Such an understanding will aid you in designing the most balanced case you can about an issue as well as present it effectively. There is always some risk, of course, that you will lose your own views as you articulate another's. That may be salutary in some instances, but certainly not all. The greatest risk occurs when you are developing a new line of argument, one you may not yet have mastered, as a counter to a well-established line of argument, one you may once have accepted yourself and still find seductive. When you articulate the clearer alternative, you risk losing a fragile hold on something of significance. Of even more concern, when you take on the point of view of readers who you believe will not value what you have to say, you may lose your voice in adopting theirs. In these instances, you would certainly want to postpone writing a Rogerian argument until this (later) stage in the writing—after you have first clarified your own views. You can adopt a Rogerian approach, that is, after you have first attempted to express your views in your own language. Such reconsideration—seeing the issues anew from a different point of view—is, in fact, the essence of revision.

The heart of Rogerian argument is to reach an understanding of an issue that accommodates both writer and reader. In many instances, the view the writer is challenging has been accepted and used by many others in their own reasoning. By inviting that view into the discussion, writers pay respect to those already engaged in the conversation and allow for discussion of reasoning based upon it. Such accommodation means that the views of the reader as well as those of the writer determine what must be discussed in any particular situation and that different readers will occasion different sets of topics to consider. The understanding that ultimately results may require both parties to reconceive the issue and to redefine what is relevant to a discussion of it. Such a reconception allows not only what Rogers calls "communication" but also a greater understanding of the fullness of the issues that concern us.

10.3 Organize for Your Readers

Once you have introduced your readers to your subject, found potential common ground with them, and indicated your willingness to pay as much attention to their ideas as you hope they will pay to yours (indeed already having done so), how can you choose from the myriad of organizational patterns available to you? Simply selecting a ready-made pattern may not work, however effective that pattern may be in some circumstances. There are no rules that will inevitably lead you to organize in a manner that works for your subject and your readers. Again, you must recall your purpose in writing and your readers' in attending to your text.

10.3.1 Designing the Overall Frame

Think of organization as a series of boxes within boxes: the overall frame of your paper sets out large portions of your argument, subsections develop each of these, and individual paragraphs and sentences make up the subsections. As you set out to write, initially you worked at all these levels at once, thinking them through, writing them to get them right, taking up your readers' concerns and their reactions to yours. Now that you have that draft—writing at step 2—you are ready to recast your arguments in the order your readers will best be able to comprehend them.

As you lay out the large frame of your paper, first recall your purpose. What work does this writing need to do? Karen's letter needed to overcome her lack of experience teaching flute sufficiently to be considered for the position; the Humane Society wanted to interest local vets in cooperating with its enterprise to help with spaying and neutering; Dworkin wanted to offer his readers enough good reasons for not prosecuting draft dissenters that they would consider acting on his proposition. Second, identify any constraints your argument itself may place on the overall progress of your paper. For instance, which parts of your case depend on other parts to make sense? Does the genre of your writing impose form, as the nature of mystery writing caused Doyle to structure "Silver Blaze" in a particular way? Third, ask how your readers can best process your case. Which parts are your readers likely to agree with, and which parts are likely to cause them to resist your conclusions? Organize your paper in such a way as to meet your readers' needs for information and reasoning as you lead them to appreciate your conclusions.

You have already seen that telling readers the story of how you discovered your ideas and conclusions more often confuses than instructs them. In laying out the large frame for your writing, then, you can help your readers understand your claims and the connections between them by clustering your ideas around a few central points. In revising her letter, for example, Karen may see it as offering her readers three central arguments: (1) She has the education necessary for the position, (2) she has some experience teaching children (even if not flute), and (3) she has personal experience on which she has reflected thoughtfully. These three points, moreover, are precisely what her readers will be looking for—education, experience, and personal care and thoughtfulness. All of her thinking about her ability to teach children to play the flute (often good, though at the moment unfocused) supports one of these three claims. By setting them out clearly and by using them to organize her letter, Karen can lead her readers to understand what she has to offer the Community School of Music and perhaps also genuinely consider her for the position—the ultimate goal of her letter.

Writing an abstract may help you to discover your central points, especially if you are writing a long argument. Try writing a paragraph in which each sentence states a central tenet of your argument. It is often easier to see how these tenets weigh against each other and lead one to the next in a short format like an abstract than in the longer version of your document where you may become embroiled in the details of a subsection. Alternatively, write headings and subheadings (without any text), or write an outline. All of these abbreviated forms help you to capture the whole picture at once, to see how the parts fit together, to construct and reconstruct your broad ideas.

Once you have identified the central tenets of your case, about which cluster all the details of your arguments, you need to order them. Above all, think of readers thinking through your case. Which arguments will they readily accept? Which arguments can you lay out so soundly that most readers would grant your conclusions? Begin there. Help your readers to enter your case gently, beginning with your common ground and interests, moving through concerns of theirs you have identified, into those of your arguments they may see as plausible, all the while establishing your credibility as a good thinker. Then move into the difficult claims, the ones you find more challenging to argue, the ones most likely to put off your readers. Your readers will be far more likely to consider a difficult or imperfect argument after they have read through sound arguing than before doing so. In fact, they may not get past an imperfect or off-putting argument to discover other, better-reasoned argumentation. It is surprisingly tempting to begin with the difficult sections of a case, moreover, partly because they are most likely foremost in your mind, the ones you want to get out of the way, and partly because they may be the most important to establish if your writing is to do the work your purpose requires it to do. Nonetheless, resist the urge. Write them first as you draft your case, but when you revise, leave them to the end.

The organization of a paper, like all the other aspects of thinking and writing you have been considering, helps define your message. Writing at all stages of the process helps you to discover what you need to say, and determining the large framework of a piece of writing is no different. By focusing on the interplay between your purpose and your readers' needs—by thinking of the communication as a cooperative enterprise— you further form (reform) your position. That position, if it is mediated throughout by a concern for your readers' needs, understanding, and emotional responses, allows both you and your readers to resolve differences, perhaps by shifting the grounds upon which those positions are based.

10.3.2 Helping Your Reader Follow Your Argument

Unfortunately, organizing your material well is usually not enough. You must also lead your readers through your arguments by helping them to see the structural patterns that inform your writing. You can be bold or subtle, but you do need to tell your readers why you are offering certain material at certain points. You can do so by offering your readers substantive cues to follow your reasoning (introductions to paragraphs and sections of an argument, transitions between parts, titles and subheadings) and by providing linguistic cues.

Consider what may happen if you fail to make connections between your points. This is a paragraph, short—and exaggerated in its lack of connectives—for illustration. It describes the hero as W. H. Auden finds him in Grimm's Fairy Tales, but it has been recast so that it progresses from point to point in simple sentences without Auden's cues to help readers make sense of those points.

> A fairy story is distinct from a merry tale or an animal story. It is a serious tale. It has a human hero and a happy ending. The progression of its hero is the reverse of the tragic hero's. He is socially obscure. He is despised as being stupid or untalented. He lacks heroic virtues. He surprises everyone by demonstrating his heroism. He wins fame, riches,

and love. He does not succeed without a struggle. His success is in doubt. Opposed to him are natural difficulties. These might include glass mountains or barriers of flame. Hostile wicked powers, stepmothers, jealous brothers, and witches are opposed to him. He might fail. He is assisted by friendly powers. They give him instructions. They perform tasks for him. He cannot do these tasks himself. He has his own powers. He needs luck. Luck is not fortuitous. Luck is dependent upon his character. It is dependent upon his actions. Justice is established. The good are rewarded. The evil are punished.

Pause for a moment to consider this paragraph without rereading it. First, how much of it can you remember? (Try writing down the details you can remember without looking back at the paragraph.) Then summarize its major and minor points, again without rereading it. Now look back over the original. Most readers are chagrined to discover how little of the paragraph they can recall and blame the writer for a "poorly organized" paragraph. But this paragraph suffers from lack of syntactic cues, not organization. Here is the paragraph again, set out to reveal its structure:

(1) It has a human hero and a happy ending.
    (2) The progression of its hero is the reverse of the tragic hero's.
       (3) He lacks heroic virtues.
          (4) He is socially obscure.
          (4) He is despised as being stupid or untallented.
       (3) He surprises everyone by demonstrating his heroism.
          (4) He wins fame, riches, and love.
    (2) He does not succeed without a struggle.
       (3) Opposed to him are natural difficulties.
          (4) These might include glass mountains or barriers of flame.
       (3) Hostile wicked powers, stepmothers, jealous brothers, and witches are opposed to him.
    (2) He is assisted by friendly powers.
       (3) They give him instructions.
       (3) They perform tasks for him.
          (4) He cannot do these tasks himself.
          (4) He needs luck.
             (5) Luck is dependent upon his character.
             (5) It is dependent upon his actions.
(1) Justice is established.

This paragraph is organized well enough. But because the original version offers no cues to help readers see the relative importance of individual points or their relation to each other, it seems a hodgepodge of isolated data. Without puzzling through the entire paragraph, readers cannot be certain, for example, which of the first four sentences guides the paragraph or why "He has his own powers" is relevant at all.

Once you understand the relative importance of the points, however, you can add substantive cues or, in this case, simply subordinate less-important sentences so that readers will know—as they are reading—which ideas guide the paragraph and how ideas relate to each other. You must be diligent, however, in subordinating the less-important ideas; simply combining points can cause even more confusion than leaving them isolated. Writing "Lacking heroic virtues, he surprises everyone by demonstrating his heroism," for example, confuses rather than clarifies the paragraph. Consider this revision of the Auden paragraph (his version) in which the ideas abstracted remain in main clauses and the others are subordinated:

> A fairy story, as distinct from a merry tale, or an animal story, is a serious tale with a human hero and a happy ending. The progression of its hero is the reverse of the tragic hero's: at the beginning he is either socially obscure or despised as being stupid or untalented, lacking in the heroic virtues, but in the end, he has surprised everyone by demonstrating his heroism and winning fame, riches, and love. Though ultimately he succeeds, he does not do so without a struggle in which his success is in doubt, for opposed to him are not only natural difficulties like glass mountains, or barriers of flame, but also hostile wicked powers, stepmothers, jealous brothers, and witches. In many cases indeed, he would fail were he not assisted by friendly powers who give him instructions or perform tasks for him which he cannot do himself; that is, in addition to his own powers, he needs luck, but this luck is not fortuitous but dependent upon his character and his actions. The tale ends with the establishment of justice; not only are the good rewarded but also the evil are punished.

> (201)

Judicious subordination allows you to guide your readers through your ideas, and provides opportunities to set up parallel structures, reminiscent of Dickens and Martin Luther King (Chapter 9), to clarify relationships further. For instance, in Auden's paragraph parallel structures underscore the contrast between the hero at the beginning and the end of his quest: ". . . at the beginning he is socially obscure . . . but in the end he has surprised everyone. . . ." You can also vary sentence length, reserving short sentences for emphasis or transitions, and you can cut the unnecessary words that clog your meaning.

Another way to show connections between ideas is by associating like points through parallel sentence structures. Here are a few patterns:

Parallel Phrases and Clauses

Reading maketh a full man, conference a ready man, and writing an exact man. And therefore, if a man write little, he had need have a great memory; if he confer little, he had need have a present wit; and if he read little, he had need have much cunning, to seem to know that he doth not. Histories make men wise, poets witty, the mathematics subtle, natural philosophy deep, moral grave, logic and rhetoric able to contend.

(Bacon 175)

Anaphora (Repeating Sentence Openings)

Perhaps it is easy for those who never felt the stinging darts of segregation to say, "Wait." But *when you have seen* vicious mobs lynch your mothers and fathers at will and drown your sisters and brothers at whim; *when you have seen* hate-filled policemen curse, kick and even kill your black brothers and sisters; *when you see* the vast majority of your twenty million Negro brothers smothering in an airtight cage of poverty in the midst of an affluent society; *when you* suddenly find your tongue twisted and your speech stammering as you seek to explain to your six-year-old daughter why she can't go to the public amusement park that has just been advertised on television, *and see* tears welling up in her eyes when she is told that Funtown is closed to colored children, *and see* ominous clouds of inferiority beginning to form in her little mental sky, *and see* her beginning to distort her personality by developing an unconscious bitterness toward white people; *when you have* to concoct an answer for a five-year-old son who is asking: "Daddy, why do white people treat colored people so mean?"; *when you take* a cross-country drive and find it necessary to sleep night after night in the uncomfortable corners of your automobile because no motel will accept you; *when you are* humiliated day in and day out by nagging signs reading "white" and "colored"; *when your* first name becomes "nigger," your middle name becomes "boy" (however old you are), and your last name becomes "John," and your wife and mother are never given the respected title "Mrs."; *when you are* harried by day and haunted by night by the fact that you are a Negro, living constantly at tiptoe stance, never quite knowing what to expect next, and are plagued by inner fears and outer resentments; *when you are* forever fighting a degenerating sense of "nobodiness"—*then you* will understand why we find it difficult to wait.

(King 81–82) (Italics added to emphasize structure)

Epistrophe (Repeating Sentence Closings)

And what, monks, is the Noble Truth of Suffering? Birth is suffering, aging is suffering, death is suffering, sorrow, lamentation, pain, sad-

ness, and distress are suffering. Being attached to the unloved is suffering, being separated from the loved is suffering, not getting what one
wants is suffering. In short, the five aggregates of grasping are suffering.

(Buddha, "The Four Noble Truths")

Combinations of Repetition

There are nine standards by which to administer the empire, its states,
and the families. They are cultivating the personal life, honoring the
worthy, being affectionate to relatives, being respectful toward the great
ministers, identifying oneself with the welfare of the whole body of
officers, treating the common people as one's own children, attracting
the various artisans, showing tenderness to strangers from far countries, and extending kindly and awesome influence on the feudal lords.
If the ruler cultivates his personal life, the Way will be established. If he
honors the worthy, he will not be perplexed. If he is affectionate to his
relatives, there will be no grumbling among his brothers. If he respects
the great ministers, he will not be deceived. If he identifies himself with
the whole body of officers, then the officers will repay him heavily for
his courtesies. If he treats the common people as his own children, then
the masses will exhort one another [to do good]. If he attracts the various artisans, there will be sufficiency of wealth and resources in the
country. If he shows tenderness to strangers from far countries, people
from all quarters of the world will flock to him. And if he extends kindly
and awesome influence over the feudal lords, then the world will stand
in awe of him.

("The Doctrine of the Mean" 105–6)

As you revise paragraphs, especially troublesome ones, consider
breaking them down into their isolated points, determining which of these
are the major ones, which the minor or supporting, and use that analysis
to rework the sentences, subordinating and patterning to clarify relationships. Then do the same with whole sections of your writing. Cue both
directly and indirectly: tell your readers that you are moving from one
point to the next and why, and consider using parallel syntax to reinforce
parallel points, however separated in your text they may be.

Exercises 10.1–10.3

1. Consider the following passage, the introduction to an article
   arguing that dogs are overlooked as models of certain virtues.
   The article was published in a scholarly, interdisciplinary journal. Explain why the author introduces his subject as he does.

How is he anticipating his readers' potential resistance to his subject?

> Writing about dogs in a scholarly essay raises a difficult set of issues concerning style and intention. Scholarship is serious, and seriousness is gravity, sobriety, productivity. Dog talk is, by contrast, a luxury, something personal and private, an aspect of leisure. Dog talk can only appear, in the context of scholarship, amusing but wasteful, extravagant, and conspicuous, an indiscretion broached only under the sign of excess or hyperbole. This is, in fact, how we treat our dogs, as extra-economical objects, nonuseful splurges, recipients of surplus, frivolous affection, things to be given and given to, things to be treated like toys.
>
> (Webb 213)

2. Rewrite Karen's letter, organizing it according to the three categories of points outlined in section 10.3.1.

3. Rewrite Ari Gantz' letter (section 2.4), bearing in mind the needs of his audience: finding a common ground, clustering individual accomplishments around a few central claims, ordering those claims and cueing readers so they can follow from one point to the next, and establishing a respectful tone throughout.

4. The following passage describes a study of the African elephant undertaken by the Ivory Trade Review Group. Subordinate less important information to more important information in the following passage to aid readers in following the main ideas.

> The study was convened in July 1988. It was completed in May 1989. The results were compelling. It happened between 1970 and 1989. Kenya's elephant population had declined from 140,000 to less than 17,000. Tanzania's population had declined from 200,000 to a little over 65,000. Uganda's population had declined from 18,000 to a few hundred. The pattern was similar in Central Africa. Overall, the elephant populations were halving every ten years. That rate of decline was ten times faster than the rate of elephant habitat loss. That happened through agricultural expansion. The rate of decline was five times greater than the increase in human populations. Most of the elephants were being lost inside national parks and deep forests. There the pressure of human population is not great. Poaching for ivory was indisputably the main reason for the decline. It dwarfed all other reasons. There needed to be a letup in the ivory trade. The loss of elephants would accelerate in the coming years. What about the global pattern of trade? Ivory has been exported by Sudan, the Central African Republic, the Congo, and Zaire. This has happened in recent years. The volume

of exports has nothing to do with the number of elephants in those countries. Laundering had obscured the ivory's true origin. Most exports were bound for the Far East. They were bound for Hong Kong, Singapore, and Japan. Hong Kong was the major entrepôt. There ivory was carved and exported to other countries. These included Japan, Europe, and America. The total export value from Africa of ivory was worth on the order of $50 to $60 million a year. Only a tiny portion of that went back to Africa. About $5 to $6 million went back. This study dispelled one major illusion. The ivory trade was worth $1 billion worldwide. It was worth virtually nothing in Africa. What was the impact of the trade on elephant populations? Two independent studies gave the same results. Graeme Caughley was with the Australian Commonwealth Scientific and Industrial Resources Organization. He predicted that elephants would become extinct throughout Africa by the year 2010. He predicted that they would become extinct in East Africa within five to seven years. This would happen if the ivory trade did not slacken. The report never saw the light of day. This study's assumptions were more conservative. This study concluded that the African elephant would be extinct within the next 25 to 30 years. This would happen with the present level of trade.

(Adapted from Western 85–88)

5. This is an example of a kind of advertising one frequently finds in magazines today. (This particular example comes from the *Family Handyman* magazine—a magazine that discusses ideas and plans for home-improvement projects.) Determine whether it is reader-based or writer-based, and explain why. You can also find material in this example for discussion of many other ideas in this book. In particular, discuss its audience analysis, use of anecdotes in the argument, clarity of the conclusion urged, kinds of appeals made, and anything else you find pertinent.

Boyfriend Wanted
By Rebecca Ann Stratton

My name is Becky Stratton. You don't know me from Adam. But, I'm a real person. I'm single now. I live near Roswell, GA. I have an associate degree in finance. And, up until 18 months ago, I was so inhibited, I hardly had the courage to say "hello" to people.

I was too tired to be romantic with my then-husband, Bernie. I'd fall asleep on the couch every night at 8:30 or 9:00. When he did take me out, he was ashamed of me. And said so in front of everyone.

When I walked, my thighs brushed together. I couldn't even cross my legs. I was fat. Not just "overweight." Fat. I was 5'4" and weighed over 200 pounds.

(Cont.)

Two years ago, Bernie went out ". . . for a paper." He never came back. But he did leave a "Dear Becky" letter on my dresser. And a week later, he filed for divorce.

I went to my doctor for help. I knew my weight was the source of my problems. But I'd tried 15 different diets. One by one. And failed at all of them.

My doctor listened carefully, then he recommended an entirely different program. This wasn't a "diet." It was a unique new weight-loss program researched by a team of bariatric physicians—specialists who treat the severely obese. The program itself was developed by Dr. James Cooper of Atlanta, Georgia.

I started the program on April 22nd. Within the first four days, I only lost three pounds. So I was disappointed. But during the three weeks that followed, my weight began to drop. Rapidly. Within the next 189 days, I went from 202 pounds to 133 pounds.

The reason the program worked was simple: I was *always* eating.

I could eat *six times every day*. So I never felt deprived. Never hungry. I could snack in the afternoon. Snack before dinner. I could even snack at night while I was watching TV.

How can you eat so much and still lose weight?

The secret is not in the amount of food you eat. It's in the *prescribed combination* of foods you eat in each 24-hour period. Nutritionally dense portions of special fiber, unrefined carbohydrates, and certain proteins that generate a calorie-burning process that continues all day long . . . a complete 24-hour fat-reduction cycle.

Metabolism is evened out, so fat is burned away around the clock. Not just in unhealthy spurts like many diets. That's why it lets you shed pounds so easily. Without hunger. Without nervousness.

And it's all good wholesome food. No weird stuff. You'll enjoy a variety of meats, chicken, fish, vegetables, potatoes, pasta, sauces—plus your favorite snacks. Lots of snacks.

This new program must be the best kept secret in America. Because, up until now, it's *only been available to doctors*. No one else. In fact, the Clinic-30 Program has been used by 142 doctors in the U.S. and Canada to treat more than 9,820 patients. So it's doctor-tested. And proven. This is the first time it's been available to the public.

There are other benefits too . . .

- There are no amphetamines. No drugs of any kind.
- No pills. No powders. No chalky-tasting drinks to mix. Everything's at your local supermarket. No special foods to buy.
- There's no strenuous exercise program.
- You don't count calories. Just follow the program. It's easy.
- It's low in sodium, so you don't hold water.
- You eat the foods you really enjoy. Great variety. Great taste.
- You can dine out.
- There's no ketosis. No bad breath odor. But *here's* the best part . . .

Once you lose the weight, you can keep it off. Permanently! Because you're not hungry all the time.

Let's face it. We all have "eating lifestyles." Our eating habits usually include three meals a day. Plus two or three snacks. We all love snacks. Especially at night.

But most diets try to force us to change all that.

And that's why they fail!

The Clinic-30 Program lets you *continue your normal eating lifestyle.* You can eat six times a day. You can snack when you wish. So, when you lose the weight, you can keep it off. For good. Because no one's forcing you to change.

Here are other patients from Georgia who entered Dr. Cooper's Clinic-30 Program . . .

- Reverend Donald F. is a 42-year-old minister who went from 227 to 179 in just four months.

  "In spite of church suppers, I've lost almost 50 pounds in four months and I'm not having a rebound gain. Both my wife and I enjoy the meals."
- Renate M. was a G.I. bride from Germany who went from 212 to 140.2 in 8½ months.

  "I believe I was a participant in every weight-reducing plan there ever was. I failed at all of them. Then, about two years ago, I started the Clinic-30 Program. And I haven't regained a pound."

And then there's me.

Bernie did me a very big favor.

Since I've become thin, my life has changed. Totally. I quit smoking. I have a good job. I love to shop for nice clothes. And I'm in control again.

I'm very particular about who I date. I really am. I'm looking for a guy who really cares for me. Who won't abuse me—physically or verbally. And who enjoys doing fun things on the spur of the moment.

Obviously, I'm excited about the program. This is the first time it's been available outside of a clinical setting. Dr. Cooper has asked Green Tree Press, Inc. to distribute it.

They'll be happy to send you the program to examine for 31 days. Show it to your doctor. Try it. If you're not delighted with the amount of weight you're losing, you'll receive a complete refund. Every penny. Even shipping and handling.

What's more, Green Tree Press won't cash your check for 31 days. You can postdate it 31 days if you wish.

Choose a day and start the program. If you don't begin losing weight within five days—and continue losing weight—you'll promptly receive your *original uncashed check.* No delays. No excuses.

Or keep it longer. Try it for six months. Even then, if you're not continuing to lose weight on a regular basis, you'll receive a full refund.

To order, just send your name, address and postdated check for $12.95 (plus $3.00 shipping/handling) to The Clinic-30 Program, c/o Green Tree Press, Inc., Dept. 941, 3603 West 12th Street, Erie, PA 16505.

(Cont.)

> ### AN IMPORTANT REMINDER
>
> *As your weight begins to drop, do not allow yourself to become too thin.*
> *It's also very important to consult your physician before commencing any weight-loss program. Show him this program. And be sure to see him periodically if you intend to take off large amounts of weight.*
>
> Green Tree Press is a member of the Erie, Pennsylvania Chamber of Commerce. Bank and business references are available upon request.

10.4 Incorporate and Cite Others' Work

As you research a subject, you discover the ongoing conversation about it—what is being said by those who are thinking and writing about it. Initially you discover where your ideas fit in, which contexts give rise to your concerns, whose questions and whose conclusions affect yours, and certainly whose lines of argument you must address. Think of it this way: you enter a room full of people talking about your subject, not lecturing one at a time to all the rest who listen politely, but speaking in small groups to others interested in the same particular questions. As you listen in on these conservations, you realize some of these folk have been talking for a very long time—a whole lifetime in some cases—and they have moved from group to group as their interests overlap. How can you join in this conversation, and what will you be able to add?

For that is precisely what you do when you write your own piece: you join an ongoing conversation. As you researched your topic, you probably did not have time to linger with each group. But the work you have already done in this text has led you to focus your efforts, and the sources you have selected will now assist in finding your place in this conversation. By citing your sources, then, you affirm your participation in this community (this "room") of shared knowledge, and your use of sources claims others' attention, since they in turn will respond to what you have to say.

Let's work through an example. You may not have sufficient knowledge of anatomy and archaeology to craft a sophisticated, original argument concerning the relationship between fossil remains of birdlike dinosaurs and modern birds, but if you have read a dozen articles, book chapters, and monographs setting out the main data and controversies, you can write a carefully reasoned argument about the *Mononykus* assigned in class. You can also respond to a question about a 1994 article in

Scientific American, and your readers can evaluate your argument in light of the sources you cite. Here's a passage from Michael J. Novacek, Mark Norell, Malcolm C. McKenna, and James Clark's article "Fossils of the Flaming Cliffs"; suppose your assignment is to use it as a prompt to evaluate certain dinosaur fossils in relation to specialized bone structures that allow most modern birds to fly and others (like ostriches, emus, and kiwis) not.

> An unexpected discovery at Tugrugeen in 1992 further amplified the proposed connection between dinosaurs and birds. We found a delicate skeleton that was identical, except for its smaller size, to one discovered by Mongolian scientists some years earlier. The animal, roughly the size of a turkey, has a remarkably gracile frame with long legs. In addition, the keel of the breastbone is very well developed. In modern birds, strong pectoral muscles that power the down stroke of the beating wing attach to this keel. Instead of long wing bones, however, this creature has stubby, massive forelimbs somewhat like those of a digging mole. The end of the arm and hand is appointed with a single, very large claw; hence, the scientific name bestowed on the animal is *Mononykus*—literally, "single claw." (The original spelling was the more etymologically correct *Mononychus*, but it turned out that a beetle had first claim.)
>
> *Mononykus* is a bizarre creature. Although it has no wings, it has several features that suggest a closer relation to modern birds than the famous primitive bird *Archaeopteryx*. In addition to the enlarged sternum, these features include an antitrochanter, a small protrusion on the pelvis at the hip joint that serves as a muscle attachment point, a continuous crest on the femur for the attachment of limb muscles, and a greatly shortened fibula, the thinner of the lower limb bones. A detailed analysis of *Mononykus* favors the view that this creature was a flightless relative of modern birds.
>
> That argument has drawn some criticism. Certain specialists claim *Mononykus* is simply a small dinosaur whose birdlike features are a product of convergent evolution. The weight of the evidence, however, does not favor convergence. . . .
>
> (67)

How you use your sources and what you cite follow from the essential features of your reading, thinking, and writing on a subject—all the things we have discussed so far. Think again about your readers. They expect some combination of your understanding of the ongoing conversation and your own contribution to it; they expect you to have done your homework and to know how to enter what you have to say into that conversation. That means you will need to consider citation in the fullest sense of integrating others' ideas into your own, paraphrasing and quoting them accurately, and then moving the reader back into your own text. That means also that you will need to consider the progress of your argument, the mechanics of quotation, and the documentation of sources. Otherwise you risk ending up with another "memory dump," only this time of other people's ideas.

10.4.1 Integrating Others' Ideas

You use source material to support your own ideas—as context, as evidence (data, examples, expert testimony), as suggestive hypotheses—and you incorporate that support just as you do other support of its kind. You frame a section of your paper, introduce the relevance of your support, and then offer it. When the support comes from someone else, you need in addition to guide your readers through that material, guide their interpretation of it, connect it with your own work, and, most important, separate it from your own ideas.

Consider how you might incorporate different parts of the passage cited on p. 267 into a text of your own.

1. As context, to situate your writing within an ongoing debate, on the order of Doyle's explaining the importance of Silver Blaze's disappearance as the most talked-about event in all of England, or as suggestive hypothesis:

   The 1992 discovery in Tugrugeen of fossil remains of *Mononykus,* possibly a flightless relative of modern birds, is helping to redefine our understanding of the connection between dinosaurs and birds. Michael Novacek, Mark Norell, Malcolm McKenna, and James Clark believe this finding, along with an almost complete skull discovered at Ukhaa Tolgod, will provide evidence important to the debate over the dinosaur-bird connection (67).

2. As supporting data:

   We are most fortunate that limestone has preserved the impression of feathers in *Archaeopteryx,* leading us to speculate on the connections between this creature and modern birds. The more recent fossil discoveries of *Mononykus* suggest different features to study. Michael Novacek, Mark Norell, Malcolm McKenna, and James Clark list features of *Mononykus* they claim suggest an even closer relation to modern birds: "In addition to the enlarged sternum, these features include an antitrochanter, a small protrusion on the pelvis at the hip joint that serves as a muscle attachment point, a continuous crest on the femur for the attachment of limb muscles, and a greatly shortened fibula, the thinner of the lower limb bones." Also, as they point out, ongoing laboratory work analyzing a complete skull of *Mononykus* may yield more similarities (67).

3. As expert testimony:

> Though some specialists hypothesize that these similarities simply
> reflect convergent evolution and not an evolutionary connection
> between dinosaurs and birds, "the weight of the evidence," claim
> Michael Novacek, Mark Norell, Malcolm McKenna, and James Clark,
> "does not favor convergence" (67). These four have explored the Gobi
> Desert for the Mongolian Academy of Sciences and the American
> Museum of Natural History, where Novacek, Norell, and McKenna are
> curators in the department of vertebrate paleontology. In addition,
> Novacek is vice president and dean of science at the museum,
> McKenna is professor of geology at Columbia, and Clark is assistant
> professor of biology at George Washington University. They contend
> that "a detailed analysis of *Mononykus* favors the view that this creature
> was a flightless relative of modern birds" (67).

As you integrate quotation or paraphrase into your text, consider (1) your frame, (2) your transition from your ideas into your sources', signaled by reference to them, and (3) your transition from your sources' ideas back into your own. Each of the sample paragraphs above sets out a rationale for the quotation or paraphrase that follows—the 1992 discovery of *Mononykus* in Tugrugeen, features of dinosaur fossils that suggest a relation between those species and modern birds, the competing hypotheses of an evolutionary connection between *Mononykus* and modern birds and convergent evolution. These lead-ins shape readers' understanding of the source material; they offer the context, that is, within which readers can interpret it. Such lead-ins, like all cues, enable readers to understand the ideas you present within the framework you create, and they help lead readers through your argument. Moreover, citing the source of a quotation or paraphrase within your text separates the voices of the conversation you are presenting—yours and your sources'. It is important to know who is speaking at each point of your text, and transitions citing sources' names help readers, without breaking the flow of your argument, to follow shifts in conversation and alert them, without the need to check your bibliography, to the range of your research. Parenthetical references mark the transition back into your voice. You then can explain how the citations further your purpose.

10.4.2 To Quote or Not to Quote

You have decided to incorporate someone else's idea into your own text. Should you quote it or paraphrase? Many people assume that if they incorporate others' ideas into their own work, they should quote them, but it is usually preferable to paraphrase. Doing so allows you to maintain a more consistent style throughout your paper and better control over the amount of space you give to that source without distorting it (e.g., by cutting off a quotation from its context). Of course, whether you quote or paraphrase, you still must credit the ideas with proper documentation.

The occasions when you might choose to quote a passage rather than paraphrase it—and these are limited to just a few—all require you to present not only an idea but also the exact expression of that idea. If, for example, you need to convince a skeptical audience that a source really does hold the view you claim it does, perhaps because it is a surprising or counterintuitive view, a paraphrase may not be sufficient to persuade. If you think your audience may not be ready to accept that a man writing in the fourth century B.C.E. really did maintain that men and women should have equal opportunity to train and study for the highest position in the ideal state (the role of "Philosopher-King"), quoting the passage from Plato's *Republic* can help in an obvious way that paraphrasing the point may not.

It is also appropriate to use direct quotation when the very words themselves are crucial to the issue. For example, when you present a difficult passage from an author in order to enter into discussion of its interpretation, you will have to direct the reader's attention to the exact words you are interpreting. While documentation can help, you cannot assume that your reader is looking at the original source along side your discussion of it.

Finally, quotation may be appropriate when the source has expressed the idea in such a powerful or striking way that paraphrasing it would diminish it. This passage from John Elder's *Following the Brush: An American Encounter with Classical Japanese Culture* provides a nice example of incorporating quotations for this reason (152–53):

> Wildness is thus an inward and essential state about which the wildness, like the garden, can remind us. In order to encourage such a wild awareness, Thoreau urges that, wherever we may find ourselves, we "live in infinite expectation of the dawn." In much the same way, Bashou strengthens our natural identity with his simple, integral picture of life within the flowering world:
>
> > *Asagao ni*
> > *ware wa meshi kuu*
> > *otoko kana*
> >
> > I am one
> > who eats his breakfast
> > gazing at the morning-glories.
> >
> > (Translated by R. H. Blyth)

Notice that Elder still explains his interpretation of these lines and how they fit into the point he is making. Quotations, even powerful ones, do not themselves explain your use of them. You need to do that.

10.4.3 Common Mistakes Integrating Others' Ideas

There are some common mistakes that result when writers fail to offer a frame for their source material or transitions between it and their own text. Read these samples to discover for yourself the difficulties readers experience as they try to make sense of quotations or paraphrases added too abruptly into a text.

A. "In addition to the enlarged sternum, these features include an antitrochanter, a small protrusion on the pelvis at the hip joint that serves as a muscle attachment point, a continuous crest on the femur for the attachment of limb muscles, and a greatly shortened fibula, the thinner of the lower limb bones" (67). Michael Novacek, Mark Norell, Malcolm McKenna, and James Clark list these features of *Mononykus* as evidence for their claim that *Mononykus* may display an even closer relation to modern birds than *Archaeopteryx.* . . .

Do not begin with a quotation or paraphrase, the supporting evidence. You need to spend too much time backtracking, explaining to the reader why you think the quotation is important, how it helps to develop your ideas, and where it came from. And once readers understand its importance, they will likely need to return to the quotation to reread it since, having been asked to read it without knowing its significance, they may have glossed over it. A greater risk is that without a context readers will misinterpret your data, as they did Karen's in the early draft of her letter. As with any writing, begin by cueing your reader and then presenting your ideas and evidence, including the quotation or paraphrase.

B. We are most fortunate that limestone has preserved the impression of feathers in *Archaeopteryx,* leading us to speculate on the connections between this creature and modern birds. The more recent fossil discoveries of *Mononykus* suggest different features to study. "In addition to the enlarged sternum, these feature include an antitrochanter, a small protrusion on the pelvis at the hip joint that serves as a muscle attachment point, a continuous crest on the femur for the attachment of limb muscles, and a greatly shortened fibula, the thinner of the lower limb bones" (Novacek, et al., 67).

The quotation comes too abruptly; as a result there is no indication of its source and its relevance to the argument. Make a smooth transition into the quotation, showing its logical connection to your essay and its original authorship.

10.4.4 Punctuating Quotations

Above all, punctuation helps guide your readers through your prose, and that is as true for quotation and paraphrase as for your own words. Begin by ensuring that your quoted material is grammatically compatible with its surrounding text. Then the formal rules of punctuation begin to make sense.

A. If your transition into a quotation is a complete sentence, follow it with a colon. That preserves the grammatical relationship of full sentence (often a general point): completion of the point (often a more specific restatement or modification of it).

> Michael Novacek, Mark Norell, Malcolm McKenna, and James Clark list features of *Mononykus* they claim suggest an even closer relation to modern birds: "In addition to the enlarged sternum, these feature include an antitrochanter. . . ."

B. If your transition is less than a sentence, follow it with a comma. Again, this rule is no different from those governing the punctuation of your own text.

> They contend, "A detailed analysis of *Mononykus* favors the view that this creature was a flightless relative of modern birds."
> "The weight of the evidence, however," claim Michael Novacek, Mark Norell, Malcolm McKenna, and James Clark, "does not favor convergence."

C. If you incorporate a quotation into the grammatical pattern of your own sentence without a break, it requires no punctuation.

> They contend that "a detailed analysis of *Mononykus* favors the view that this creature was a flightless relative of modern birds."

D. Paraphrases should not cause you difficulty in punctuation; you punctuate them as you would any other text in your own words. The only difference is that you follow the paraphrase with a parenthetical citation that delays the end of the sentence and therefore also the punctuation.

> Michael Novacek, Mark Norell, Malcolm McKenna, and James Clark believe this finding, along with an almost complete skull discovered at Ukhaa Tolgod, will provide evidence important to the debate over the dinosaur-bird connection (67).
> Also, as they point out, ongoing laboratory work analyzing a complete skull of *Mononykus* may yield more similarities (67).

E. Quotations are enclosed in quotation marks only if they form
   part of your text. If you quote a passage longer than about four
   lines, indent it ten spaces to signal that the words are someone
   else's. Periods and commas come before the quotation marks—
   always. (Look over the citations above for examples.) Semicolons
   and colons come afterwards—always. (They contend that "a
   detailed analysis of *Mononykus* favors the view that this creature
   was a flightless relative of modern birds"; others, however,
   suggest convergent evolution.) Question marks and exclamation
   marks vary; they come after the quotation marks when it is the
   whole sentence (rather than just the quotation) that is a question
   or exclamation, and they are enclosed when the quoted material
   is itself the question or exclamation. The only exception to these
   rules occurs when you follow a quotation with a parenthetical
   citation. The parenthetical reference is considered part of the
   sentence, and it therefore delays the punctuation. (They contend
   that "a detailed analysis of *Mononykus* favors the view that this
   creature was a flightless relative of modern birds" (67), but
   others suggest . . . .)

When you integrate the work of several sources, your paragraphs
must sort out the relationships. Consider this paragraph from Doug Brent's
article "Young, Becker, and Pike's 'Rogerian' Rhetoric: A Twenty-Year
Reassessment," which refers to several articles and books, quoting some
passages, paraphrasing others, and simply referencing yet others.

> Young, Becker, and Pike's overarching goal, a rhetoric of social coop-
> eration founded on dialogic principles, is as important now as it was in
> the 1970s. Although the "dialogic communication" movement is no
> longer in the forefront of rhetorical inquiry, it has faded not because its
> goals have been superseded but because they have become so accepted
> that there is little need to argue for them. Connors, Ede, and Lunsford's
> *Essays on Classical Rhetoric and Modern Discourse,* for instance, is a re-
> cent and highly influential collection that is everywhere informed by
> the conviction that the purpose of rhetoric is not simply to persuade
> but to discover knowledge in a cooperative dialectic between rhetor
> and audience. John Gage's essay in that collection, "An Adequate Epis-
> temology for Composition: Classical and Modern Perspectives," speaks
> for many contemporary rhetoricians:
>
>> Rhetoric can be viewed as dialectical . . . when knowledge is seen as
>> an *activity,* carried out in relation to the intentions and reasons of
>> others and necessarily relative to the capacities and limitations of
>> human discourse, rather than a *commodity* which is contained in one
>> mind and transferred to another.
>>
>> (156)

Rhetoric is designed not just to move another to a predetermined position but to "resolve real questions of disagreement" (158).

This paragraph introduces the central question for this section of Brent's article (how important is Rogerian rhetoric in the 1990s?), recalls a central tenet of his essay so far (communication as dialogue), cites general evidence for his claim that this tenet is widely accepted, quotes a representative spokesperson, and concludes—with a combination of paraphrase and quotation—on his central point of affirmation (the communal nature of rhetorical inquiry).

10.4.5 Documentation

When do you mention a source for ideas? After you have read widely on a topic, many of the ideas in your sources begin to play off one another. Imagine an iceberg floating in the water, the tip showing above the surface buoyed up by the vast bulk of the ice beneath it. The tip is like your paper, the ideas and arguments that end up on the page; the vast bulk is like the reading and planning and thinking that prepared you to write that paper. The preparation buoys up your paper. Not all of this preparatory reading needs to be acknowledged in the same way. Some ideas you will discard as perhaps interesting but not relevant to your own paper. Others will be fundamental to your own thinking. These are the ones you cite, whether or not you quote or paraphrase them.

Acknowledge sources of inspiration. Incorporate ideas when they are necessary for you to make your case in the way you have chosen to make it—research that you need to support your claims, work that suggests avenues of investigation, ideas that provide context for your work or lead you in new directions, and, indeed, some arguments that run counter to your own. But beware of these: do not bring up an argument just to tear it down. (Why bother?) You may use it, however, to demonstrate that you understand the argument or, as Dworkin did, to suggest the best argument against your case or, as we discussed in Chapter 3, as a technique for developing your own argument.

Documentation makes possible the ongoing process of scholarship. Citing references shows readers whose work has influenced your own and suggests places to find further information. Therefore, citations must include all the information necessary for readers to locate your sources. Form and order allow for abbreviations, a kind of shorthand. Different disciplines prefer different styles—different shorthands—and the context of a piece determines which style you adopt. Many publishers use the *Chicago Manual of Style* since it addresses the recasting of manuscripts into print. Academics use APA style (American Psychological Association), prefered by social scientists; one of the styles set out in scientific societies' manuals (for instance, those of the Council of Biology, the American Chemical Society, or the American Mathematical Society); or MLA style (Modern Language Association), used in the humanities. MLA style is a system of parenthetical citations in your text that are more fully explained in a Works Cited list at its end. You have been learning the parenthetical system as you have worked through this book. At the close of your essay attach a separate sheet titled "Works Cited" that lists all the works you have cited in your text alphabetically by the author's last name. Here are sample forms to follow for offering all pertinent information briefly.

Book
Rogers, Carl. *On Becoming a Person.* Boston: Houghton Mifflin, 1961.

Book with more than one author
Rendall, Steve, Jim Naureckas, and Jeff Cohen. *The Way Things Aren't: Rush Limbaugh's Reign of Error.* New York: The New Press, 1995.

Book with an editor
Tweeney, Ryan D., Michael E. Doherty, and Clifford R. Mynatt, eds. *On Scientific Thinking.* New York: Columbia UP, 1981.

Book in translation
Terence. *The Comedies.* Trans. Betty Radice. New York: Penguin, 1976.

Book in second edition
Matthiessen, Peter. *Wildlife in America.* 2nd ed. New York: Viking, 1987.

More than one book by an author
Matthiessen, Peter. *Sand Rivers.* New York: Viking, 1981.
———. *Wildlife in America.* 2nd ed. New York: Viking, 1987.

Introduction, preface, or foreword in a book
Bevington, David. Introduction. *The Complete Works of Shakespeare.* Ed. by Berington. 4th ed. Glenview, Ill.: Scott, Foresman, 1992.

Article in a book
Lopez, Barry. "Gone Back to the Earth." In *A Forest of Voices.* Ed. Chris Anderson and Lex Runciman. Mountain View, CA.: Mayfield, 1995. 195–201.

Article in a periodical
Brent, Doug. "Young, Becker, and Pike's 'Rogerian' Rhetoric: A Twenty-Year Reassessment." *College English* 53 (1991): 452–66.

Article in weekly or monthly periodical
Novacek, Michael J., Mark Norell, Malcolm C. McKenna, and
    James Clark. "Fossils of the Flaming Cliffs." *Scientific American*
    Dec. 1994: 60–69.

Article in newspaper
Cooper, Claire. "States Term Limit Law Challenged in U.S. Court."
    San Francisco Examiner 21 July 1995: A1.

Publication of a Corporation, Foundation, or Government Agency
Committee on Earth and Environmental Sciences of the Federal
    Coordinating Council for Science, Engineering, and Technology.
    Our Changing Planet. Washington, D.C.: National Science Foun-
    dation, 1994.

Publication without an author
"The Doctrine of the Mean." *A Source Book in Chinese Philosophy.*
    Trans. Wing Tsit Chan. Princeton: Princeton UP, 1963. 97–114.

Film
Indochine. Dir. Regis Wargnier. With Catherine Deneuve, Vincent
    Perez, and Linh Dan Pham. Paradis Films et La generale
    d'Images, 1992.

Lecture
Kripke, Saul. "Naming and Necessity." Lecture at Princeton Uni-
    versity, 20 Jan. 1970.

The Newest Frontier: Electronic Materials

Standard formats for citing electronic materials (i.e., from such sources
as the World Wide Web, E-mail, On-line databases and CD-ROMs) have
not yet achieved the conventional status that procedures for citing other
materials enjoy. However, a number of good proposals are currently cir-
culating, any one of which could reasonably be followed. In general, the
principle underlying whatever format is selected should be the same as
with non-electronic sources: citations should provide clear and unambiguous information sufficient to enable a reader to find an original source.
When providing electronic addresses (e.g., URLs for the World Wide Web),
it is especially important to record the address accurately (including all
punctuation), or the record will not be retrievable by someone trying to
follow your citation. Dates given in citations for electronic sources are
generally dates at which the person making the citation assessed the
source, thus indicating how recently the material was available in the
cited form.

Style manuals such as the *MLA Handbook* and the *Chicago Manual of
Style* are beginning to offer some help, but other books provide much
greater detail concerning the variety of electronic media. One book that

many electronic style sheets acknowledge is by Xia Li and Nancy Crane (Li and Crane). Their web site (see below) mentions that a revised edition is forthcoming.

Various proposals and models for citing electronic information can be accessed on the World Wide Web. We found much information about citation styles by trying a web-search (via Netscape) using the terms *electronic style sheet* and *citing electronic information.* Here are just a few of the useful online resources we found. In listing them, we are following Li and Crane's format:

"JWA Information on Electronic Citation," *Journal of World Anthropology,* Online. Available: http://wings.buffalo.edu/academic/department/ahthropology/jwa/citation.shtml. 21 August 1996.

Li, Xia, and Nancy Crane, "Bibliographic Formats for Citing Electronic Information," Online. Available: http://www.uvm.edu/~xli/reference/estyles.html. 21 August 1996.

Samford University Library, "Citing Electronic Sources," Online. Available: http://davisweb.samford.edu/citation.htm. 21 August 1996.

St. Lawrence University Library, "Citing Electronic Resources," Online. Available: http://www.stlawu.edu/library:http/citing.html. 21 August 1996.

Walker, Janice R. "MLA-Style Citations of Electronic Sources," Online. Available: http://www.cas.usf.edu/english/walker/mla.html. 21 August 1996.

Exercise 10.4

Evaluate the ways in which the following passages incorporate material from sources. What is the reason in each case for incorporating a source—as context, data, expert testimony, or some other reason? Do they incorporate the sources successfully? Should they quote where they paraphrase, or paraphrase where they quote? Are transitions into quoted material smooth or abrupt, and is punctuation correct? Is it appropriate not to cite a source for claims here unacknowledged?

1. China's treatment of political dissent has played some role in the discussion of most-favored nation trading status, while the exploitation of children for labor has gone largely unnoticed. As Irving Epstein pointed out in "Child Labor and Basic Education Provision in China," "The possibility that Americans may be

unwittingly subsidizing the forced incarceration of political dissidents who participated in the Tiananmen uprising has provoked appropriate domestic outrage. But it is equally probable that juvenile offenders, placed in the same circumstances, are being equally exploited" (232). A report listing 70 penal institutions supplying labor for the production of goods to be exported mentioned two juvenile delinquency institutions, as well as seven "reeducation through labor" institutions a significant proportion of whose inmates are juveniles (232).

2. The finding of the bodies of the four women, by contrast [with coverage given the murder of Jerzy Popieluszko], was a back-page item in the [*New York*] *Times,* and in all four of the media institutions in our sample the accounts of the violence done to the four murdered women were very succinct, omitted many details, and were not repeated after the initial disclosures. No attempt was made to reconstruct the scene with its agony and brutal violence, so that the drama conveyed in the accounts of Popieluszko's murder was entirely missing. The murder of the four churchwomen was made remote and impersonal.

The *Time* account, for example, after giving the names of the victims, says, "Two of the women had been raped before being shot in the back of the head." The *New York Times* account, shown in table 2-2, is also quite succinct. The Rogers Commission report pointed out that one of the victims had been shot through the back of the head with a weapon "that left exit wounds that destroyed her face." The Rogers report also noted that those present at the disinterment found "extensive" wounds and that "the bodies were also bruised." Raymond Bonner's account in *Weakness and Deceit,* noted that

In the crude grave, stacked on top of each other, were the bodies of four women. The first hauled out of the hole was Jean Donovan, twenty-seven years old, a lay missionary from Cleveland. Her face had been blown away by a high calibre bullet that had been fired into the back of her head. Her pants were unzipped; her underwear twisted around her ankles. When area peasants found her, she was nude from the waist down. They had tried to replace the garments before burial. Then came Dorothy Kazel, a forty-year-old Ursuline nun also from Cleveland. At the bottom of the pit were Maryknoll nuns Ita Ford, forty, and Maura Clarke, forty-nine, both from New York. All the women had been executed at close range. The peasants who found the women said that one had her underpants stuffed in her mouth; another's had been tied over her eyes. All had been raped.

We may note the failure of *Time* and the *New York Times* to mention the bruises (which both of these publications mentioned and repeated as regards Popieluszko); the failure to mention the destruction of Jean Donovan's face; the suppression of the degrading and degraded use of the nuns' underwear; the failure to give the account of the peasants who found the bodies.

(Herman and Chomsky 61–62)

3. Many people, upon first exposure to Japanese sumo wrestling, express amazement at the enormous size of the wrestlers (*rikishi*). "Rikishi eat only two meals a day, and experience has taught that food is better absorbed this way" (69). According to Tsutomo Kakuma, chairman of the Sports Watching Association (an organization of and for amateur sumo fans), these guys actually want to get fat, and even work at it, eating a special diet suited for the purpose. Nonetheless, you may be surprised to learn that the average businessman is more likely to be over-weight, as Kakuma points out. "There are lots of *rikishi* with a good layer of fat on them, but under that are hidden muscles to rival Hercules. You may think your stomach is no more than a modest paunch, but how much muscle do you have? According to one survey, a businessman 172cm tall and weighing 75kg has a higher percentage of fat than a chunky wrestler 178cm tall, weighing 138kg. In other words, the businessman is the one who is overweight. Businessmen do not get enough exercise, so they become overweight as their muscles weaken, even though their appearance may not change. In other words, sumo wrestlers are not necessarily the ones with the excess fat problem." (70)

4. On August 10, 1938, I sailed from New York on the Polish liner *Batory* on my way to Vilna. Nineteen thirty-eight was not an auspicious year to travel to Eastern Europe for business or pleasure. All that year the premonitions of war poisoned the air as if the suffocating aroma of sulfur had already been unloosed. In March Adolph Hitler had invaded Austria and annexed it. Then he turned on Czechoslovakia under the pretext of protect-ing the "rights" of the German-speaking population who had lived for centuries in a part of Bohemia called Sudetenland.

The Czech government resisted the Nazi demands and late in May the Germans responded with a massive concentration of troops on the Czech border. The Czechs, in turn, ordered a partial mobilization of their army, and the British warned Germany that they would intervene in the event of a European conflict. Hitler backed down and the first Czech crisis petered out. The war, which had seemed imminent and inevitable, did not erupt. It was suspended for only a moment in historical time. In August, when I left New York, the second Czech crisis was beginning to heat up. The summer of 1938 was definitely not an auspicious time to go to Poland.

(Dawidowicz 3)

Appendix

Solutions to Selected Exercises

4.1 Identifying Arguments

1. argument
   conclusion: *It would be best to prohibit pigs as pets.*
   premise indicator: *since*
   conclusion indicator: *all in all*

3. argument
   conclusion: *You can believe what he says about finance.*

5. argument
   conclusion: *He must have been innocent.*
   conclusion indicator: *so*

7. non-argument

9. argument
   conclusion: *It is right to prosecute serious wrongdoing regardless of who the wrongdoer is.*
   conclusion indicator: *I can quote the law as a great proof . . .*

11. argument
    conclusion: *If a person is not to stifle his human feelings, he must practice kindness towards animals.*
    premise indicator: *for*

13. argument (Most of this passage provides a context for the argument, which has two premises):
    conclusion: *The various schools of Buddhism can be seen as expressive of different roads to the same goal.*
    conclusion indicator: *thus*
    premise 1: *Enlightenment is beyond all thinking.*
    premise 2: *If enlightenment is, by its very nature, beyond all*

*thinking, then no one expression of it can claim to be
exhaustive.*

15. argument
conclusion: *These plans are not such a good deal.*

17. non-argument

19. argument
conclusion: *Masturbation is not a substitute for "normal" sex.*

4.2 Diagramming Arguments

1.

He must have been innocent.

If Nixon were really guilty of   But it didn't.
all those crimes, then Congress
would have impeached him.

3.

You can believe what he says about finances.

He's a recognized financial commentator.

5.

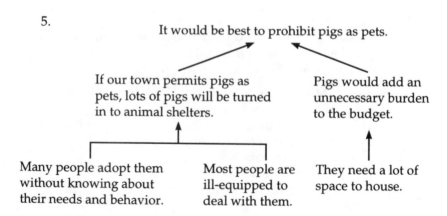

It would be best to prohibit pigs as pets.

If our town permits pigs as   Pigs would add an
pets, lots of pigs will be turned   unnecessary burden
in to animal shelters.   to the budget.

Many people adopt them   Most people are   They need a lot of
without knowing about   ill-equipped to   space to house.
their needs and behavior. deal with them.

9.   The pious is what I am doing now, to prosecute
the wrongdoer, be it about murder or temple
robbery of anything else, whether the wrongdoer
is your father of your mother or anyone else; not
to prosecute is impious.

Zeus is the best
and most just of
the gods.

Zeus bound his father
because he unjustly
swallowed his sons.

Zeus's father
castratred his father
for similar reasons

11.   If a person is not to stifle his human feelings,
he must practice kindness toward animals.

He who is cruel to animals becomes
hard also in his dealings with men.

13.   The various schools of Buddhism can be seen as
expressive of different roads to the same goal.

Enlightenment is
beyond all thinking.

If enlightenment is, by its
very nature, beyond all
thinking, then no one
expression of it can claim
to be exhaustive.

15.   People 50 to 80 can obtain better insurance
through traditional plans than they can get
through the special senior plans.

Frequently, someone with a
questionable medical history
and insurability problems can
buy significant coverage for
less than these plans cost.

Unlike these plans, the
coverage often offers
benefits payable from
the first day, on the full
amount of the policy.

5.1 Ambiguity

II. A. ambiguous:
- All glittering things are non-gold.
- Some glittering things are not gold.

C. ambiguous:
- Letterman hosted more shows that were shocking than Carson did.
- Letterman's shows are more shocking than Carson's were.

E. ambiguous:
- He participates in religious rituals and activities, shares certain beliefs, etc.
- He is reliable or regular in his habits/activities.

G. This one is not truly ambiguous—since we know that one grammatically possible meaning is not a real possibility in context. The two readings would be:
- Those who oppose the plan are expected to put up a big fight.
- Dead people ("stiffs") are expected to oppose the plan.

I. ambiguous:
- The reason she didn't marry is that she's a widow.
- She married, but not because she's a widow.

K. unambiguous

M. ambiguous:
- What price will a Grammy fetch if you sell it?
- What price is it worth paying to receive one?

O. unambiguous:
"Almost" and "results guaranteed" do not lead to different interpretations: presumably this just means that if you are one of the unlucky few whose loved one cannot be located, you'll get a refund.

Q. ambiguous: ("trying to plug the leak")
- Trying to fix the roof.
- Trying to stop the reports from getting out.

III. Eliminating Ambiguity
A. • alternative wording: *In what section of town did you get infected?*
- additional wording: *Where did you get infected? I didn't see any poison ivy on the way.*

- context: *Ranger looking at a map of the hiking trail, desiring to locate the poison ivy.*

C. - alternative wording: *The meaning of the word "obfuscation" is "confusion."*
   - additional wording: *When I looked up the meaning of obfuscation the result was confusion, and that is a much simpler word to use.*
   - context: *looking up a word in a dictionary and writing down the definition*

E. - alternative wording: *While flying past it in a helicopter, I saw the space shuttle on the ground at Cape Canaveral.*
   - additional wording: In this case, it's best not to retain the original wording, since the dangling modifier is the source of the ambiguity.
   - context: *A reporter in a helicopter, who has just explained that the space shuttle was rumored to be in flight despite the fact that no flight for it had been announced, declares the rumor false, since "I saw the space shuttle as I flew past Cape Canaveral."*

5.2 Missing Premises

I. A. (c) is best: it is the weakest claim that provides sufficient support for the conclusion. (a) is too strong: it says that all redheads are short-tempered, much more than is needed to support the "probably" in the conclusion. (b) is too weak: "some redheads" doesn't support a conclusion that claims that being a redhead shows that he is *probably* short-tempered. (d) is close, but since the claim is about a male, (c) is both weaker than (d) and sufficient to do the job, and therefore preferable.

II. Write Out Missing Premises
   A. 1. A country is less democratic to the extent that its citizens are unable to vote.
   2. Those who vote only when bilingual ballots are available do not understand English language ballots well enough to vote without translation to their native language.

   C. 1. Homosexuals have something to hide.
   2. People with something to hide do not make good security risks.

   E. 1. In order to be equally protected by law, all people must have reasonable access without cost to the knowledge of what the law says.

2. The best place to make what the law says freely available is in public libraries.
3. People do not have reasonable access to knowledge of what the law says unless the laws are stated in language that ordinary people can understand.

G. 1. If the state may fix the rate of tax on disseminating information, then it may set the tax high enough that some people could not pay it.
2. If the state sets the tax on disseminating information high enough that some people could not pay it, then the state would be infringing the right of free speech.

III. The author is assuming that what made the bombing of Hiroshima a mistake was the presence of *American* citizens who could not leave the targeted region. While it is controversial among Americans today whether the atomic bombing was morally justified, it is striking that this author's reason for thinking it a mistake refers not to all innocent victims, but only Americans. More than 100,000 Japanese people—most of whom were not connected in any way to the military—were killed in the Hiroshima blast, and thousands suffered horribly in the aftermath. In this light, the assumption that the mistake was the killing of "our" innocent people is rather incredible.

6.4 Deductive Validity

I. Valid or Invalid?

1. valid	7. valid	13. invalid	19. invalid
3. valid	9. invalid	15. invalid	
5. valid	11. invalid	17. invalid	

II. Scenarios

1. Even if it were true that social change always produces violence (something we might not want to accept), and if we grant (what seems correct) that violence is always regrettable, it still doesn't follow that social change is regrettable. When the American colonists freed themselves from British rule, it took a war to accomplish the task. Nonetheless, the social change that resulted is not regrettable.
3. It is true that he will be admitted to the theater only if he has a ticket, and also we might imagine he has one, but saying this in no way excludes the possibility that there are other require-

ments for admission as well—such as wearing clothing. So even if these premises are true, if we imagine he is naked, the conclusion may well turn out to be false.

5. All we need to imagine here is that someone else is elected and that person is not as disastrous for the economy.

III. Logical Analogies

1. You can't pass a law against dangerous driving because no one can draw a sharp line between dangerous and nondangerous driving.

3. All professional water polo players are human beings. Paul McCartney is a human being. So Paul McCartney is a professional water polo player.

5. Each of us will die if we have a terminal disease. Each of us will die. So each of us has a terminal disease.

7. Because torture followed by death is harsher than mere torture, we should maintain mere torture as a punishment.

9. Inappropriate: Valid Argument

11. Inappropriate: Valid Argument

13. A president will be reelected only if he is very popular in the year preceding the election. Ronald Reagan was very popular in 1987, a year before the election. So Ronald Reagan was reelected in 1988.

15. Abraham Simpson is the father of Homer Simpson, and Homer is the father of Bart Simpson, so Abraham is the father of Bart.

7.1 Analogies

I. A. *Primary subject matter:* repression and its relation to resistance (in Freud's theory).

Analogue: the expulsion of the interrupter and the placement of the chairs against the door to keep him out.

Function of the analogy: to illuminate the concepts of repression and resistance—to help us get a grasp on what these mean.

Evaluation: The analogy succeeds as well as we can tell without delving into psychoanalytic theory. The analogue is certainly familiar (much more so than the primary subject matter), and it remains vivid because it is not a worn-out analogy. One danger of the analogy is that it may encourage us to personify the psychological forces within us, e.g., by leading us to think of the repressed item as having desires of its own.

C. *Primary subject matter:* While the outcome of the land battle was uncertain until it was in fact achieved, the outcome of the battle at sea was never in question.

Analogue: the disanalogy between a football game and a vehicle crossing a bridge.

Function of the analogy: This is a double analogy: Churchill uses the analogy between a football game and the battle on land on the one hand, and the battle at sea and a vehicle crossing a bridge on the other hand, to argue for the claim that the outcome of one battle was certain, the other uncertain.

Evaluation: Clever as the contrast of two different analogies is, one might wonder whether we should accept Churchill's conclusion on the basis of this argument. Churchill claims that the seafaring resources of Great Britain were superior to the U-boat attack, which was so gradual that these superior resources had time to be deployed. For this reason, he argues, the German defeat was certain. That seems a strong point. On the other hand, one reason that the battle on land was uncertain in a way that is not just a matter of ignorance was because of the element of human decision and potential error, factors that can confound the presence of superior force. Of course, they are also present in the case of a sea battle.

E. *Primary subject matter:* the world and whether it has a creator.

Analogue: machines—especially the ability to infer causes of a certain sort (intelligent creators) of machines from their design (from the "adjustment of means to ends").

Function of the analogy: to provide an argument for the existence of a creator of the world, similar to, though much greater than, human intelligence.

Evaluation: This is a difficult one, about which people have disagreed. Here is one possible critique of it. The inference to an intelligent creator depends on the principle that from similar effects you may infer similar causes. Clearly, applying this principle is risky, since the notion of "similar effects" is vague. In particular, applying it in this case is questionable, since the extent to which the effects really do resemble each other is questionable. After all, the ability to infer an intelligent creator of machines is based on the assumption that because certain configurations of materials are not found in nature, we can be assured that they are human productions. When we conceive of the entire world as one great machine, however, we can no longer assume that certain configurations cannot be natural (and therefore require an intelligent creator) because it is the entirety of nature of which we are now speaking! That throws the analogy into doubt. To put the point a bit differently: we can infer a nonnatural cause of natural events only if natural causes are insufficient explanations (after all, that's why we infer a watchmaker from a watch), but nothing in this argument shows us why we should treat naturalistic explanations as insufficient. (It doesn't show us, that is, why we should infer a tree maker from a tree when we could do quite well with seeds, soil, and so forth.)

7.2 Generalization

I. A. This is a generalization from a sample.

Generalization: Violent and nonviolent people are chemically different.

Sample: 2 sets: 24 matched pairs of violent and nonviolent siblings, and 192 men, half extremely violent, half controls matched for age, race, etc. From the statement that Walsh "spends his spare time working with prisoners" we may infer (with some hesitation) that the samples of violent individuals were taken from those imprisoned for violent crimes.

Problems: We don't know whether there are other factors produced by the method of selecting the sample that have not been discounted. For example, prisoners eat a fairly uniform diet (especially if they are in the same prison), and this may help explain the presence of some trace elements in their hair.

C. This is a generalization.

Generalization: Many hypothermia researchers feel able to (are willing to) employ data acquired from Nazi experiments on unconsenting concentration camp subjects.

Sample: 45 research articles published since 1945 that cite Nazi data.

Problems: The generalization is itself vague: How many is many? Knowing how large the population of hypothermia researchers is, and what percentage of them is willing to use this research, would be more informative. We do not know how many researchers are actually included within the sample: on the one hand, typically scientists publish more than one article on the same general topic, and frequently publish a series when important data are found. On the other hand, many scientific studies are co-authored, so 45 articles may represent more than 45 researchers. So it's hard to say how large the sample really is from this way of characterizing it.

E. *Generalization:* Students who take special classes to improve SAT scores cannot expect to do better than they would have done without the classes.

Sample: 1500 Harvard freshmen, divided into two groups: those who did and those who did not take the special classes prior to taking the SAT.

Problems: The sample is not relevant to the generalization. What needs to be compared is a sample of students before and after taking this class. After all, what is claimed for such classes is *improvement* in scores, not a particular score or even relation to average scores. Comparing Harvard students who did with those who did not take the class does not tell us whether those who did take it improved over what they would have scored without the class.

7.3 Explanation

I. A. *Puzzle:* The evidence for evolutionary development of organisms is to some extent compatible with creationist accounts—e.g., organisms that are well-adapted to their environments. Therefore, the dispute between evolution and creation cannot be settled by showing the evolutionary adaptiveness of various species.

Hypothesis: Evolutionary theory is the superior account of the origin of species.

Data: Darwin sought data that would exhibit the kinds of oddities and incongruencies best explained by the existence of evolutionary history. I.e., he looked for data that would be improbable unless evolution were correct.

Evaluation: This is an example offered by Gould to show how careful searching for data that is improbable unless a hypothesis is true is crucial to deciding between competing hypotheses. His point is well taken and the example is a good one.

C. *Puzzle:* Why orb-weaving spiders shed their legs when injected with venom.

Data: speed of shedding, death of those who do not shed, components known to cause human pain.

Hypothesis: Spiders feel pain.

Evaluation: For the data to support this hypothesis, we need some auxiliary assumptions: A1—these spiders have a neural apparatus similar to the apparatus enabling humans to feel pain in response to these chemicals and A2—intervention of conscious state (pain) is the simplest explanation of how these spiders might be caused to shed their legs (as opposed, for example, to direct signal to spine without conscious intervention). These are considerable assumptions that probably do not hold up.

II. Jenner

A. Jenner's hypothesis: An attack of cowpox confers immunity to smallpox. He predicted that if this hypothesis were true, then Phipps would be immune to smallpox following his bout of cowpox. Auxiliary assumptions include the following:

1. The smallpox matter with which Phipps was inoculated had not lost its potency.
2. What Jenner did really inoculated Phipps, and he accurately observed whether Phipps had cowpox and whether he contracted smallpox.
3. Persons who are inoculated and do not contract even a mild case of smallpox are immune.

B. Even if the prediction comes out true, the hypothesis might still be incorrect, for there is such a thing as a natural immunity. Phipps may have had a natural immunity to smallpox, independent of the cowpox inoculation. In fact, natural immunity to smallpox was apparently rare, and so Jenner's hypothesis had a higher prior probability than the alternative.

IV. Semmelweis

A. *Hypothesis* (H): patients become more susceptible to childbed fever when they are alarmed by the priest on his way to deliver last rites.

Prediction: If H, then if the priest refrains from walking through the First Division on his way to deliver last rites, the mortality rate for childbed fever in that division will decrease.

Auxiliary Assumption 1: The patients won't learn of the priest's presence in some other way.

Auxiliary Assumption 2: Everything else in the patients' treatment and environment remains the same.

The prediction turns out to be incorrect, thus disconfirming H. Here is the argument:

If H, then if the priest refrains from walking through the First Division on his way to deliver last rites, the mortality rate for childbed fever in that division will decrease.

The mortality rate did not decrease.

Therefore, H is false.

B. *Hypothesis* (H): Cadaverous matter spreads childbed fever (CF) during examinations.

There are actually three arguments confirming the cadaverous-matter hypothesis:

1. If H, then washing hands in chlorinated lime before examinations will reduce the incidence of CF.

   Washing hands before examinations does reduce the incidence of CF.

   H is confirmed.

2. If H, then the incidence of CF for midwives should be lower.

   The rate for midwives is lower.

   H is confirmed.

   (Auxiliary Assumption for 2: Midwives don't touch cadaverous matter.)

3. If H, then women who are not examined but are present in the same ward should have a lower incidence of CF.

   Unexamined women in the same ward do have a lower incidence of CF.

   H is confirmed.

   (Auxiliary Assumption for 3: the women do not come into contact with cadaverous matter in some other way, such as via air or dirty linens.)

C. Not only could he be wrong, but he was! "Cadaverous matter" is too restrictive. There is nothing special about the fact that stuff spread by the medical students came from *cadavers*. It might also come from living, infected people. Semmelweis himself discovered this later. After disinfecting hands with lime, the students examined a woman with festering cervical cancer, and then went on to examine 12 more women, with only routine washing (no lime). Eleven of the 12 died of childbed fever, leading Semmelweis to the new conclusion that the infectious material (he called it "putrid matter") can also be derived from living organisms.

8 Fallacies

1. This combines straw man with illegitimate emotional appeal: evolution is caricatured and then refuted by appealing to human fears that we may not really be any better than monkeys (you don't want to be related to monkeys, do you?).

3. This is a straw man: Elders never suggested showing kids *how to* masturbate, though her unfortunate phrasing—"teaching masturbation" as part of a safe sex program—left her open to misunderstanding.

5. Both *ad hominem* (calling the judge a hypocrite) and slanted language ("scumbozo," "straining at a gnat," "plays God," "technicality") are present in this one. Notice also the improper appeal to authority: Ecclesiastes is not authoritative on the causal question of whether the death penalty is an effective deterrent.

7. The argument is deductively valid, but it starts with a questionable premise: even if every word is a name of something, it doesn't follow that a sentence is a list of names. Analogously, a painting composed of nothing but dots can be much more than a collection of dots—for example, a picture of something! Similarly, a sentence composed of nothing but names may still do more than merely listing.

9. The argument equivocates on "preventive detention." First it means detaining "someone who is preparing to commit a crime (such as a man going around a parking lot trying car doors)," which seems reasonable; by the end of the argument it means detaining "anyone suspected of harboring criminal intentions," which may turn out to be someone who is not preparing to commit a crime.

11. This is a *post hoc* fallacy: nothing here shows that it is Idaho's new law that has produced the noticed result.

13. This is a faulty charge of improper appeal to authority. Although there is some merit in considering the potential bias of someone who has devoted his life to an activity (because he would be less likely to admit it if the activity were not particularly valuable), and should keep us on our guard in simply accepting his authority on a question like this, it ignores the important point that if anyone is qualified to comment on the value of a certain kind of life, it is going to be someone who has dedicated himself to it.

15. There is no fallacy here. Phrases like "cook the meat" are graphic and indelicate, but they are not slanted just because they raise emotions or may offend some people. We may not

like to think of the electric chair as a cooker, but if that's what it does, then that's what it does. In some contexts, such a description is both appropriate and accurate.

17. This passage—from a public school history text—is fallacious in two general ways. Supposing we are to infer from this example what the legislative process is like, the sample is both small and unrepresentative (a writer traveling around for a day with a legislator would undoubtedly influence the events he was observing). The second fallacy is slanted language— slanted throughout toward presenting the State Assembly and this particular legislator positively. For example, without knowing what bill Assemblyman Torres introduced, we are told it will "improve" school meals—how could you object to that? An assemblywoman "explains" a bill, "everyone asks questions," "citizens share their opinions"—one has the impression there is an open and honest inquiry into an issue about which people have no prior opinions or on which there are no interested parties applying any pressure. The slant begins looking as if it might be outright falsification when Torres goes to dinner with doctors and *"tells them* about several health bills"; in all likelihood they know perfectly well about the bills and are there to lobby him one way or another. In that case, they are probably telling him about the bill—they may even have had a part in writing it! The propaganda value of the piece is high when we learn that Torres thinks *everyone* should take a turn in office. Do you think he'll step aside to let you take your turn?

19. The argument equivocates on "your own." You can own the paper as property, and also you can author it. The paper becomes yours by buying it, but if you misrepresent its authorship, you still plagiarize.

21. You can plausibly interpret this passage in terms of more than one fallacy label. It could be viewed as begging the question— appealing to the catalog as proof of the catalog's believability assumes what you set out to prove. It also can be viewed as improper appeal to authority; the catalog cannot be the place to look to determine whether the catalog is authoritative on graduation requirements.

23. Of course, it has been many years since the Celtics won a championship, but this is nonetheless a case of ridicule taking the place of argument. Bob is made to look stupid, but no reasons for thinking the Celtics can't win are offered.

25. This argument suppresses evidence. (It can also be seen as a faulty analogy.) If the ice caps were floating in the water, as the analogy suggests, the point would be reasonable. But most of

the ice in the world is on land, so their melting would add to the total volume of the oceans, leading to an estimated catastrophic rise of 200 feet (Rendall, Naureckas, and Cohen 17).

27. The language in this ad suggests in a number of ways (without actually saying so) that this creme will make breasts grow larger and change shape. The claim that this product "has been used by thousands of women with great success" makes it sound as if some kind of evidence for FORM U's efficacy is being offered. Of course, no reason is provided to think that breasts can be enlarged simply by using a cream, though everything in the ad points in that direction and no other hint is given of what the cream could be for. The ad thus invites you to draw the wrong conclusion. Perhaps the right conclusion is that if you rub this cream on your breasts, they'll look gorgeous (maybe because they'll look shiny?).

29. This is a reasonable appeal to authority, though the ad omits mention of how large a percentage of the doctors who smoke this is—that is, how many doctors continue to smoke, despite the evidence.

31. Improper appeal to authority (the authority of the common person, also known as the "bandwagon"—everyone's doing it).

33. If you recast the thrust of Marvell's argument, you can see that at least part of the persuasive power of the poem depends on a fallacious argument:

If we had enough time, then coyness would be fine.
But we don't have enough time.
_____

Therefore coyness is not fine.

This is a case of denying the antecedent—a formal fallacy. (It's still a lovely poem.)

35. A funny cartoon, but if we infer anything about the value of vegetarianism from it, we are substituting ridicule for reasons. Of course, its original context—a book by humorist Dave Barry—is one in which just about everything is spoofed and readers know that we are being invited to laugh at ourselves and everyone else. Appreciated in that context, we understand that no serious refutation is intended, so there is no fallacy.

9.3 Sentence Combining

I. There are, of course, many ways to do these. Here are some sample answers that work:

A. Lorenzo de' Medici, called "Lorenzo the Magnificent," was a patron to Florentine artists.

C. Sitting alone on the beach reading yesterday's paper, Fred suddenly looked alarmed.

E. Scientists study comets—essentially dirty snowballs formed at the birth of the solar system—to understand conditions when the sun and planets came into being.

G. Spotting the horizontal sewer grate outside the American Museum of Natural History a little past 5 A.M., they quickly tether a voracious-looking papier mache alligator to it.

I. Actor, poet, playwright, theater shareholder, naturally learned, astute observer of people and places, Shakespeare had what Dryden called "the largest and most comprehensive soul" of modern or ancient men.

III. A. Relatively informal style—lots of short sentences; longer ones have coordinate sentence structure. Diction is simple, occasional slang ("chums," "wench"). The style is appropriate to the meaning of the passage, as it helps maintain the personal feeling, directly expressing the author's feelings.

C. The short coordinate clauses in Mailer's passage are quite effective in producing the feeling of the very thing he is discussing: fight metaphors. Before long you feel you are being jabbed or clubbed with quick shots exemplifying the passage's point stylistically. The words he chooses reinforce this feeling of brief, but powerful punches.

E. A modern high style. Lots of prepositional phrases bury the action in abstract nouns. Verbs are usually linking. Not much jargon or technical terminology makes the passage a bit easier to read than many in this style, but it is still difficult to pin down exactly what these guys are saying. One has the suspicion that when put into plain, simple words, it won't amount to too much.

G. This is a personal, informal style: sentences have a simple, coordinate structure (nothing is subordinated) following subject—verb—object pattern. About half the sentences use *I* as subject. Only the diction is sophisticated.

10.4 Incorporating and Citing Others Work

1. This passage uses the quoted material as expert testimony on a point about which we do not hear much in the press. Thus, it

may be appropriate to quote rather than merely paraphrase here because a reader might not be as willing to accept the point otherwise (though that judgment may vary according to purpose and audience for the writing). Transition into the quotation is smooth, and punctuation is correct.

3. Just about everything that can go wrong with use of sources does go wrong here. A quotation without proper introduction makes for an abrupt change and consequent need to backpedal to explain who the author is and why we ought to listen to him. Were the point better integrated (e.g., if placed after the point that *rikishi* eat a special diet), it could just as well have been paraphrased. The long quotation that comes at the end is improperly punctuated: the lead-in should be a colon, not a period, and the citation should be placed before the final period (excess fat problem" [70].) And finally, the quotation is too long to be quoted within the paragraph—it should have been indented.

Bibliography

Aristotle. *Nichomachean Ethics.* Trans. Martin Ostwald. Indianapolis: Bobbs-Merrill, 1962.

—. "Rhetoric." *The Basic Writings of Aristotle.* Trans. W. Rhys Roberts. Ed. Richard McKeon. New York: Random, 1941.

"Astrograph." *Redlands Daily Facts* 2 Feb. 1988: B5.

Auden, W. H. "Introduction to *Tales of Grimm and Anderson.*" *Forewords and Afterwords.* New York: Random, 1973.

Austad, Steven. "The Adaptable Opossum." *Scientific American* (Feb. 1988): 98–104.

Austen, Jane. *Pride and Prejudice.* New York: Knopf, 1991 (1813).

Bacon, Francis. "On Studies." *A Selection of His Works.* Ed. Sidney Warhaft. Toronto: Macmillan, 1965. 174–75.

Baker, Russell. "Collegiettes." *New York Times Magazine* 23 Oct. 1977: 13.

Bhumitchitr, Vatharin. *Thai Vegetarian Cooking.* Bangkok: Asia Books, 1991.

Bloyer, Gordon. Letter. *USA Today* 18 July 1995: 10A.

Bok, Sissela. *Lying: Moral Choice in Public and Private Life.* New York: Vintage, 1989.

Boyer, Gregory A. Letter. *Los Angeles Times* 5 June 1995: B4.

Brent, Doug. "Young, Becker, and Pike's 'Rogerian' Rhetoric: A Twenty-Year Reassessment." *College English* 53.4 (Apr. 1991): 452–66.

Buddha. "The Four Noble Truths." *Thus Have I Heard: The Long Discourses of the Buddha: Digha Nikaya.* Trans. Maurice Walshe. Boston: Wisdom, 1987.

Bunch, Bryan. *The Science Almanac.* Garden City: Anchor, 1984.

California History: The Study of Our State. Glenview: Scott, Foresman, 1983.

Carroll, Lewis. *Alice in Wonderland.* New York: Three Sirens Press, 1900.

Chicago Manual of Style. 14th ed. U of Chicago P, 1993.

Churchill, Winston. *The World Crisis.* London: Butterworth, 1923.

Cohen, Richard. "A Communications Gap When It's Man to Man." *Washington Post* 1980: B1+.

Cooper, Claire. "States Term Limits Law Challenged in U.S. Court." *San Francisco Examiner* 21 July 1995: A1.

Copi, Irving. *Introduction to Logic.* 7th ed. New York: Macmillan, 1986.

Corbett, Edward P. J. *Classical Rhetoric for the Modern Student.* 2nd ed. New York: Oxford UP, 1971.

Cousins, Norman. "Dehumanization." *Saturday Review* (20 Sept. 1975): 4.

Dawidowicz, Lucy S. *From That Place and Time: A Memoir 1938–1947.* New York: Bantam, 1989.

Delwiche, Aaron. "Examples: Newt Gingrich." *Propaganda Analysis Home Page* Online. Available: http://carmen.artsci.washington.edu/propaganda/newt.htm. 20 August 1996.

Dickens, Charles. *David Copperfield.* Vol. 1. New York: Collier, 1917.

Didion, Joan. "Holy Water." *The White Album.* New York: Simon, 1979. 59–66.

"The Doctrine of the Mean." *A Source Book in Chinese Philosophy.* Trans. Wang-Tsit Chan. Princeton: Princeton UP, 1963. 97–114.

Doheny, Kathleen. "Forget Tourniquets for Snakebites—Head to the ER." *Los Angeles Times* 8 Aug. 1995: E1–2.

Doyle, Sir Arthur Conan. "The Adventure of Silver Blaze." *The Strand Magazine* 4 (1892): 83+.

Dworkin, Ronald. "On Not Prosecuting Civil Disobedience." *New York Review of Books* (6 June 1968): 14–21.

Elbow, Peter. *Embracing Contraries.* New York: Oxford UP, 1986.

—. *Writing with Power.* New York: Oxford UP, 1981.

Elder, John. *Following the Brush.* Boston: Beacon, 1993.

Epstein, Irving. "Child Labor and Basic Education Provision in China." *International Journal of Educational Development* 13.3 (1993): 227–38.

Feyerabend, Paul. *Science in a Free Society.* London: Verso, 1983.

Feynman, Richard. *Surely You're Joking, Mr. Feynman!* New York: Norton, 1985.

"Florida Governor Seeks to Free 'Mercy Killer' for Court Appeal." *Los Angeles Times* 23 Aug. 1985: A9.

Flower, Linda. *Problem-Solving Strategies for Writing.* 4th ed. Fort Worth: Harcourt, 1993.

Freud, Sigmund. "The Origin and Development of Psychoanalysis." *American Journal of Psychology.* Trans. Harry W. Chase (1910): 181–18.

Fuller, Lon L. "The Case of the Speluncean Cave Explorers." *Harvard Law Review* 62 (1949): 616–45.

Gandhi, Mohandas K. *An Autobiography.* Trans. Mahadev Desai. Boston: Beacon, 1957.

Garibaldi, Joseph. *MLA Handbook for Writers of Research Papers.* 4th ed. New York: MLA, 1995.

Gibson, Walker. *Persona: A Style Study for Readers and Writers.* New York: Random, 1969.

Gould, Stephen Jay. *The Panda's Thumb.* New York: Norton, 1980.

Groddeck, Georg. *The Book of the It.* London: Vision, 1949.

Hammond, Ruth. "Child Labor in the Third World." *Utne Reader* 63 (May 1994): 20.

Hempel, Carl G. *Philosophy of Natural Science.* Englewood Cliffs: Prentice-Hall, 1966.

Heritage, John, and David Greatbatch. "Generating Applause." *American Journal of Sociology* 92 (July 1986): 110–57.

Herman, Edward S., and Noam Chomsky. *Manufacturing Consent: The Political Economy of the Mass Media.* New York: Pantheon, 1988.

Hitchcock, David. *Critical Thinking: A Guide to Evaluation.* Toronto: Methuen, 1983.

hooks, bell. *talking back: thinking feminist, thinking black.* Cambridge: Harvard UP, 1987.

Howe, Irving. Introduction. *If Not Now, When?* By Primo Levi. Trans. William Weaver. New York: Penguin, 1985. 3–16.

Hume, David. *Hume's Dialogues Concerning Natural Religion.* Ed. Norman Kemp Smith. Oxford: Clarendon, 1935.

Ivins, Molly. *Molly Ivins Can't Say That, Can She?* New York: Vintage, 1991.

"Jenner, Edward." *Britannica Online.* Version 96.2. May, 1996. Online: Encyclopedia Britannica. Available: http://www.eb.com:180/cgi bin/g?DocF=

micro/302/1.html&bold=on&sw=Jenner&sw=edward&DBase=Articles&
hits=10&context=all&ParagraphType=1&indexremove=off&bl= #first_hit:
21 August 1996.

Johnson, Samuel. "The History of Rasselas, Prince of Abissinia." *Rasselas and
Other Tales*. Ed. Gwin J. Kolb. New Haven: Yale UP, 1990.

Kahane, Howard. *Logic and Contemporary Rhetoric*. 5th, 7th ed. Belmont, CA:
Wadsworth, 1988, 1995.

Kakuma, Tsutomu. *Sumo Watching*. Trans. Deborah Iwabuchi. Tokyo: Yohan,
1993.

Kant, Immanuel. *Lectures on Ethics*. Trans. Louis Infield. New York: Harper,
1963.

King, Martin Luther. "Letter from Birmingham Jail." *Why We Can't Wait*. New
York: Mentor, 1963. 76–95.

Lanham, Richard. *Analyzing Prose*. New York: Scribner, 1983.

Lehman, Susan. "A Matter of Engineering." *The Atlantic* 265 (Feb. 1990):
26–29.

Levi, Herbert W., and Lorna R. Levi. *Spiders and Their Kin*. New York: Golden,
1990.

Li, Xia, and Nancy Crane. *Electronic Style: A Guide for Citing Electronic Information*. Westport: Meckler, 1993.

—. *Electronic Styles: A Handbook for Citing Electronic Information*. Medford, NJ:
Information Today, forthcoming.

Lipson, Benjamin. *How to Collect More on Your Insurance Claims: A Money
Saving Guide to Greater Protection and Bigger Returns on Your Insurance
Claims*. New York: Simon, 1985.

Magurshak, Dan. "The 'Incomprehensibility' of the Holocaust." *Echoes from the
Holocaust: Philosophical Reflections on a Dark Time*. Ed. Alan Rosenberg and
Gerald E. Myers. Philadelphia: Temple UP, 1985. 421–31.

Mailer, Norman. "The Ali-Frazier Fight." *Life* 70.10 (19 Mar. 1971): 18+.

Marquez, Gabriel Garcia. *One Hundred Years of Solitude*. Trans. Gregory
Rabassa. New York: Avon, 1972.

Marvell, Andrew. "To His Coy Mistress." *The Poetical Works of Milton and
Marvell with a Memoir of Each*. Boston: Houghton, [1880].

McEvedy, Colin. "The Bubonic Plague." *Scientific American* (Feb. 1988): 118–23.

"Mercy Death." *Los Angeles Times* 1 May 1986: A18.

"The Message of Miracles." *Time* 145 (10 Apr. 1995): 64–68.

Mohr, Richard D. "Gay Basics: Some Questions, Facts, and Values." *The Right
Thing to Do*. Ed. James Rachels. New York: Random, 1989. 147–64.

Moore, Kathleen Dean. *Inductive Arguments: A Field Guide*. Dubuque: Kendall/
Hunt, 1989.

Morgan, Byron. Letter. *The Sun* [San Bernardino, CA] 27 Apr. 1995: A11.

Munson, Howard. *The Way of Words: An Informal Logic*. Boston: Houghton,
1976.

Nixon, Richard M. "Text of Senator Nixon's Broadcast Explaining Supplemen-
tary Expense Fund." *New York Times* 24 Sept. 1952: A22.

Novacek, Michael J., Mark Norell, Malcolm C. McKenna, et al. "Fossils of the
Flaming Cliffs." *Scientific American* 271.6 (1994): 60–69.

O'Brien, Carla. Letter. *Los Angeles Times* 5 June 1995: B4.

Orwell, George. "Politics and the English Language." *A Collection of Essays.* Garden City: Doubleday, 1954. 162–77.

The Oxford Annotated Bible With the Apocrypha. Ed. Herbert G. May and Bruce M. Metzger. Revised Standard ed. New York: Oxford UP, 1965.

Perkins, David. *Knowledge as Design.* Hillsdale, N.J.: L. Earlbaum Associates, 1986.

Pinker, Steven. *The Language Instinct: How the Mind Creates Language.* New York: Harper, 1994.

Plato. "Euthyphro." *The Trial and Death of Socrates.* Trans. G. M. A. Grube. Indianapolis: Hackett, 1975. 3–20.

—. *Republic.* Trans. Francis M. Cornford. New York: Oxford UP, 1945.

Plunkett, Robert L. "Vow for Now." *National Review* (29 May 1995): 48.

Potok, Chaim. *Wanderings: Chaim Potok's History of the Jews.* New York: Fawcett Crest, 1978.

Radner, Daisy, and Michael Radner. *Science and Unreason.* Belmont, CA: Wadsworth, 1982.

Raeburn, Paul. "Stiff Sentence." *Omni* (Feb. 1988): 28.

Rendall, Steve, Jim Naureckas, and Jeff Cohen. *The Way Things Aren't: Rush Limbaugh's Reign of Error.* New York: New Press, 1995.

Robbins, John. *Diet for a New America.* Walpole, NH: Stillpoint, 1987.

Rogers, Carl. *On Becoming a Person.* Boston: Houghton, 1961.

Rollin, Bernard E. *Animal Rights and Human Morality.* Buffalo: Prometheus, 1981.

Rosenhan, D. L. "On Being Sane in Insane Places." *Science* 179 (19 Jan. 1973): 250–58.

Russell, Bertrand. *Human Knowledge: Its Scope and Limits.* New York: Simon, 1948.

Salinger, J. D. *Catcher in the Rye.* Boston: Little, 1951.

Sather, Edward I. Letter. *The Sun* [San Bernardino, CA] 10 Apr. 1990: A5.

Schafer, Arthur. "On Using Nazi Data: The Case Against." *Dialogue* 25 (1986): 413–19.

Shakespeare, William. "Hamlet." *The Complete Works of Shakespeare.* Ed. David Bevington. 4th ed. Glenview: Scott, Foresman, 1992.

—. "The Merchant of Venice." *The Complete Works of Shakespeare.* Ed. David Bevington. 4th ed. Glenview: Scott, Foresman, 1992.

Singer, Peter. *Animal Liberation: A New Ethics for Our Treatment of Animals.* New York: New York Review, 1975.

Skyrms, Brian. *Choice and Chance.* 3rd ed. Belmont, CA: Wadsworth, 1986.

"Study Finds SAT Coaching Waste of Time." *The Sun* [San Bernardino, CA] 10 Feb. 1988: A3.

Subhuti. *Sangharakshita: A New Voice in the Buddhist Tradition.* Birmingham, Eng.: Windhorse, 1994.

Szasz, Thomas. *Law, Liberty, and Psychiatry.* New York: Macmillan, 1963.

—. *Sex By Prescription: the Startling Truth about Today's Sex Therapy.* Garden City: Anchor, 1980.

Vannoy, Russell. *Sex Without Love.* Buffalo: Prometheus, 1980.

Velasquez, Manuel G. *Business Ethics: Concepts and Cases.* Englewood Cliffs: Prentice-Hall, 1988.

Viscusi, W. Kip, and Wesley A. Magat. *Learning About Risk: Consumer and Producer Responses to Hazard Information.* Cambridge: Harvard UP, 1987.

Vos Savant, Marilyn. "Ask Marilyn." *Parade Magazine* 26 Mar. 1995: 12.

Webb, Stephen R. "Pet Theories: A Theology for Dogs." *Soundings* 78 (June 1995): 213–37.

Western, David. "When the Forest Falls Silent." *Elephants: The Deciding Decade.* Ed. Ronald Orenstein. San Francisco: Sierra Club, 1991. 83–96.

Wilson, Edward O. *On Human Nature.* New York: Bantam, 1982.

"Your Body, Your Health." *Ladies Home Journal* (Feb. 1988): 91–93.

Index